SOE
IN FRANCE 1941 - 1945

SOE
IN FRANCE 1941 - 1945
An Official Account of the Special Operations Executive's 'British' Circuits in France

Major Robert Bourne-Paterson

Frontline Books

SOE IN FRANCE
1941-1945
An Official Account of the Special Operations Executive's 'British'
Circuits in France

First produced as 'The "British" Circuits in France, 1941-1944'
by Major Bourne-Paterson, London, 30 June 1946.

This edition published in 2016 by Frontline Books,
an imprint of Pen & Sword Books Ltd,
47 Church Street, Barnsley, S. Yorkshire, S70 2AS,
based on file reference HS 1/122 at The National Archives, Kew and
licensed under the Open Government Licence v3.0.

Preface Copyright © John Grehan
Text alterations and additions © Frontline Books

The right of John Grehan to be identified as the author of the preface has been
asserted by him in accordance with the Copyright, Designs and Patents Act 1988.

ISBN: 978-1-47388-203-4

CIP data records for this title are available from the British Library

For more information on our books, please visit
www.frontline-books.com
email info@frontline-books.com
or write to us at the above address.

Printed and bound by CPI Group (UK) Ltd, Croydon, CR0 4YY
Typeset in10.5/13.5 Palatino

Contents

Preface

By John Grehan

It was more an act of defiance than considered strategic planning when Winston Churchill uttered the oft-quoted phrase to Hugh Dalton, the Minister of Economic Warfare, to 'Set Europe ablaze'. The date was 22 July 1940, just seven weeks after the British Expeditionary Force had been chased off the beaches of Dunkirk and exactly one month after France had signed an armistice with Germany.

The skies over Britain were filled with the drone of German aero engines and the population braced itself for the day Hitler's troops stormed the beaches of the South Coast. Little could either Dalton, Churchill, or even Lord Hankey, who had prepared the ground for sabotage and guerrilla warfare a year earlier, have envisaged in the summer of 1940 just how successful and effective an organisation the newly-formed Special Operations Executive (SOE) would become over the course of the following four years.

From the outset, France was viewed as being the country where the opportunity to develop and support resistance groups would be most likely to succeed. As might be expected, the initial efforts at establishing resistance groups, or circuits as they became called, proved difficult. The apparent strength of the German forces, and Britain's comparative weakness, offered little incentive to any French man or woman to risk joining any organisation associated with the latter. Indeed, all of the early circuits were penetrated by the Gestapo, whose brutal methods were rightly feared by the occupied population.

Yet the SOE persisted in infiltrating its agents into France, and, as the war turned increasingly in favour of the Allies, so more French people were encouraged to join the ranks of the resistance movement, in all its forms. As hope of an Allied victory transformed into certainty, so the efforts of the SOE agents and sub-agents grew in scale and audacity, with roads and railways being blocked and blown up, power stations sabotaged, and convoys attacked.

As Allied troops prepared for D-Day in the UK, so SOE planned for the Normandy landings in France. Stock piles of weapons, ammunition and explosives were hidden, orders issued. Even as the great armadas of ships and 'planes were heading over the Channel on 5 June 1944, across France the resistors began their programme of widespread destruction. Communication lines were cut and means of transportation disrupted, preventing the Germans from mounting a coordinated counter-strike against the Allied beachheads. France at least, had indeed been set ablaze.

The highly secretive nature of the SOE, combined with a somewhat less than methodical approach to record-keeping and the intentional and accidental destruction of a vast quantity of documents, has meant that an accurate assessment of the achievements of the organisation has proven difficult to produce. No doubt well aware of this, Major Bourne-Paterson attempted to record as much about the SOE's British circuits in France as he was able.

A peacetime solicitor, Major Robert Bourne-Paterson became one of the Special Operation Executive's planning officers in F Section. His service in this organisation led to his involvement with some of its most famous operatives – individuals such as Violet Szarbo GC, whose will he was a witness to. Through his work in compiling this account Bourne-Paterson has been described as being the SOE's 'first historian'.

Bourne-Paterson's 'history' is reproduced here in the form that it was originally written. Aside from correcting obvious spelling mistakes or typographical errors, we have strived to keep our edits and alterations to the absolute minimum. A direct consequence of this policy is that there are inconsistencies in the text. The surname Grand-Clément, for example, appears both in this style as well as a single word. Likewise, the accent is often omitted (as is the case in many place names). We have not attempted to correct such errors or standardise the text; that is not the purpose of this book. That said, it is important to point out that a small number of short appendices containing personal information on those who assisted the circuits during the war have been omitted in order to comply with the terms of the Open Government Licence. This detail can of course be viewed by a researcher in an original copy of the report held at The National Archives, Kew.

Such alterations aside, what follows is, in effect, a condensed history of SOE's 'British' circuits in France compiled by a staff officer inside the organisation, and it is reproduced here for the general public for the first time since it was written.

John Grehan
Storrington
July 2016.

Foreword

1. The compilation of the attached notes has been a race against time, and time, regrettably has won. This has meant that certain circuits and a number of very gallant officers have not been mentioned at all and, although I hope and believe that this does not adversely affect the general picture of what the British circuits set out to – and did – accomplish during the fight for the liberation of France, my apologies are due to them.

2. Another consequence is that this record is not exhaustive. It is not possible to say, because a man or a circuit is not mentioned in these pages, that he or it never existed. Nor must it be assumed, because no Decoration is set against an officer's name, that he did not in fact receive one.

3. This subject of Decorations, incidentally, is an extremely sore one in France, where the slowness of the British in awarding Decorations to French members of British circuits is not understood. It is a surprising fact that up to February 1946 no British Decoration had, for instance, been awarded to any member of the *Farmer* circuit in Lille. Franco-English goodwill is at times subjected to surprising stresses.

Major Bourne-Paterson
London
30 June 1946

Introduction

General.

1. The S.H.A.E.F. view of Resistance in France is, briefly, that it rendered valuable services from the Military point of view, but that it was only able to do so as a result of the supplies, directives and Command organisation which it received from London (either direct or through the North African organisation which was set up at an intermediate stage and was finally responsible for an important area in Southern France).

2. This Command Organisation was built up in various ways:

   (1) By a system of self-contained circuits, stalled, supplied and controlled by the French Section (F. Section) of S.O.E. These circuits were purely British in the sense that control lay entirely in British hands and the French had no say in the running of the circuits. The first officer was sent to the Field by this Organisation in May 1941.

   (2) Somewhat later the de Gaulle Forces Françaises Libres (F.F.L.), later to become the Forces Françaises Combattantes (F.F.C.), were in position to organise their own circuits. S.O.E. formed a liaison section (R.F. Section) and undertook to provide Training, Supplies and Communications for the French Circuits.

   (3) Towards the end of the Clandestine period, Tripartite Missions were organised to go to selected areas to co-ordinate the activities of the circuits already working in these areas. These generally consisted of a French, a British and an American officer.

(4) From D-Day onwards teams of three, consisting of two officers (one French, the other either British or American) and a Radio operator, were sent to selected groups to assist them in organising guerrilla action against the Germans. Approximately 100 of these teams, known as Jedburghs, were sent to France by S.O.E.

(5) The British effort also included the sending of S.A.S. (Special Airborne Services) Detachments to France. Some of these were British, others of French Nationality, but all were equipped and trained in Great Britain.

3. The present book deals only with No. (1) above, the "British" Circuits in France.

The British Circuits in France.

4. The purpose behind the work of these circuits was the encouragement of sabotage in Occupied Europe. In this respect France presented a special case, since after the events of May and June 1940 only half of the country was actually occupied by the Germans, although in the remainder it was abundantly clear that the Vichy Government was at the mercy of the invader, who could choose his own time to put on pressure.

5. The distinction, however, did involve a difference in so far as the work of S.O.E. was concerned. Whereas in the Occupied zone "discreet" explosions could be countenanced, there could be no such licence in the Unoccupied zone; there, fires might mysteriously light themselves, bearings might run hot, but things must not "go bang in the night."

6. A word that was very popular in the early stages was the word "insaisissable" as applied to sabotage.

7. In fact, in the early stages the objectives put before F. Section organisers were somewhat nebulous: "insaisissable" sabotage, "discreet" bangs, "organisation" of resistance were supremely indefinite terms.

8. The last, in particular, possessed dangers all its own. The British organiser was very carefully trained in matters of security, and he was

told that the only secure method was to build up what was known as a "circuit" by a system of small self-contained cells, very much on the method known to be adopted by the Communist Party. The emphasis was on efficiency, security and smallness of numbers.

9. "Organising Resistance," or any similar omnibus term, on the other hand, implies large numbers and centralised organisation. It was tried, by Lucas in Paris[1] in late 1941 and early 1942, by David in Bordeaux[2] in late 1942 and early 1943, and in both cases it brought its own Nemesis. The time was not yet ripe.

10. At the same time the very indefiniteness of the objective in the early period tended to defeat itself. The organiser recruited his men and found himself unaware of what to do with them.

11. And so the system grew up of smaller, more compact circuits with definite limited objectives; something to bite on, and something well within the capacity of the numbers which could be recruited with safety and efficiency.

12. In the early stages the objectives were economic, and targets were chosen for their capacity to impair the industrial effort of occupied France in support of the German economy. Little by little the emphasis shifted and the targets became more and more military. They remained however, sabotage targets, but the railway line, the telephone cable and the canal had replaced the factory.

13. There were two types of activity which quite definitely formed no part of what it was intended that an F. Section circuit should perform, and into which, equally, they were pitch-forked by the logic of events in the later stages.

14. Firstly they were not "Intelligence" circuits. They were there for action, and the passing of Intelligence was a waste of time and – more valuable still – of vital wireless space. Besides, the collection of information was in other hands. The outstanding series of Intelligence reports which came out of Bordeaux in mid-1943 and from Le Havre in early 1944 are magnificent exceptions which prove the rule. At a still later stage, just before the Normandy landings, S.H.A.E.F. being

dissatisfied with the amount of Intelligence actually available, asked that S.O.E. organisers be instructed to report back all items of military intelligence. This was firmly resisted by S.O.E., where it was realised that radio operators in the Field were already working almost beyond endurance; a compromise was reached and S.O.E. organisers were asked to report back a specified number of major types of Intelligence.

15. The copious reports on V.1 sites by the Farmer circuit and the Mitchell circuit, and the tactical Intelligence by Verger just behind the battle near Thury Harcourt are good instances of what was accomplished in this new sphere. Pedlar also, by his speedy reporting of Von Kluge's new Headquarters near Verzy, caused a further and rapid dislocation of that harassed General's plans.

16. Secondly, the F. Section circuits were sabotage circuits, and not designed for guerilla warfare and still less for open warfare. The original intention had been that the British circuits should occupy themselves exclusively with sabotage, while the French paid special attention to the "Insurrection Générale," but inevitably as time went on the British circuits, by their experience and their excellent communications took their part in the guerilla phase. This phase remained, of course, essentially a French one, the British rôle being that of co-operation with the French organisations, a task of which the British officers involved acquitted themselves with almost ambassadorial distinction.

Why "British"?

17. A word is perhaps needed to explain the existence of "British" as opposed to "French" circuits in the Field. The difference is one of Control and Organisation, since quite clearly the working members of both types of circuit were French.

18. S.O.E. was already in existence when General de Gaulle raised the Free French banner in June 1940, and a section had already been formed for the organisation of subversive activity in France. This was already active in the Field by the time the Free French Organisation was sufficiently developed to undertake similar activities in mid-1941.

19. Inevitably, as soon as this point was reached, the Free French claimed the exclusive right to control subversive activity in France, but for various reasons (in particular, unfortunate experiences of French lack of security, as in the abortive Dakar operation) it was decided to maintain the "British" circuits side by side with, but entirely distinct from, those controlled by the Free French, S.O.E. providing a liaison service with Free French Headquarters, and acting as universal provider of facilities for training, transport and supply.

20. This arrangement continued until D-Day, when "British" and "French" circuits merged in the F.F.I. under the command of General Koenig working through E.M.F.F.I. (État-Major des Forces Françaises de l'Intérieur), a joint Franco-Anglo-American headquarters staff in London.

21. There were obvious disadvantages in this duality, but there were also great advantages, particularly in the earlier clandestine stage. Against the over-lapping of effort and the lack of co-ordination which the existence of two entirely separate organisations inevitably occasioned must be set, first of all, the enormous gain from the security point of view. This followed in part automatically from the fact that the Germans were always chasing two organisations instead of one, and also from the fact that the security of the British organisation was itself superior to that of its opposite number.

22. Another advantage lay in the fact that the British organisation had no Politics and was able to concentrate on its objective, the expulsion of the enemy, without the political distractions which tended to assail all purely French Resistance movements. The personnel of the British circuits was extremely varied, running right across French society without distinction of class and type, and the lack of political bias in the officers sent out to control those circuits[3] enabled Frenchmen of widely differing backgrounds to co-operate wholeheartedly in the liberation of their country, conscious of the fact that there was no political afterthought in the circuits' activities.

23. Finally its system of command was much more supple and its communications much speedier.

Post-Liberation Developments.

24. By the combination of all these factors it is certain that the British organisation was the more efficient in the clandestine period. (Indeed over the whole period May 1941-September 1944 the British organisation (F. Section) delivered more material to the Field than its French counterpart.) All of which has its present repercussions. There was, and still is, a deep and abiding jealousy of the F. Section or Buckmaster[4] circuits, and a deep interest in the doings of everyone connected with them both on the part of the Deuxième Bureau and also on the part of the Communists. The Communists, in particular, suspect the Amicale, "Libre Résistance," 3 Rue de Marivaux, Paris (Secretary Marcel Taurent-Singer), which has been formed of ex-members of the "Réseau Buckmaster," of being a body of pronouncedly Rightist tendencies and a danger to themselves. In so far as its existence tends to disprove the Communist assertion of a quasi monopoly of Resistance activity, they are undoubtedly correct.

25. (There is considerable irony in this attitude of the Communists. During the Resistance period the most frequent clashes of opinion between the British and the French organisations arose precisely over the question of supplies to the Communists. The B.C.R.A.[5], under the leadership of Colonel "Passy," with only half an eye on the immediate objective and the remainder of their gaze fixed on the post-war political scene, were resolutely opposed to providing help to the Communists in any shape or form. The British, with but one objective, the ousting of the Hun from France, were willing to, and did, supply the Communists upon certain well-defined conditions. These conditions were, on the whole, well observed, and the Communists played their part in the final attacks on the occupying forces. Indeed, in the South-West, the Spanish Communists bore the brunt of the early fighting while the raw French levies were being trained and armed. Elsewhere the quality of Communists' co-operation depended on the personality of the local commander, discipline from the centre being extremely nebulous.)

26. It had long been realised in London that vigorous measures would have to be taken to prevent members of British circuits being victimised, as without such measures they were fair game both for the jealous Communists and for the antagonistic B.C.R.A. One of these measures

consisted of the formation of a mission – the Judex mission – composed of F. Section officers from Headquarters, which toured France between September 1944 and March 1945. The purpose was to make personal contact with the Field circuits, preferably in company with the British officers who had worked with them, to congratulate them on their achievements, and above all to make sure that they took the correct administrative steps to have themselves accredited to the liquidation services of the D.G.E.R..

27. An office was also opened in Paris which continued to function in full till December 1945 and on certain financial matters till March 1946.

28. The Judex tour revealed such an intense and enthusiastic pro-British feeling that F. Section, in co-operation with the British Council, made plans to organise the visits to England of selected parties of Frenchmen and Frenchwomen who had worked with the British and the French circuits during the Resistance period. Two of these visits took place before the winding up of S.O.E.

29. In the final stage, the interests of F. Section group members is being looked after by "Libre Résistance," of which further details will be found, under "Paris," at paragraph 119.

30. F. Section in all sent 393 officers to France. 119 of these were arrested or killed by the Germans. Of those arrested only seventeen came back.

NOTES TO INTRUDUCTION:
[1] See Paris, para. 7, *et seq.*
[2] See Bordeaux, para. 5, *et seq.*
[3] As to the officers themselves, they were sent in for the most part by parachute, but some were landed by aircraft or from surface vessel or submarine. As most Frenchmen arriving in England tended to gravitate to de Gaulle, the proportion of French officers sent by S.O.E, to F. Section circuits was low; the majority were more-or-less bilingual Britons, who were reinforced by some French Canadians and, in the latest stages, by a certain number of Americans, following upon the arrival of O.S.S. on the S.O.E. scene.
[4] The British circuits were organised and controlled by F. Section of S.O.E. under the command of Colonel Buckmaster.
[5] Bureau Central des Renseignements de l'Armée, the London organisation which on moving to France became the D.G.S.S. (Direction Générale des Services Spéciaux) which, in turn, became the D.G.E.R. (Direction Générale d'Études et Recherches).

Abbreviations

The use of abbreviations has been avoided as far as possible.
The following occur:

A.S.	Armée Secrète
B.B.C.	British Broadcasting Corporation
B.C.R.A.	Bureau Central des Renseignements de l'Armée
B.O.A.	Bureau des Opérations Aériennes
C.F.L.	Corps Francs de la Libération
C.G.T.	Confédération Générale du Travail
D.G.E.R	Direction Générale d'Études et Recherches
D.G.S.S	Direction Générale des Services Spéciaux
D.M.R.	Délégué Militaire Régional
E.M.F.F.I.	État-Major des Forces Françaises de 1'Intérieur
F.F.C.	Forces Françaises Combattantes
F.F.I.	Forces Françaises de l'Intérieur
F.F.L.	Forces Françaises Libres
F.T.P.	Francs-Tireurs Partisans
F.T.P F.	Francs-Tireurs Partisans Français
F. Section	The British Section of S.O.E. dealing with France
G.M.R.	Garde Mobile de Réserve
Helmsman	A special type of Intelligence mission
Jedburgh	A team of two officers and a radio operator sent to help selected Resistance groups
M.U.R.	Mouvements Unis de Résistance
O.C.M.	Organisation Civile et Militaire
O.F.A.C.M.	Organisation Franco-Anglaise du Capitaine Michel (the Lille Group)

O.G.	Operational group
O.R.A.	Organisation de la Résistance dans l'Armée
P.S.F.	Parti Social Français
P.T.T.	Postes, Télégraphes et Téléphones
R.F. Section	The Liaison Section of S.O.E. with the French
S.F.H.Q.	Special Force Headquarters
S.H.A.E.F.	Supreme Headquarters Allied Expeditionary Force
S.O.E.	Special Operations Executive
U.N.R.R.A.	United Nations Relief and Rehabilitation Administration
W.O.	War Office: The name by which the British organisation is known in Lille and in certain other places

Part I

The Old Occupied Zone

The Paris Region

BRITISH CIRCUIT ACTIVITIES IN THE PARIS REGION

1. There are three easily distinguishable periods in the work of the British Circuits in the Paris region:

2. The first dates from June 1941 when Baron Pierre de Vomecourt was parachuted to the field. This was the early period, when the Free French

1

were not yet in the running, and a number of Frenchmen, who had been acting as liaison officers between the British and French armies, went to France to work with British Circuits. De Vomecourt returned to England in March 1942, returned to France again in April, and was arrested in the same month.

3. A second major effort was made at the beginning of October 1942 with the sending to the Field of Major F.A. Suttill, who, in his turn, built up an extremely powerful organisation. All went well until June 1943, when the circuit, which had this time become *the* major objective of the Gestapo, was penetrated and liquidated.

4. In October 1943 a pick-up operation brought back to this country a Frenchman, R. Dumont-Guillemet, who had already been working with a British organiser in the field, and so was eligible to work for F. Section and without the necessity of having to be passed over to the Fighting French. In February 1944 he returned to France to organise a circuit which successfully survived until the liberation of the region at the end of August. He was also instrumental in re-establishing contact with the Lille group.

5. Paris was also the Headquarters of a group specialising in pick-up operations by Lysander aircraft.

6. Finally mention must be made of another British circuit under Major Frager (Louba) which, although its major activities were carried out far from Paris, had its headquarters there, and exercised a great influence on the fortunes of the organisation as a whole.

Baron Pierre de Vomecourt's Organisation.
Operational name of organisation: The Autogyro Circuit.
Operational name of organiser: Etienne, and later Lucas and Sylvain.
Name by which known in the Field: The above, with the addition of Pierre.

7. Baron Pierre de Vomecourt is one of the most exceptional men to go to the field.

8. In these early days, as opposed to later on when missions became

very precise, organisers were sent to France with the wide and potentially all-embracing mission of "organising resistance."

9. Pierre was especially well fitted for this task. Determined, efficient and very intelligent, he had a mass of contacts in France in all walks of life. So, when he was parachuted in May 1941 it was as a first-class organiser of whom much was expected. His "region" was the Occupied Zone.

10. And he did accomplish much more indeed, than would be thought possible, considering the difficulties under which he worked.

11. He very quickly observed that his work had two distinct sides, the formation of small completely dependent groups for sabotage and the large-scale organisation of an uprising to coincide with an Allied landing. For this latter purpose he foresaw an organisation upon a Departmental basis (sub-divided into cantons), and by February 1942 progress in its setting-up had been made in the Sarthe, Haute-Saone, Doubs, Vosges, Meurthe-et-Moselle, Finistere and Eure-et-Loir Departments, and in their neighbourhoods of Rouen, Le Havre, Evreux and Tours.

12. This constituted his own group, but he had also made contact with groups already existing, and had persuaded them to enter into a "fusion," two conditions precedent of which were that all requests for finance and material should pass through himself and that he should have complete control of all subversive work carried out by all or any of the organisations.

13. The following groups were reported as about to enter the "fusion":

Liberte.
Groupement Neo-Socialist.
Elements P.S.F.
Groupement Alsacien.
An unnamed association in the region of Rouen.

Liberation Nationale had not yet decided, but were reported to be favourable.

14. The strengths of the groups were as follows:

Liberte, not precisely known, but about 6,000.
Liberation Nationale, between 2,000-3,000.
Groupement Neo-Socialist, about 3,500.
Groupement Normandie, about 2,000.
Groupement Alsacien, about 2,000.
P.S.F. approximately 6,000.
Pierre's own group, about 2,000.

15. Pierre had also organised the elements of an Intelligence service, and, in particular, had well-placed contacts in the S.N.C.F. and the Controle Fluvial who were willing to work with him.

16. As to immediate sabotage, small mobile groups had been formed, but activity was hampered by lack of materials. One goods train had, however, been blown up and burnt, the turntable at Le Mans had been obstructed by overturning a large locomotive into it, shunting gradients had been tampered with and minor forms of sabotage, such as hot-boxes, were being constantly applied.

17. On the organisational side, then, a great deal had been done. On the material side, unfortunately, Pierre had been dogged by difficulties of communications. Originally the only means of sending messages to London was through an operator in the Chateauroux district. This was obviously unsatisfactory since each message and its reply necessitated a long journey and two crossings of the Demarcation line. Ultimately this position was rectified by the sending of an operator to the Occupied zone, but worse was to befall, since this operator was arrested soon after he had passed his first message, and the Chateauroux operator disappeared at about the same time.

18. In desperation, for lack of communications means lack of material and – worse still – of money. Pierre contacted a Polish organisation in touch with London. He soon found, however, that this group had been penetrated by the Gestapo and he was forced, therefore, to limit his messages to arrangements for his visit to England. The Germans connived at his departure with the object, on his return, of making a more complete haul of his collaborators.

19. In London the value of what he had set on foot and of the political contacts he had made were quickly realised and meetings were arranged for him on a very high level. More difficult was the question of deciding what to do next in the practical sphere, since it was evident that the Gestapo knew all about him and were just waiting to pick him up.

20. Finally, Pierre's own view prevailed. He pointed out that his lieutenants were also in danger and that he must go back and warn them. Furthermore, that if he did not go back, British prestige would suffer an irremediable blow and the organisation which he had built up would disintegrate.

21. With many misgivings his point of view was accepted, and in April 1942 he was parachuted back to the Field. In the same month a courier from him was caught on the Demarcation line and his own arrest followed.

22. So ended our first large-scale effort to build up an organisation in the Occupied Zone. With Pierre were arrested, of the officers who had been sent from England, Albert, his second in command[1], Gaston, who had set up a small independent organisation in Caen[2], and Jean[3]. His radio operator[4], as has been noted, had been arrested previously. The one survivor was Benoit[5], who succeeded in making his way out through Spain and was later to fulfil three other missions in France with great distinction.

23. Pierre had also recruited his two brothers. One of them, Baron Jean de Vomecourt (Constantin), who lived in Eastern France, had already organised teams among the railway men for the purpose of cutting all rail communications from Germany to France at the critical moment. The other, Baron Philippe de Vomecourt (Claude), operated in the Unoccupied Zone, where he was engaged in setting up the counterpart of Pierre's organisation. He escaped arrest (at this time), but Constantin was caught, taken to Germany and died there.

24. (Pierre himself returned to England after eighteen months spent in Fresnes and eighteen months in Oflag IVC. His full name and address figure in Appendix E, as do those of Benoit, who is also now in Paris.)

25. Meanwhile, Benoit had succeeded in making his way back to London. In spite of the fact that the Gestapo were known to have his description and that he had been closely involved in the Gestapo-sponsored operation by which Pierre had returned to London, he was convinced that he could successfully return to the Field, although he realised that it would be suicide to remain more than a few days in Paris. It was therefore arranged that he and another officer should drop together in the Unoccupied Zone and make their way to Paris, where Benoit would introduce the new arrival[6] to his contacts in the city.

26. This part of the plan was successfully carried out at the end of May and Alexandre was on a fair way to setting up a circuit. But on his way back from Lyon, whither he had gone to fetch a radio operator, he was arrested in Limoges on the 15th August, 1942, and imprisoned.

27. The same end-of-May operation, however, brought another fine officer to the Paris area[7]. A pre-war resident of Paris, a racing motorist, he was confident of building up a circuit by means of his own pre-war friends. In this he was successful, and when Benoit met him in July, his circuit was in being and ready, on receipt of materials, to take action against its targets. In this, however, he also was completely held up for lack of wireless communication with London, the position only being rectified by the despatch to him by Lysander aircraft of an operator[8] in March 1943.

28. In July 1942 an assistant[9] for Sebastien landed at Antibes, but unfortunately was arrested with Alexandre at Limoges.

29. Meanwhile, towards the end of April 1942 a radio operator[10] had left England for Paris, travelling via Gibraltar and Lyon. Hearing on the way of the arrest of Pierre and the break-up of his organisation, he was diverted to the region of Tours, where he made contact with an organiser[11] and established himself in August 1942.

30. On the 1st October a first-class organiser, Major Suttill (Prosper) was dropped blind near Vendome, accompanied by an assistant, Lieutenant Amps (Jean). He had been given three addresses in Paris to which he could go, and he was to meet there soon after his arrival Mlle. Borrel[12], who was to act as courier to his circuit. She also had acquaintances in the

Paris area. Jean having proved unsatisfactory, Monique took his place with distinction.

Major Suttill's Organisation.
Operational name of circuit: The Physician Circuit.
Operational name of Organiser: Prosper.
Name by which known in the Field: Prosper or Francois.

31. Among the contacts which Major Suttill had been given was one supplied by the Carte organisation (see under Major Frager below) named Germaine Tambour. She proved an excellent person, and the members of the Carte group proved a valuable milieu for Intelligence, access to Ministries, Safe Houses, False Papers, &c.; they also included an action group.

32. Apart from this Prosper created a similar organisation of his own, the word "organisation" being used in the sense that he himself was in contact with all the groups, while they themselves were not aware of each other's existence.

33. Communications with London in the early period were, as usual, extremely difficult. Some messages were passed through the Indre at Tours above mentioned, and on occasion use was even made of an operator in the Bordeaux area, with whom Prosper was in periodic contact by courier.

34. On the 1st November a radio operator, Captain (later Major) Gilbert Norman, (Archambaud, Aubin), was parachuted to the Tours circuit already mentioned. By the middle of the month he had contacted Prosper and started working as his Lieutenant: he had early troubles in making radio contact with London, but by March 1943 he was passing messages regularly.

35. Prosper showed himself an organiser of outstanding enterprise and ability, and once communications had been put on a satisfactory basis the circuit went ahead by leaps and bounds. So much so that, in spite of the ever-present scarcity, a second wireless operator was sent to him at the end of December 1942[13]. This man continued to work for him until June 1943, when he returned to London.

36. By June 1943 the organisation of the circuit was as shown in Appendix (A). It will be noted that it covered twelve departments, had thirty-three grounds ready for the receipt of men and materials and by the 1st June had received 254 containers of stores. In June 1943 it broke all records by receiving 190 more containers between the 12th and the 21st of the month.

37. This was, however, too good to last. Precisely what happened is not clear, since neither Prosper himself, nor Monique, nor Archambaud, his two lieutenants, has returned to tell the tale. We do know that the three heads of the circuit just mentioned all disappeared about the 24th June, that George Darling, carrying out a reception of stores near Triechateaux, was surrounded and killed and that Culioli and Suzanne (Mme. Ruddelat, a courier sent from England), also at a stores reception, were surrounded and wounded at the same period. It is known that the extent and activities of the Prosper circuit had for a considerable time been a matter of the utmost concern to the Gestapo – indeed, the Prosper circuit had officially become their "objective number One."

38. This was a major success for the Gestapo and a further conclusive demonstration of the truth, well-known but difficult to abide by that large circuits (at any rate at this period) carried the seeds of their own insecurity.

39. To repeat, what happened exactly is not known. But, as in all these cases the hand of suspicion has pointed at various members of the Circuit. Gaspard[14] (see Appendix B) has been suspected of having had something to do with the arrests, but he arrived in England in May 1944, where the Security services investigated his case: the evidence was purely circumstantial and he must be taken to have been cleared. Against Paul (see Appendix B) the case is blacker, but he has never been available for examination: he is reported to have led the Gestapo straight to a Reception operation in an area outside his own, in circumstances which leave little doubt that he was working for the Germans.

40. The greatest mystery of which it is necessary to have some knowledge concerns Archambaud. His work, as radio operator and as lieutenant to Prosper, was superlative, and the fine record of activity

which the circuit holds is in large measure due to his enthusiastic co-operation and technical skill. His training record is good and his security-mindedness in the Field exemplary. And yet – he is almost universally believed to have sold out to the Germans after his arrest. His wireless set continued to communicate with London after the date on which Prosper, Monique and he had disappeared, and it is not known – and never will be – whether he was, in fact, free, whether he was working under duress or whether his set was being worked by somebody else. He *appears* to have broken down, but it is difficult to assess his case on the evidence available: nothing has ever been *proved* for or against him.

41. The circuit had been very active one, and a summary of these activities is at Appendix B. It had also served another important purpose: it had been the means, through its contacts, through its channels of communications or through the facilities for reception which it represented, of enabling a number of organisers to establish themselves in France, to retain communication with headquarters, or to spend the initial difficult forty-eight hours in security before moving on to their own areas.

42. In its first capacity it provided the original contact for Achille, on his way to Sebastien, in its second it was for a long time the only means of communication for the two circuits in the Lille and St. Quentin area, in its third it provided the Reception Committee, which received (among others) the ubiquitous Benoit, when, in April 1943, he returned to France for the third time to carry out a mission in the Troyes region. The circuit also maintained a constant liaison, for purposes of mutual assistance, with two other British circuits, that of Ernest[15] in the Meaux District and of Robin[16] in the neighbourhood of Chalons-sur-Marne.

43. Unfortunately, the circuit had been too useful, and the liaison with the other groups had been too close. The circuit in Chalons was cleaned up at the same time, and although Lieutenant Fox in Meaux survived till the beginning of September, his arrest without any doubt formed part of the same series of operations.

44. Sebastien and his group were also liquidated about a month later; not in this case through any too close connexion with the Prosper

organisation, but as a result of his radio operator having been caught transmitting by the German D/F-ing service. Lille and St. Quentin (where Captain Trotobas and Major Bieler were also in contact with Prosper for communication with London) were fortunately untouched.

45. Nantes and Angers, however, were not so lucky. In November 1942, Alexandre and Fabien had been released by the French on the occupation of the Z.N.O. by the Germans, and had made their way to Angers where Alexandre had family connexions. Here they had built up a small but efficient group which had received three or four deliveries of material. At Prosper's request Alexandre then started doing the same thing in Nantes, while Fabien continued in Angers. Good progress was being made when Alexandre was trapped in Paris at the beginning of August. Fabien, for his part, had two brushes with the Gestapo in Angers in close succession, fled to Paris and on the 23rd June, 1943, returned to London by Lysander.

46. To all intents and purposes, then, the only F. Section circuits remaining in being at the end of July 1943 in the old Occupied Zone were the Farmer and Musician groups in Lille and St. Quentin, the Tinker (Benoit) group at Troyes, and the Donkeyman (Major Frager) group.[17] A small group existed in Tours, without much importance, but with, happily, a competent radio operator who was able to continue transmitting for his own and the Lille and St. Quentin circuits.

47. The seriousness of the setback lay now, not so much in the cessation of sabotage activities against the enemy, as in the fact that each of the suppressed circuits, large or small, had a number of targets, generally against army communications, which they had fully prepared for action on D-Day. It became necessary to rebuild, and to rebuild quickly.

48. Before further describing this process, it is necessary to go back to describe three circuits which played an important part in the activities of the Paris area. These are the Bricklayer, Donkeyman and Farrier circuits.

Major Antelme's Organisation.
Operational name of organisation: The Bricklayer circuit.

Operational name of organiser: Renaud.
Name by which known in the Field: Renaud or Antoine.

49. Major Antelme's mission was an unusual one for F. Section of S.O.E., but he himself was an unusually gifted man. He left England on the 18th November, 1942, in order to make contact with certain political elements in France, and, by direct approach to the heads of the different groups with whom he made contact, to ascertain their views and requirements. This work brought him into touch with prominent politicians, including Herriot and Reynaud, and he also made important connexions with individuals of importance in the banking and business world.

50. He was received by the Tours organisation already mentioned and immediately went to Irene (Lise De Baissac) in Poitiers, through whom he met his first influential contact, M. Rambault of the Banque de France, at that time Directeur General de l'Escompte for France and clearing officer between France and Germany, Italy and Spain.

51. On the 4th January, 1943, Antelme left for Paris, where he established his Headquarters.

52. Here he was soon in communication with Prosper and David (organiser in Bordeaux), both of them at this time out of touch with London and in dire need of money. The latter need he was able to meet through the help given to him by Maitre Savy. At a later stage he was able to make financial arrangements on a large scale and thereby to help, not only Prosper and David, but also the various smaller circuits in the Occupied Zone.

53. He also organised independent circuits in Le Mans and Troyes. The Le Mans circuit was placed under the command of a locally recruited organiser, Emile Garry,[18] and given a London-sent radio operator, Madeleine Princess Inayat Khan; Troyes was put into the capable hands of Benoit (Major Cowburn), who arrived in April 1943, accompanied by a radio operator,[19] to take charge of it.

54. Major Antelme was also instrumental in putting David in touch with the Grand-Clement organisation in Bordeaux with a strength of 3.000 men.

11

55. All this, of course, was in addition to his political mission, on which he reported to Mr. Eden and Lord Selborne on his temporary return to England in March 1943.

56. Not content with this he also brought back to London two plans which might have had a profound effect on the course of an invasion of France by the Allies. The first was designed to ensure adequate supplies of French currency for the invading armies: it really comprised two plans, one of them to be worked through M. Alexandre Celier, President du Conseil d'administration of the Comptoir National d'Escompte de Paris, whereby the managers of their branches within a 100 km. wide coastal belt would secrete and deliver to the Allied armies an important stock of notes which they would keep for that purpose. As an alternative, Major Antelme had got in touch with M. Panouillot de Vesly, Inspecteur des Finances, who was also prepared to see that a large supply of bank notes remained in coastal areas in the hands of the "Tresoriers Payeurs."

57. The other plan concerned the feeding of the Invading Troops, and for this purpose Major Antelme had been in contact with M. Duthilleul, Assistant Director of "Ravitaillement" for the Sarthe Department. This man declared himself able to set up in each of thirty Departments an organisation, which would be capable of supplying the troops with meat, bread, potatoes, vegetables, preserved food and chocolate. Reports showed that these commodities were in plentiful supply in the strategic area, and it was estimated that the food situation in France would easily provide for the feeding of an invading army of 500,000 men without prejudice to the civilian population.

58. These plans were in the development stage when Major Antelme was forced by the disasters in the Prosper circuit to return to England. He returned to the Field at the end of February 1944, but was immediately arrested.

Major Frager's Organisation.
    Operational name of organisation: The Donkeyman circuit.
    Operational name of organiser: Jean-Marie.
    Name by which known in the Field: Louba, Paul or Jean-Marie.

59. In early 1942 one of our organisers in the South of France had made contact with an organisation, known as the Carte organisation. In mid-1942 an officer from this organisation came to London and in July 1942 returned to the Field accompanied by an officer from Headquarters. It was decided to give the Carte organisation the fullest support.

60. In January 1943, however, the organisation was split in two by internal strife: part of it, under Paul, its second-in-command, broke away owing to the impracticable nature of Carte's own ideas and practices. At the end of January 1943 Paul arrived in London.

61. His views being accepted, it was agreed that the "solid" (as opposed to the "mystic") part of the organisation, which he represented, should be incorporated in F. Section's activities and for administrative purposes split in three: the first and second zones, comprising South-East France from the Mediterranean to Haute-Savoie, would have two British officers in charge, while the third, which extended from Chalon-sur-Saone to Paris and across to Nancy and the Eastern Frontier of France, was to be developed by Paul (now to be known as Jean-Marie) himself. In April 1943 he returned to the Field to start work.

62. Crippled at the outset by arrests, progress at first was slow, but it was sure. In August 1943 we received a report from him that his groups were prepared to carry out derailments at 151 points on receipt of orders. In October 1943 he returned to London and reported that areas under his control included Dordogne, Jura, Lorraine, Mantes, Montauban, Normandy and the Yonne Valley. Between June and August 1943 his groups had received nineteen operations comprising 247 containers.

63. They had been helped in this by the fact that in May 1943 they had been sent a British officer[20] to act as liaison with London. It had also been possible to detach a radio operator to them; this was Lieutenant Clech, who with the dissolution of the Le Mans circuit (the organiser had returned to England) had become available. Captain Jones put in some excellent work until November 1943, when he was arrested.

64. Reference will be made later to Paul's circuit's activities in 1944.

65. Paul, although intensely patriotic and undoubtedly sincere, had methods distinctly his own. Prosper distrusted him and would have nothing to do with him. Paul in his turn was deeply suspicious of the officer in charge of the Lysander service for F. Section, and denounced him to London as a double agent. And it was mainly to produce evidence to this effect that he came to London in October. Much of this evidence was based on information which Paul had received from a German Intelligence agent Colonel Heinrich, with whom he was in contact and whom he sincerely believed to be anti-Nazi, although this was more than doubtful. (In fact, this same Colonel was instrumental in arresting Paul in August 1944.)

66. This Lysander circuit was in charge of Flying Officer Dericourt.

Flying Officer Dericourt's Organisation.
Operational name of organisation: The Farrier circuit.
Operational name of organiser: Gilbert.
Name by which known in the Field: Gilbert or Claude.

67. An experienced civil air-lines pilot, Gilbert was first interviewed by F. Section in October 1942. In January 1943 he was parachuted to the Field after training as a Lysander expert, and for more than a year provided the only such link between London and the F. Section circuits in the Field. During this time he carried out fifteen operations, all of them successful, an outstanding record. By these operations thirty-three agents were sent to the Field and a large number exfiltrated.

68. In the middle of 1943, however, suspicions were cast on the good faith of Gilbert, who was alleged by Jean-Marie to be opening his courier and passing on information to the enemy. This latter accusation was based on Jean-Marie's contact with Colonel Heinrich. It was also backed up by three other sources:

(1) Squadron Leader Yeo Thomas, who stated that a B.O.A. agent had reported that the agent in charge of operations in the Angers district had caused the arrest of two men and a woman whom he had received.
(2) A similar (though slightly different) report by a member of the Deuxieme Bureau. (3) A returned S.I.S. agent stated that Gilbert

had talked indiscreetly on his return to France, and the Gestapo had consequently sought an interview with a view to using him as an agent.

69. As a result Gilbert was recalled to the United Kingdom on the 8th February, 1944, on the pretext of consultations. Paul reiterated his accusations, but repeated interrogations of Gilbert failed to produce conclusive evidence one way or the other: neither the two men nor one woman, who were supposed to have been denounced, could be traced, nor could Gilbert be shaken.

70. As no conclusions were reached, other interested Departments considered that Gilbert should not be returned to the Field. He remained on S.O.E.'s payroll until he resigned from the R.A.F. and joined the French Air Force about August 1944.[21]

71. Operationally, therefore, the result was that after the beginning of February 1944 F. Section had no regular Lysander service to the Occupied Zone. Gilbert's assistants (one of whom had paid a visit to London) were still in the Field and prepared to operate, but no operations were actually carried out in view of the security doubts which weighed on the circuit as a whole.

72. Consideration of this period would be incomplete without making mention of the sending on the 22nd July, 1943, of Major Bodington for a month to the Paris area for the purpose of assessing the damage done by the arrests in the Prosper circuit and of taking measures to reorganise the sound elements. He was accompanied by Flight Lieutenant Agazarian as radio operator, but the latter was arrested shortly after their arrival at a contact given by Archambaud. Contact was, however, made with Cinema, from whom it was clear that the whole Prosper circuit was destroyed, with the exception of his own, the Hirson group and an O.C.M. (Organisation Civile et Militaire) group under Marc O'Neill with whom Prosper had just been put in touch by David, the F. Section organiser in Bordeaux. With the disappearance of Prosper, David took this group in hand himself, sending to Marc O'Neill one of his own radio operators, Captain Defence (Dede), who continued to work in the Paris area until approximately December 1943.

15

73. As an aftermath of all these events there followed a rather trying period in which the only bright features were the continued survival of the Donkeyman organisation and of the imperturbable Benoit at Troyes.

74. Attempts were made, as soon as the necessary personnel was available, to send new organisers to the Field to found new circuits in the most important area running from Tours to Paris and Northwards to Lille. A number of organisers were ready to go to the Field in December 1943 and January 1944, but owing to bad weather were unable to leave until February. For a number of them the Reception arrangements were to be carried out by Phono, but it transpired later that his organisation had also been penetrated and these efforts came to naught and a number of organisers were lost. By a stroke of ill-fortune Major Antelme was one of them.

75. In August 1943 David (Major de Baissac) of Bordeaux had returned to England just before the Grand-Clément collapse in Bordeaux. He was held in London, and instead of being allowed to return to Bordeaux was given a mission in Normandy. He was ready to leave again for the Field in October 1943 but the weather was so bad that he did not finally reach France till February 1944.

76. Another organiser had also reached London in October 1943, René Dumont-Guillemet.[22] As he had many contacts with the Germans he did not wish to be away from France for more than a week or two, but bad weather took a hand in his case also, and he, too, did not finally return until February 1944.

77. In the meanwhile further efforts were being made to build up circuits in the area which the Gestapo believed they had cleared of F. Section influence, and which both they and we knew to be crucial in relation to the battle to come. They were encouraged to believe that we were unaware of the extent of their penetration, and deliveries of stores were continued to circuits known to be Gestapo-operated, in order to give time for new recruits to establish themselves. And new organisers were sent to the Field to receptions arranged by an extremely efficient organiser operating in the old Unoccupied Zone,[23] and, to a large extent, with contacts provided by Baron Philippe de Vomecourt of whom mention has already been made and who now reappeared upon the scene.

78. By these various means, in the early months of 1944, new organisers began to work in the following areas:

> Captain Benoist in the region of Nantes and Rambouillet.
> Major Hudson in the region of Le Mans.
> Captain Wilkinson in the region of Orleans.
> Lieutenant Dedieu in the region of Chartres – Dreux.
> Lieutenant Henquet[24] in the region of Blois and Vendome.
> Major Dumont-Guillemet in the region of Paris and Meaux.
> Major De Baissac in the region of Normandy.
> Captain Mulsant[25] in the region of Nangis.
> Lieutenant Bassett[26] in the region of Creil.
> Major Bodington in the region of Epernay and St. Dizier.

79. De Vomecourt himself worked South of the Loire in the neighbourhood of Salbris.

80. A new organiser accompanied by a radio operator and a courier had also been sent to the Tours area, but this party was arrested soon after their arrival. This set-back apart, the new measures worked well, and with Major Frager's organisation becoming extremely active in the Yonne and Cote d'Or and Major Cowburn's successor continuing his good work in Troyes, the Battle area was by D-Day fairly completely surrounded by F. Section circuits.

81. It is obviously impossible, in the scope of a work such as this to enter into comprehensive details of all these circuits. They were all active in varying degrees in the events leading up to the liberation of the region from the Germans. Together, during 1944 they received over 6,300 containers of arms and explosives. They were all of them briefed in the same way, namely to organise attacks on well-defined German communications targets; some of them were able to go further and organise Maquis activity and guerrilla warfare where local conditions were favourable to this type of activity.

82. Of the 13 circuits finally established in what may loosely be called the Paris zone, the majority were based on points outside Paris itself. Three, however, were more particularly Parisian than the others, those of Major Frager, Major Dumont-Guillemet and Captain Robert Benoist.

Major Frager's 1944 Organisation.

83. Reference has already been made to Major Frager's presence in London in October 1943 and to the arrest during this period of Captain Jones, British liaison officer to the group, and of his radio operator, Lieutenant Clech: his courier Suzanne (Vera Leigh) was also arrested at the same time.

84. Provision was therefore made for a new radio operator[27] to be sent to his group and a Lysander-trained expert[28] was also despatched. The latter however, never made contact with the circuit and he was next heard of in Fresnes prison.

85. Frager had laid claim to organised groups in areas as far apart as Dordogne, Calvados and Meurthe et Moselle, and it had been agreed that he should limit himself to the valley of the Yonne (Yonne and Côte-d'Or) in the interests of security and practicability. In the main this agreement was loyally observed, though an exception was made for two local Normandy groups operating in the regions of Mantes and Orbec.

86. From reports received, Frager's organisation has a very fine record of activity, and although there is an ever-present danger that such reports may contain exaggerations, verification has been obtained that the main actions reported by the group did in fact take place. Frager even went so far as to secure a *constat d'huissier* of the damage done by a sabotage attack on the Cellophane works at Mantes, and this was photographed and sent to London.

87. Frager reported very considerable harassing action after D-Day, and on the 21st July he stated that he had 700 men armed in the Yonne, 300 in the Joigny area, 200 Villefranche–Châteaurenard, 120 Joigny–Toucy, 96 Auxerre, 180 Aillant–Charny–Toucy and 150 at Avallon. There was also a number of unarmed F.F.I. groups.

88. Unfortunately he continued to keep in contact with Colonel Heinrich, and an escaped P.O.W. named Thompson, who was working with Frager, reported that Heinrich arrested him in Paris on the 3rd August, 1944. He was sent to Germany and executed at Buchenwald in September. His second in command, Roger Bardet, succeeded him in the command of the Yonne and Côte d'Or.

89. In the course of the battle of Normandy, Frager's organiser for that area was over-run and sent immediately to London. This man, Jean Kieffer (known as Raoul and Michel), produce a most impressive report of harassing activity against the German Army; the writer has inspected three bridges destroyed by these groups and considers the report well-founded and that these groups did extremely good and valuable work. They were, in fact, the only groups in their district (Orbec-Lisieux) who had been really active, but, as has so often happened, they did not reap their just reward and found themselves supplanted after the liberation by the usual crowd of "Résistants de Dernière Heure." The reverse of the medal is not so pleasant. Both Bardet and Kieffer are accused of having been double-agents. This point is dealt with later.

Major Dumont-Guillemet's Organisation.

Operational name of organisation: The Spiritualist circuit.
Operational name of organiser: Mickey, Conte or Armand.
Name by which known in the Field: Armand and (in Lille) Hercule.

90. Dumont-Guillemet had been working in contact with Captain Sidney Jones, whom he had known before the war, and in October 1943 the latter sent him to England. The original intention was that he should report and return after a brief stay, but, in fact, it was not until February that he returned to France.

91. By this time Captain Jones had been arrested, but Dumont-Guillemet was confident that he could make his way by means of his own personal contacts, and in spite of the fact that his long absence must have made the Germans, with whom he had many business contacts, suspicious of him.

92. So on the 6th February, 1944, he was dropped blind, near his own estate in Indre et Loire, accompanied by a radio operator.[29]

93. His list of objectives was an unusual one. First in priority was the capture of one of the leading German technicians engaged in the construction of rocket sites and apparatus on the French coast. Secondly, he had persuaded us that under his leadership an attack on Fresnes prison was practical politics provided air cover was available. His third target was the Bosche Lavelette works. Finally (and in the end the most

important of the four) he was to be responsible for renewing contact with the Farmer circuit in the Lille region.

94. Each of these in the conditions prevailing was a task of the greatest difficulty, and more particularly so in view of the shortness of time available and the fact that the circuit had to be constructed *ab initio*. But the contact with Lille was established, and the kidnapping of the Rocket technician was on a fair way to success, when the Germans at the last moment removed their man into a highly-fortified chateau where it was impossible to follow him.

95. At this period the delivery of material to areas near Paris and to the North and East of it was becoming increasingly difficult, and this was always a limiting factor. So much so that it was found that the only way to get stores to Lille was to run them from the Paris area by lorry.

96. This contact with Lille, which was maintained unimpaired right to the end, was probably the most important single achievement of the circuit. The Lille group was strong, determined and efficient, but would have disintegrated without the contact, advice, instructions and finance which Dumont-Guillemet represented for them. Tangible results of this contact were represented by a mass of well-directed sabotage against German communications and a mass of information, particularly of rocket emplacements, which came flowing in from Lille: this, combined with the information which Dumont-Guillemet's own contacts provided, earned him a special message of congratulation from S.H.A.E.F.

97. In the Paris region he had 6,500 men, 1,500 of whom he hoped to arm, while maintaining contact with the rest for later action. He permitted no politics in his group, and his security seems to have been excellent, there being only one arrest reported. This was no doubt very largely due to his skill in maintaining liaison with the Gestapo and in having advance information of their activities.

98. The group included a further 200 men, organised into sabotage groups, which were extremely active before the liberation. It also comprised 250 gendarmes in the Paris suburbs whose main rôle was the prevention of the destruction of installations of use to the Allies.

Further measures of the same type were concerted through the Mayors of certain Paris Arrondissements with whom he was in contact.

99. At the end of August Dumont-Guillemet left Paris for the purpose of organising the reception of Paratroops in the region of Meaux. His intention was to install 500 of his men in complete secrecy in the countryside, in order to be ready for action when the time came. On the 27th August they were to make their way out of Paris as unobtrusively as possible and with definite orders not to fire a shot. These orders were not carried out, and his men arrived at Forfry after having been in constant action for over three hours. They had forty German prisoners with them. Soon after, seven German tanks appeared and inflicted very heavy casualties on Dumont-Guillemet's men before they could be induced to retreat. After the battle, the Germans behaved with unspeakable brutality to the wounded, burning 25 of them alive (including two nurses).

100. Dumont-Guillemet himself was lucky to escape with his life, having been forced to hide in a river bed for over six hours in close proximity to a German tank, and subject during the whole of the time to the attacks of leeches, with which the water was infested.

101. Immediately upon the Liberation Dumont-Guillemet contacted the American authorities, and was able to provide them with extremely valuable information on Gestapo personalities and German plans for counter-Allied espionage activities.

102. He has been awarded the D.S.O., the Legion d'Honneur and Croix de Guerre.

103. The third of the "Parisian" groups is that of Captain Robert Benoist.

104. Captain Benoist before the war was a racing motorist of international reputation. A friend of Grover-Williams, he had been recruited by him and became his right-hand man. At the time of the break-up of the circuit he had himself been arrested by the Gestapo, but had escaped from the Gestapo car by throwing one at his captors out of it at a sharp bend and by leaping out on top of him. He made good his escape and was brought back to London by Lysander in August 1943.

105. It may perhaps have been an error to send so well-known and recognisable a man as Robert Benoist back to the Field after what had happened, but he himself was so insistent and so confident that he could get away with it that in October 1943 he returned to France.

106. His mission (Paris obviously being too hot for him) was to build up an organisation in the Nantes area and in particular to attack the H.T. Pylons crossing the Loire at Ile Heron. He was to use for this purpose the wireless operator Hercule (Dubois), who was believed to be still working in the Tours area. Unhappily, Hercule had been arrested shortly before Benoist arrived.

107. He was able, however, to prospect the ground, and on his return to London in February 1944 to report, declared himself still able to carry out his mission. He was given a radio operator, Mlle. Denise Bloch, and left again for the Field in March.

108. By the end of May he reported all his Nantes objectives ready. He also reported that he was in touch with a group of 2,000 F.F.I. near Rambouillet, for whom he asked for arms and instructions. These were sent, and his groups carried out several actions in the insurrection period. He also reported a group of 10,000 men in the Compiegne area as being under his orders, but the grounds he proposed for the receipt of stores for them were all in an area to which the R.A.F. could not fly.

109. But early in July there was a wave of arrests among his groups. First, the Gestapo surrounded the Group Headquarters in the country near Dourdan, where they arrested three persons, including the radio operator. The fourth, another racing motorist named Wimille, escaped. Almost immediately afterwards Benoist himself was arrested in Paris. He was executed in September 1944 at Buchenwald.

110. There is no doubt that he had been betrayed, and suspicions of this betrayal have lain against his brother, Maurice Benoist. The writer does not know if these suspicions still persist, for on the 29th May, 1945, an official party representing British Headquarters at a memorial service to Robert Benoist were somewhat embarrassed to find Maurice Benoist among the chief mourners.

111. A brief summary is attached of the main features of the other circuits of the Paris region and at Appendix A of the more noteworthy actions they undertook.

112-113. There are two additional matters to which some reference must be made, since they are still the cause of a certain amount of heart-burning on the part of a number of completely honest people in Paris an elsewhere. It will be remembered that Major Frager vehemently accused Flying Officer Dericourt of working with the Germans, that, as a result of these accusations, Dericourt was recalled to the United Kingdom, that investigations failed either to prove or disprove the allegations, but that, as a measure of prudence, he was kept in England. The point requires bearing in mind that his case is not completely closed even now, since his name has occurred in at least one report made by a captured Gestapo agent. There have been recent rumours that, as a result, the French were about to reopen the case. Unfortunately, the writer of these notes is not in a position to confirm or deny this report, and it is suggested that reference should be made to the Embassy in the event of any questions arising in connection with Flying Officer Dericourt's circuit.

114. The second question is closely allied to the first, since Major Frager's circuit is involved, and since here also a question of working with the Germans is concerned. Both Frager and Dericourt openly stated that they were in contact with the Germans – as indeed most intelligent organisers were to a greater or less degree – but it is only in Dericourt's case that suspicion has arisen that he had been working *for* the Germans.[30] But what is incontestable so far as Major Frager's circuit is concerned is that both his second in command Bardet (known as Roger) and Kieffer (known as Raoul or Michel, who headed his Normandy groups) have been arrested by the French as double-agents. Their cases have been most obscure, and they have both been arrested and released more than once. But the evidence seems to point to their having worked with the Germans as early as 1942. Bardet's case is the blacker of the two and it may yet be established that he was responsible for the arrest of a British officer and his radio-operator in Toulouse, as well as for that of Captain Jones and Lieutenant Clech, which he has already admitted. It is also possible that the suspicions

against Dericourt in Major Frager's mind were inspired at first hand by Bardet and at second hand by the Gestapo to divert attention from their own activities. Prosper's remark that anyone in contact with Frager sooner or later found himself in trouble may not have been wide of the mark, although not for the precise reason which Prosper had in mind.

115. At present, however, these cases are *sub judice* and no definite conclusions can be drawn.

116. Soon after the liberation of Paris representatives of London Headquarters set up an office in Paris, first at the Hotel Cecil (rue St. Didier) and subsequently at 37 Boulevard des Capucines. This office finally closed on the 10th December, 1945, although an officer from London was still working in Paris as late as mid-March 1946 on the settlement of amounts due to French nationals in repayment of sums advanced by them to British circuits during the occupation.

117. The bulk of the work of this office lay in seeing that the French members of the British circuits were properly accredited for administration purposes to the D.G.E.R., since, for example, the responsibility for Pensions for these people is a French one. This has proved a long and tedious process, partly owing to the difficulty of obtaining the necessary particulars of all the French men and women who had really worked with the British circuits, and partly owing to administrative deficiency within the D.G.E.R. (the number of files that they have "lost" has been phenomenal).

118. Furthermore, although officially the British circuits were incorporated for all purposes in the F.F.I. under the command of General Koenig, this has not sufficed really to allay the anti-British bias which permeated the D.G.E.R. as an inheritance from the B.C.R.A.; and this was only too apt to express itself in a "you worked for the British, then let them take care of you" attitude in their dealings with F. Section circuit members.

119. It was this attitude which had a considerable influence in the formation, in self-defence, of "Libre Resistance," the Amicale of members of the Buckmaster circuits. This body exists for the benefit of

all those who worked with the British circuits and now has a large membership. It acts, now that the Boulevard des Capucines office is closed, as the semi-official liaison with the D.G.E.R.

120. Officially it has no politics, but in fact it is very definitely anti-Communist. One of the powers behind the throne is Pierre de Vomecourt (his brother Philippe may also be expected to exert an appreciable influence, but he is at the moment very busy with U.N.R.R.A.). For a long time Dumont-Guillemet stayed aloof, but some months ago he was strongly urged to accept the Presidency. This he did not precisely do, but the present holder is M. Picard, a great friend of his and a member of his circuit during the Resistance period. Of the Vice-Presidents, Pierre Seailles was in command of the Farmer circuit in Lille in its later stages; the Secretary, Marcel Jaurent-Singer, did very good work in the neighbourhood of Chalon-sur-Saône before and during the Liberation.

121. (*N.B.* – M. Marcel Durand now holds no official position in "Libre Resistance." He was until recently secretary and in this capacity has been responsible for a very large volume of work successfully completed. He is still carrying on this work, although without any official function.)

THE LE MANS AREA

122. Captain (later Major) C.S. Hudson was first dropped into France in September 1942 to organise a circuit in the Clermont-Ferrand area. Arrested in October, he spent over a year in French prisons until in January 1944 a mass escape was organised from the prison at Eysses, and Captain Hudson, Baron Philippe de Vomecourt and 52 others gained their freedom.

123. In April 1944 Captain Hudson dropped again to the Field accompanied by a radio operator.[31] Shortly afterwards he was joined by two more officers and a courier.[32]

124. His mission was to build up a circuit in the Sarthe from contacts which de Vomecourt was to provide for him. Initial lack of contact prevented a start being made until the end of the month.

25

125. Preparations went steadily ahead, but were still incomplete by D-Day. On D-Day Captain Hudson took what he himself describes as a wrong decision, and set up a large Maquis in the Foret de Charnie, another under Alcide in the Foret de Berce and a third near Coulans.

126. On the 15th June the Charnie Maquis was attacked and dispersed. All the radio material was lost, also 3 cars, 1 million francs, bicycles, arms and materials.

127. From this moment they were without communications with London.

128. Deciding that the Maquis principle was impossible, a system of small groups was now set up:

A. An extremely active group towards Chateau du Loir under Alcide.
B. A group under Claude Husault just S.E. of Le Mans, busy on telephone cables, ambushes and railway sabotage.
C. A group under Gaston which kept cutting the Le Mans–Alencon, Le Mans–Mamers and Fresnay–Mamers cables, the latter having been reported as most important.
D. West of Le Mans: Specially occupied with the cable to Laval and Rennes and the telephone line via Loue. Both of these were cut at the time of the American offensive towards Rennes.
E. A group in Mayenne under André Drouot, undertaking the usual guerrilla activities.
F. A new group in formation round Chateau du Loir.

129. All railway lines were frequently cut, one particularly successful operation taking place on the Le Mans–La Suze line, where two ammunition trains were held up.

130. Telephones were the main objective, and Le Mans was practically isolated. The German military telephone exchange was blown up and completely destroyed just as it was being completed.

131. Road sabotage was greatest in Alcide's area. His report mentions:

11 Overhead telephone lines put out of action.
3 Underground cables (Le Mans to Paris, Orleans, Angers).
4 Railway lines at 16 different points.

132. Ambushes took place on 11 roads; total ambushes numbered 110. 55 enemy vehicles were destroyed and one German General killed. In all 300 Germans were killed and 300 wounded. 8,000 Germans were led into American hands.

133. When Hudson established contact with the American Armies he organised 12 Intelligence Missions, using part of Alcide's groups.

134. The Special Force Detachment report on Hudson states: "He has been working with the 5th Armoured Division, giving them the disposal of German units, also the movement of units. G-2 is getting his information daily, which is vital."

135. Altogether an extremely competent job, carried out under great difficulties.

136. Major Hudson was awarded the D.S.O.

THE ORLEANS AREA

Captain G.A. Wilkinson's Organisation.
  Operational name of organisation: The Historian Circuit.
  Operational name of organiser: Etienne.
  Name by which known in the Field: Etienne and Georges.

137. Captain Wilkinson, elder brother of E.M. Wilkinson arrested in August 1943, was parachuted to the Field on the 5th August, 1944, as organiser to a circuit in the Orleans area. The initial contacts were to be given to him by Philippe de Vomecourt.

138. This was an important area, in which since the break-up of the Prosper circuit German repressive measures had effectively checked attempts to build up a Resistance movement. Etienne, however, was successful in organising the reception of arms on a large scale and in establishing groups of saboteurs and guerrillas for action on D-Day.

139. He was also successful in choosing a really excellent second in command.[33] This man was already a member of a French organisation, but, in despair at their failure to supply him with arms, threw in his lot with Etienne and proved a loyal and whole-hearted helper, and, after Etienne's arrest on the 28th June, an extremely efficient and capable commander of the circuit.[34]

140. As in all cases where the organiser did not come back from Germany, news of the Circuit's activity is sparse. But the record in Appendix A of what it did carry out between D-Day and the end of July is testimony to its excellence. In addition to the actions there noted, it provided reception arrangements for a party of S.A.S. who were parachuted in the area, and it was planning the liberation of the prisoners in Orleans Gaol.

141. The circuit's record of operations, too, is impressive.

1944	Operations	Containers	Packages
May	2	23	15
June	17	397	134
July	24	520	178

142. Further information, particularly as to the Maquis activities of the circuit, can be obtained from Pierre Charie.

143. The wireless operator to the group was Miss L.V. Rolfe (Nadine), who was arrested early in August, after having worked extremely well, first with Etienne and then with Charie.

144. Another officer sent from London was an American, Lieutenant Studler.

THE CHARTRES-DREUX AREA

Lieutenant G. Dedieu's Organisation.
    Operational name of Organisation: The Permit Circuit.
    Operational name of Organiser: Jerome.
    Name by which known in the Field: Jerome and Gerard.

145. Lieutenant Dedieu was first recruited in February 1942 by an

organiser working in the neighbourhood of Loches. Among other F. Section organisers, he came into contact with Philippe de Vomecourt. He worked between Lyon and St. Etienne and between Limoges and Vichy.

146. Arrested on the 31st October, 1942, he was sentenced to four year's imprisonment, but escaped with de Vomecourt and others from the prison at Eysses and reached England on the 9th March, 1944.

147. On the 7th June he returned to the Field with a radio operator Adele (Madame Jullian) and was received by de Vomecourt. His mission was to build up a circuit in and around Amiens, but the contacts which he had been given failed to materialise. He therefore returned to make contact with de Vomecourt again, a matter of some difficulty as in the meanwhile the latter's Maquis had been attacked, and he had changed his ground. Jerome had also tried to get in touch with other groups in Paris, but without result.

148. When contact was finally made with de Vomecourt, they agreed, and London approved, that he should take over from him Eure et Loir, Eastern Orne and Northern Loir et Cher.

149. Here he contacted the D.M.R.[35] (Sinclair) and they agreed a programme of stores deliveries which brought them 372 containers of arms and explosives between the 9th July and the 11th August.

150. Maquis groups were formed as follows:

Nogent le Rotrou, 90-150 men.
Dreux, 3 Maquis of 200-300 men in all.
Cloyes.
Beaumont les Autels, 300 men.

151. Other groups were formed in Chartres, Chateauneuve en Thunelas, Clevilliers, Denonville, Boisville le St. Pere, St. Olat, Bonneval-Chateaudun, Longuy, Jainville.

152. These groups contributed to an impressive record of sabotage and military operations, including the taking of Nogent le Rotrou, Dreux, Chateaudun and Bonneval, and the occupation of Chartres. Their

outstanding sabotage achievement was the blowing up of the Railway viaduct at Cherisy, after twenty bombardments by the R.A.F. had failed to destroy it. This operation earned for the group the congratulations of S.H.A.E.F.

153. Jerome was only in his area a month and a half. He reported that more progress might have been made if Sinclair had possessed more character and had chosen his subordinates better; also if he himself had been able to come earlier to an agreement with the local F.T.P. chief.

154. Jerome's mission, however, was extremely successful, and a very good illustration of the value, to local groups already established, of the help in technical matters and in communications which the British organisation was capable of providing.

155. Jerome's team, in addition to Adele, consisted of two assistants and instructors, Lieutenant R.G. Bruhl (Beaumetre), known as Barnabe, and Lieutenant R.C. Shearn, known as Septime. 157. Jerome was most unluckily killed in an air accident on the 1st Barnabe's greatest exploit was his attack in person on the Bretoncelles bridge, dressed in uniform and accompanied by his men in an S.S. truck.

156. Lieutenant Shearn was killed on a later mission in the Far East.

157. Jerome was most unluckily killed in an air accident on the 1st February, 1945: he was Mentioned in Despatches.

LOIR ET CHER

158. In the final stages this Département, which was of considerable importance from the point of view of enemy communications, was covered, as far as the British were concerned, by two circuits under two very capable leaders, that of Robert (Lieutenant Henquet, an American officer), North of the Loire, and that of Antoine, Baron Philippe de Vomecourt, South of the River.

159. This convenient arrangement was not, however, reached without a certain amount of friction.

160. Antoine (as is recorded elsewhere) had started his resistance career in conjunction with the British organisation in May 1941 and, first under the *nom de guerre* of Lionel and later that of Gauthier, had been very active until his arrest in November 1942. After over a year in prison, he escaped in January 1944 and came to England. In April 1944, after a brief refresher course in England, he returned to the Field by Lysander.

161. His mission was a multiple one. Like his brother before him, he had many contacts throughout France and he declared himself able to establish two other organisers, Albin in Sarthe and Etienne in Loiret, and to build up an organisation of his own in Loir et Cher with Headquarters at Salbris.

162. In any circumstances this was a tremendous task for any man, and in the particular circumstances of time and locality in which it was set, almost superhuman. But Antoine is a man of boundless enthusiasm and boundless energy and he duly installed Albin and Etienne and, also, for good measure, Jerome when the latter got "lost" and was put to work by Antoine in Eure et Loir. Antoine also reported, not long after his arrival, that he had additional groups available in Seine et Marne, Oise, Eure and Maine et Loire and a maquis group in Indre. These were to be handed over to other organisers.

163. London, knowing its Antoine, had laid very special emphasis on the necessity for all these circuits to work absolutely separately. There was to be no centralisation of command under Antoine's direction, a danger which was implicit in his strength of character and in the record of his previous organisation in Southern France. This agreement was on the whole loyally observed, but Antoine's acquiescence was severely tried when, a short time after his arrival in the Field, London despatched Robert to assume the direction of so much of Loir et Cher as lay North of the Loire, and the fat was definitely in the fire when some of Robert's groups began receiving stores operations just South of the river.

164. There were some very stormy interviews and London had to be heavily paternal before an armistice was declared and the Northern and Southern halves of the Département went their separate Ways.

Lieutenant Henquet's Organisation.
Operational name of organisation: The Hermit circuit.
Operational name of organiser: Robert.
Name by which known in the Field: Robert.

165. As an American officer, Robert's file is not available, but some of the activities of his circuit are reported in Appendix A. A pointer to Robert's great efficiency as an organiser is also given by the record of stores operations which the circuit carried out:

1944	Operations	Containers	Packages
June	9	248	99
July	14	519	196
August	2	72	47

Baron Philippe de Vomecourt's Organisation.
Operational name of organisation: The Ventriloquist circuit.
Operational name of organiser: Antoine.
Name by which known in the Field: Antoine and Saint Pol.

166. Landed by Lysander on Easter morning, 17th April, 1944, near Chateauroux, an operation carried out by Olive of Hector's organisation, Antoine and his radio operator, Muriel Byck, went, by way of Madame Dauprat-Sevenet's house near Loches, to Salbris.
Here he quickly started getting contacts and grounds and less than a month after his arrival had received arms and ammunition on five or six different grounds.

167. The stores operations carried out by the group were:

1944	Operations	Containers	Packages
May	12	125	59
June	6	90	32
July	26	525	201
August	14	327	128
September	7	266	116

168. This, in addition to the finding of contacts for Albin, Etienne and Jerome, was extremely good going.

169. Antoine was able to organise small groups all over Southern Loir et Cher with some success and about the end of May his London-sent assistant, Captain Makowski (Dimitri or Maurice), prepared a large Maquis at Soumes. Capitaine Lastrie (a French officer known as Alex) became chief saboteur and explosives instructor. In addition Vauguay (known as Colomb) was put in charge of all Resistance in Cher and was provided by Antoine with a radio of his own.

170. By D-Day the circuit had received some fifty plane-loads of materials and had been responsible for the reception of eight officers parachuted from London.

171. When the D-Day messages came through, Antoine and his men were able within an hour to blow up all communications in their sector in Loir et Cher and to send ammunition and explosives into Cher to blow up two railways crossing that district.

172. From D-Day to the Liberation no trains were able to travel normally on any of the railway lines through Loir et Cher and Cher. One munitions train took eight days to cover eighty kilometres, the Germans repairing the line as they went on. This same train was attacked three times by Antoine's men. Similar conditions prevailed throughout the zone.

173. Communications with London were sometimes difficult. Muriel Byck, who had worked well, died from a stroke as the result of a heavy bombing attack on Salbris. Three days later she was replaced by Lieutenant Counas, but he proved an unsatisfactory operator. Luckily a third operator became available and two local volunteers were trained for the work.

174. In Loir et Cher the group carried out some twenty to thirty major ambushes. Their losses amounted to approximately twenty men, including, unfortunately, Dimitri, who was wounded, tortured and killed. His death was to some extent avenged by his own Soumes Maquis which was able to ambush a German column and kill or wound some 150 Germans for the loss of five men killed fighting and four others tortured and shot afterwards.

175. Two tanks were blown up on the road between Romorantin and Vierton.

176. In Cher the groups were smaller but very efficient and under Colomb's immediate leadership they held or blew up all the Loire bridges from Briare to Nevers. (There is a slight inaccuracy here. One of these bridges, at St. Thibault near Cosne, was destroyed at General Patton's orders, by the local circuit under the leadership of an F. Section officer, Captain Le Prévost (Licencié).) Antoine pays special tribute to Alex, whom he describes as the finest and most courageous man he had the pleasure of meeting. He personally blew up 13 bridges and burnt 34 German planes, put out of action one 60-ton crane and took part in five or six major engagements.

177. One Maquis was attacked in force by the Germans, but was able to draw with only two casualties.

178. Among many instances of personal courage, Antoine cites the exploit of a lady, known as Zizi, and his own A.D.C., who took a lorry through the German lines into the Maquis, loaded it up with ammunition and explosives and brought it back through the German lines to the place where it was required.

179. Antoine concludes his report with the relation of a personal experience which shows the high esteem which the British officers working with French Resistance had earned for themselves. Antoine, with becoming modesty, fails to add that his route through this vineyard lay uphill and that owing to the nature of vineyards there was not the slightest chance of his running in anything but a straight line until he reached the top. He fails also to add that he himself is by no means a young man and that his own survival must be accounted in the nature of a miracle: "I was shot at and had to run through a vineyard under heavy fire. I passed near a farmer, who called out, 'Vas-y, petit.' He got a bullet through his neck, while I escaped without a scratch. He was an elderly man and when he was carried back to his wife, she said, 'Il vaut mieux que ce soit lui que l'officer anglais.' That sentence shows what 80 per cent. of the French people thought of our work. I am pleased to say that the man recovered and that I was able to thank him personally in the name of our organisation."

CALVADOS AND ORNE

180. After the break-up of the Prosper organisation in June 1943 and the events which followed it, the British had no action group in Normandy,

and although S.O.E. had not been officially advised of the location of the impending invasion, it was obvious that in any case Normandy would be an extremely important area.

181. August 1943 saw the return to England of Major Claude De Baissac and one of his chief lieutenants J. Dandicolle from the Bordeaux area, where De Baissac had built up a large organisation, which a month later almost ceased to exist owing to the Grand-Clement treachery.

182. With some difficulty he was persuaded not to go back to mop up the remains, but instead to devote himself to the organisation of a large and important area, comprising the Departments Manche, Calvados, Orne, Eure et Loir and those parts of Eure and Seine et Oise lying to the North of the Seine.

Major De Baissac's Normandy Organisation.
Operational name of Organisation: The Scientist Circuit.
Operational name of Organiser: Denis.
Name by which known in the Field: Denis and Michel.

183. Although De Baissac (Denis) and Dandicolle (Rene) were ready to return to France in October 1943, they were prevented from doing so by bad weather, and it was not until the end of January 1944 that Rene was dropped to a Reception Committee organised by Captain Peuleve (Jean) in Correze. From there he was to make his way North to prepare the initial contacts for his chief.

184. In mid-February Denis followed him, accompanied by his radio operator Vladimir[36]. Their landing point was even further afield, near Auch in the extreme South West, an illustration of the difficulties at this time of the infiltration of agents into the old occupied zone.

185. Rene had already made the first contacts, and on them the construction of the circuit began. Denis worked with characteristic energy and – be it said – with characteristic obstinacy, which led him to start his organisational efforts in coastal districts, where he had been given no targets and where the R.A.F. could not deliver stores. In his briefing all his targets had been set well back from the coast, as it was evident that no resistance organisation could long survive in the battle area itself.

186. He very wisely decided, as the weather had made him four months late on schedule, to concentrate on the organising and arming of the maximum number of small groups throughout his sector. In spite of the R.A.F.'s inability to deliver in coastal areas, in the Paris area and in the Seine valley, his group organised 30 receptions between the 27th April and the 5th August in which they received 777 containers and over 300 packages.

187. In one aspect of his work Denis must be counted unlucky. Like Prosper before him and Guerin in Seine et Marne, he was keenly aware of the services which a well-organised clandestine circuit could provide for incoming parachute troops. In common with other organisers part of his instructions were to reconnoitre large grounds, which could be secured and held for 48 hours while the incoming airborne troops established themselves. In spite of close guarding by the Germans in this area, Rene on the 30th June reported his organisation as complete and ready to receive paratroops on his 5 controllable grounds.

188. Unfortunately this service was never used, and much effort was in consequence wasted.

189. In April 1944 Lise de Baissac, known in her previous mission in Poitiers as Irene and now as Marguerite, arrived in the Field by Lysander. The original intention was that she should go as courier to Major Brooks, an organiser working on a line Lyon, Montauban, Toulouse, but she was temperamentally unsuited for the Trade Union (C.G.T.) atmosphere of his circuit. She obtained permission to join Denis in Normandy and did so in May. She proved of immense assistance to him, handling delicate contacts, of which there were many, in an extremely capable and diplomatic manner.

190. With increasing difficulties of communication Denis decided to cut his circuit into two, giving Rene direction of Calvados and Manche and occupying himself specially with Orne and Eure et Loir.

191. For Denis conditions were especially difficult, as in addition to ordinary communication troubles, he was well-known to the Gestapo and to a number of double-agents. His organisation, however, was ready for D-Day and went into action. To his dismay he found that his

were the only groups which in fact did so. This isolation would have made it easy for the enemy to have liquidated them, and Denis decided, therefore, to come right out into the open in order to attract other groups to him. This dangerous course proved successful, and contact was made with a number of groups whom he helped with arms and material, notably a powerful F.T.P. group in Rennes under Commandant Loulou (real name Tangui).

192. Of this group Denis wrote: "I was pleasantly surprised to find that the F.T.P.F. were recruited among very young men of all social classes, with a great many students; that politics were never mentioned and that they had only one motto: 'Kill the Boche'."

193. As might be expected (he is a man of very decided views) there were many political difficulties. The following is taken from a report made on his return to London of his contacts with various F.F.I. leaders:

194. "Source worked for a month with M. Laboureur and also contacted Michelin (who is in touch with United Kingdom) and General Allard. The latter had apparently been appointed by the F.F.I. as 'Général responsable pour la Mayenne.' Source had been giving money and arms to Laboureur when, one day, the latter said to him: 'I will put you in contact with my chief,' to which Source replied that he considered himself to be the chief. Laboureur said: 'I am part of the état major of the F.F.I.,' whereupon Source congratulated him. A few days later, when Source was out of the district, Laboureur made a tour of inspection of Source's groups, introducing himself as 'Colonel Laboureur, responsable pour la Mayenne,' and instructing groups not to follow Source's orders, not even to listen to him, as he was British and had nothing to do with the F.F.I. Two days later, Source met Laboureur and General Allard and told them, in no uncertain terms, that he did not approve of Laboureur's ungentlemanly action in inspecting his groups in his absence; and, secondly, Source pointed out that he was a member of the F.F.I., having been appointed by General Koenig in person to the position he held. General Allard replied that that was impossible, as he was in charge of the area and was receiving his orders from Paris. He knew Laboureur and Allard were good men and willing to fight and the obvious thing seemed that they should throw in their lot together. It was arranged that General Allard should send his personal lieutenant

to Source, so that they could arrange the work together. In the meantime, Source wired London for instructions and was informed, 'General Allard has no right to say you are not part of the F.F.I. which you are, and Orbit is the personal delegate of General Koenig. If you have any trouble, we count on you and Orbit to settle it.' Allard's assistant for Calvados and the Orne, Captain Marsouin, came to Source, but the latter said that he had received instructions from London to the effect that he (Source) was a member of F.F.I. and that the only person in that area whose orders he was to follow was Orbit, personal delegate of General Koenig. They therefore could not work together, and decided to part."

195. One result of all this was that Denis was *persona non grata* with Gaullist circles both in London and Paris, and this dislike was pushed to such a length, that when two Jedburgh teams were being sent by the French from London to work in Rennes region, they were despatched to a Gaullist circuit 75 miles away from the place where they were to work, and found that the people who received them had instructions not to let them contact Denis, notwithstanding that he was already receiving material, and was in contact with Loulou, in precisely the area in which their activities were to lie.

196. Against such a background Denis's was a great achievement. In view of the character of his organisation his groups did not take part in any one big action, but they were extremely active in that type of small-scale activity, which, if repeated often enough, hamstrings an army equally effectively. Latterly he retired into Mayenne, where with a central base centred on the group of villages round St. Mars du Desert and St. Aubin du Desert mobile groups were supplied and enabled to operate over a very wide area.

197. Denis estimated that more than 500 vehicles had been put out of action by his groups. Against railways he was unfortunate in that most of his own targets coincided with localities bombarded and put out of action by the R.A.F. The combined effect of bombing and sabotage kept all the Railways N. of Laval into Manche out of action from D-Day onward. As to guerrilla activity this was incessant.

198. Denis's circuit is notable also for two other things:

1. A very valuable series of messages with items of tactical intelligence (bombing targets. H.Q., etc.) which came back from his area, including an appreciable number of targets from just behind the German lines. These came from Rene, who had installed himself with Vladimir at St. Clair in the Thury Harcourt area. Rene continued sending back these extremely useful messages until on the 7th July he and his party were surprised by the Germans, and after a struggle in which five Germans, including three officers, were killed, Vladimir was killed and Rene taken prisoner.

2. The help that he was able to give to others, through the excellence of his own organisation. (*a*) Denis personally received a uniformed party of S.A.S. under Major Blackman, and made all arrangements for guides and helpers and placed his intelligence service at their disposal. (*b*) When the Jedburgh teams above mentioned did finally get in contact with him, he put them in touch with Loulou and they were at last able to go to their place of work. (*c*) He personally received Captain J.B. Hayes (Eric) parachuted for a special mission in the Avranches–St. Hilaire du Harcouet area, and provided him with the initial contacts through whom his mission was successfully accomplished. This mission was the famous Helmsman mission, which gave its name to all subsequent missions of a similar kind. An account will be found at Paras. 202-205. This mission without any doubt had an important effect on the St. Lo breakthrough and the Battle of Brittany.

199. Possibly the best assessment of Major De Baissac's mission is that made by Major Blackman, commander of the S.A.S. party already mentioned. He writes: "By his energy and untiring perseverance, together with his exceptional planning and organising ability, he undoubtedly had a large share in facilitating the American advance through the province of Mayenne. He shouldered grave responsibilities, and had many difficult decisions to make. To my certain knowledge he risked his life three times, and accounted for a considerable number of the enemy. He was at all times fearless, and treated his own personal safety with utter contempt."

200. This officer quoted as examples of De Baissac's great courage the following instances:

1. "On one night in mid-July Major De Baissac was receiving a supply dropping from England. The stores being dropped were of vital importance to the maquis in the area, and to my section of the 1st S.A.S. Regt. At the same time that the stores were dropped the Germans arrived on the scene. Major De Baissac had merely a handful of men with which to engage the strong enemy patrol. Nevertheless he put his personal safety and chances of escape last and characteristically welcomed the opportunity of engaging the enemy, although heavily out-numbered and with inferior weapons. There followed an action of approximately twenty minutes in which Major De Baissac set an example of the highest gallantry. He was everywhere where the situation was most dangerous and critical. By his enthusiasm, dash and drive he either killed or wounded the majority of the German patrol, and finally forced it to withdraw. The importance of this action was that not only had the enemy been killed, but the precious stores saved with which to continue further operations.

2. "On one occasion the Germans came to his house and used the round floor while he himself was in the first floor using it as an H.Q. and a small store containing wireless sets and arms. One small mistake by Major De Baissac would have resulted in catastrophe not only to his own party but to the whole maquis organisation in the area. Before the Germans left this house Major De Baissac was a richer man in enemy information and enemy weapons. Even driven back to his own H.Q. as had happened on this occasion, he had continued to act offensively against the enemy."

201. He added that these incidents were no mere isolated cases, but specimens of De Baissac's day by day activities.

THE HELMSMAN MISSION

202. The origins of the Helmsman Mission are to be found in the visit of an officer from London H.Q. to the American Armies in the Field. They were for the moment stationary before St. Lo, and their plans for a break-through were severely hampered by an almost complete lack of ground information on the area to a depth up to 50 miles behind the enemy's front line. They asked if S.F.H.Q. could not provide someone

who could be dropped in the appropriate area, and who would brief a number of observant local inhabitants to make their way by different routes towards the American lines, observing all they saw and reporting on enemy dispositions on arrival.

203. The officer chosen for this mission was Captain J.B. Hayes, who had already carried out two missions in the Field. He accepted the mission at very short notice and on 10th July was dropped not far from Arromanches.

204. On arrival in the field for his third mission he was received by Denis, and was immediately introduced to Emile and Rene Bergon. i/c resistance for S. Manche. He was also given as courier and lieutenant Jules Lemanileve. He proceeded to Fougerolles, where he contacted the local leader Julien Derenne, who took him to a Maquis south of S. Hilaire du Harcouet. He obtained four recruits here, and briefed them to leave on the 13th July, 1944. He renewed contact with Bergen and Lemanileve, and sent two more volunteers off on the 14th July at La Haye Pesnel, three more were briefed for the 15th July. Next, he proceeded from his German occupied farm to Ducy and sent off five more men for the 16th, 17th and 19th July. Bergon supplied him with a second courier, Andree Blandin, who produced ten volunteers from Bergon, six of whom were sent off the 18th July, three more were produced and went off the 19th July, two more were sent off the 20th July. Four of the original men returned owing to various difficulties of passing the lines, and Eric therefore decided to have a line of static observers to be overrun by the Allied forces, and then briefed six more men on the 20th July. Thirty agents had now been briefed, and he closed that part of the mission and proceeded to Avranches, but the local group was passive. Bergon, however, produced four more volunteers, who were to act as static observers, two near Coutances and two near St. Malo de la Lande. On the 26th July he went to Torigny, but found the group had been penetrated, and cut contact. On the 28th July he briefed two men from Granville to operate in the Lengronnes area. On the 31st July the Americans seemed to be near and Bergon produced seven more contacts; two were briefed for Champrepus, one Villiers, two St. Saveur de Calvados, two Torigny. He now terminated recruiting, having despatched thirty-one agents and installed sixteen static observers. Contact was made with the Americans and Eric placed himself at their

disposal. Orders came from London for a second mission in the Mayenne to organise road blocks, and to send a man to carry out a Helmsman mission near Argenton – Alencon. Lemanileve was despatched on this mission, as the Americans wanted Eric, and after giving all his information he was sent back to the United Kingdom, the advance being too rapid to re-infiltrate him.

205. Evidence of the value which the Armies attached to the successful carrying out of Eric's mission is found in the fact that the name Helmsman became the name by which all subsequent missions of this type were known, of which there was a considerable number. Organisers on the ground in addition were all asked to leave behind, in the areas about to be overrun by the Allied advance, observers on the lines of the static observers left in place by Eric.

SEINE ET MARNE

206. In November 1943 there came to London from Troyes Monsieur P. Mulsant, who for some months previously had acted as right hand man in that town to Major Cowburn. He had stayed on long enough to hand over the Troyes circuit as a going concern to Major Cowburn's successor, and had then crossed over to England; not before time, since he was pretty thoroughly "blown" in his own area, partly through the indiscretions of the Gaullist organisations there (and particularly of their leader Wauters whom Mulsant described as "le roi des crétins"), and also because of the arrest of Monsieur Hulet, an important contact whom Mulsant had introduced to Sebastian (Captain Grover-Williams), and who had been arrested at the break-up of Sebastien's circuit.

207. With him came Nenette (Madame Fauge), courier to the circuit, whose security was also compromised, as she had been forced to meet too many people in escorting a party of American airmen to safety, and Honore (Flight-Lieutenant Barrett) the circuit's wireless operator.

208. Mulsant had contacts in other parts of France and considered that he would be able to work in the Lyon, St. Etienne or Haute Loire regions.

209. But the essential thing at this period was to build up a series of circuits in the hinterland of the probable battle in Normandy, and

42

Mulsant (now known as Guerin) agreed that he would establish an organisation in Seine et Marne, basing himself on Paris where Major Cowburn gave him a series of contacts.

210. After a brief training he was ready to return to France in January 1944, but owing to bad weather did not actually get there till March. He was accompanied by Honore (now known as Stephane or Charles) as radio operator, and was later joined once more by Nenette as courier (also known as Mimi).

Captain Mulsant's Organistion.

Operational name of Organisation: The Minister circuit.
Operational name of organiser: Guerin.
Name by which known in the Field: Guerin and Paul.

211. Owing to the shortness of time available, his groups concentrated exclusively on D-Day targets. From the beginning he made good and rapid progress, his first ground for receiving material was proposed to London on the 1st April, on the 17th April he successfully arranged the reception of three officers[37] going to a neighbouring area, by the 20th April he had established contact with the Préfet of Seine et Marne: progress is illustrated by the number of successful operations which he carried out:

In April 1944   2 operations comprising 20 containers.
In May 1944   3 operations comprising 38 containers.
In June 1944   5 operations comprising 96 containers.
In July 1944   2 operations comprising 51 containers.

212. Stephane, who had already shown his quality at Troyes, proved once more an extremely capable operator, and in addition to passing Mulsant's traffic was also handling messages for the Clergyman, Diplomat and Farrier circuits. He also found and trained a local radio operator, Raoul Cooreman, who under the *nom-de-guerre* of Raoul passed his tests and became second operator to the circuit.

213. In May an assistant, Rigobert, was sent to the group. His real name was Lieutenant J.L. De Ganay (known as Jean-Louis); he knew the district, well as his family had estates there, and was convinced that the

country could be organised for the reception of paratroops on a large scale.

214. In June 1944 there arrived in London, Roger Veillard, a lawyer of Melun who had been Mulsant's most efficient lieutenant and extremely useful to him, more particularly in the multifarious contacts which he possessed in the area. He had had to leave the Field for reasons of security, had come out through Spain and reported on his arrival that Mulsant's organisation was healthy and powerful.

215. It consisted at the time of Veillard's departure of 8 groups at Rozay en Brie, Meaux, Nangis, Bray sur Seine, Donnemarie en Montois, Melun, Fontainebleau and Montereau. Preparations had been made for defending an area bounded by the towns Rozay, Nangis, Donnemarie, Vulaines, St. Juste, Corbieres, Vaudoy for large scale deliveries of parachute troops, 500 men being available. Preparations for dealing with the circuit's D-Day targets were going actively ahead.

216. On D-Day the organisation went into action – effectively as the list in Appendix A shows. The apple of its eye, of course, was the controlled area and the 5 grounds for the reception of large bodies of paratroops, and these, in the event, were not used. But in more mundane matters, such as railway, and canal and telecommunication sabotage, it played its part and played it with enthusiasm and technical skill; when it attacked a railway, it attacked the most important line available and blocked it by derailing a train in a tunnel, by far the most effective method. Their actions were typical of Mulsant, their organiser and inspiration, who was a really first-class man.

217. But in the middle of July they ran into trouble, and in a most unnecessary and regrettable manner. Round about the 15th of the month a uniformed party of S.A.S. were dropped into the Foret de Fontainebleau, had become isolated and Mulsant considered it his duty to go to their assistance. In so doing he, Stephane and another member of the circuit[38] were arrested. The impending arrival of the S.A.S. party had not been reported to Mulsant (the S.A.S. were an independent organisation and co-ordination was not always perfect), and it is a very sad irony that the group, which was, par excellence, organised for the reception of parachutists, should have met disaster

precisely through the unannounced arrival of uniformed parachutists in their area.

218. These arrests were followed by many others and by the seizure of many arms dumps. Rigobert, Nenette and Raoul survived, but Rigobert was not of the calibre to pull what was left of the organisation together. Under Mulsant he had done good work (he had been personally responsible for blowing up a dam at Chalifert and the Paris–Coulommiers–Sezanne Railway), but his real disposition was more that of a regular soldier than that of a member of a resistance group. It is incontestable that the Gestapo was looking for him, and he went into hiding. He later made efforts to form a small Maquis, but was unable to accomplish anything really effective before the arrival of the Americans on the 28th August.

219. In the meanwhile Roger Veillard had completed a brief training in England, and on the 17th August he dropped into France to a Donkeyman (Major Frager's organisation) reception, with a view to contacting Raoul and picking up the threads of the organisation. He failed to make contact with Raoul, and in any case the time at his disposal was too short for anything effective to be done. He behaved with great energy, however, took part in some skirmishes in the Provins area, with his men occupied Donnemarie and held it against counter-attack till the Americans arrived, was arrested by and escaped from the S.S., was arrested by and liberated on London intervention from a certain Captain Sains (known as Duval) of the F.F.I. of whom he fell foul, and whom he accused of incapacity and worse, and is at the present moment apparently in danger of being expelled from the Paris Bar for "excesses" during the Resistance period. These "excesses" are probably imaginary, but Veillard is a very conceited man with pronounced political ambitions and apparently a highly-developed capacity for making enemies. His rank in the British Army when dropped from the aircraft was Lieutenant; as soon as he touched the soil of France he became a full-blown Commandant, much, incidentally, to the surprise of the simple souls of the Donkeyman reception committee!

220. Captain Mulsant and Flight-Lieutenant Barrett were both executed in Germany.

221. They both obtained a Mention in Despatches. There is little doubt that had they returned they would have obtained decorations more in accord with the exceptional services they rendered.

222. Captain de Ganay, after proceeding with the Americans as far as Verdun, was wounded by a bomb splinter and returned to London. Later he worked in the Far East and has now returned to Paris.

THE TROYES AREA

223. In April 1943 the first British organiser, Major Cowburn (Benoit), arrived with his radio operator Flight-Lieutenant Barrett (Honore), to establish a circuit in the Troyes area.

Major Cowburn's Organisation.
Operational name of Organisation: The Tinker circuit.
Operational name of Organiser: Benoit and then Germain.
Name by which known in the Field: Germain.

224. Major Cowburn had already carried out two missions with distinction. In Troyes his work was of classic quality. His mission was the normal one for the period: he was to organise attacks against railways, such attacks not to be actually carried out until specific orders were received, and against certain other specified objectives. On his return to England in September 1943 he was able to report an organisation built up on extremely sound lines, in possession of the necessary materials, with a dozen small teams, living next-door to their railway targets and ready to act against them immediately on receipt of orders.

225. His immediate objective, the extremely important Creney Transformer Station, had proved too hard a nut to crack, the guards being equipped with searchlights and dogs and the transformers themselves being surrounded by high wooden walls.

226. But one valuable scalp dangled from his belt. On the 3rd July, 1943, he had personally led a party of six men in an attack on the Express locomotives in the Troyes engine sheds. He himself had personally made up the 48 charges and his party placed them on the cylinders of

12 locomotives in or near the sheds. At the first explosion the Germans had arrived in force and commenced investigations inside the running-shed, but by a fortunate chance the remaining explosions took place at half-hourly intervals and the Germans were kept at a respectful distance throughout the night. So much so that at dawn the Garrison Commander esteemed it necessary to arrive on the scene to upbraid his timorous troops. Mounted on the footplate of one of the few remaining locomotives just outside the sheds, he was just about to begin a scathing indictment of their lack of courage, when the last charge exploded in a nearby engine. The intrepid officer in his turn beat a hasty retreat.

227. Major Cowburn also reported almost the only recorded instance of the effective use of itching powder, a quantity of this substance having been introduced by a local manufacturer into a consignment of shirts for the German submarine service. It would be pleasant to be able to record this as one of the "unexplained causes" for which at least one U-Boat had failed to return to Base.

228. Notable among Major Cowburn's helpers were M. Vassard, Procureur de la République at Troyes, Madame Mielle, proprietress of the "Bonne Fermière" Restaurant at Precy-Notre-Dame, M. Buridan, farmer at Nogent s/Aube, M. Avelines, of St. Savine, and, above all, Pierre Mulsant, son-in-law of a leading local industrialist, who became his extremely efficient and enthusiastic second-in-command.

229. In September 1943 Major Cowburn returned to London – he was too well-known to the Gestapo to stay longer – leaving (as he usually did) an organisation in being behind him. The agreement was that a new organiser should be sent from London to replace him, and Pierre Mulsant remained on the scene to keep things going and to hand over when the time came.

230. In October 1943 the new organiser was ready and Captain (later Major) Dupont took over from Mulsant, who went to London in November accompanied by Mme. Fauge (Nanette) who acted as courier to the circuit.

Captain Dupont's Organisation.
Operational name of organisation: The Diplomat circuit.

Operational name of organiser: Abelard.
Name by which known in the Field: Abelard and Yvan.

231. With its new name the Tinker circuit began to take a new form, slightly more flamboyant, slightly less clandestine and more obviously destined for the insurrectional period. Approximately two months after his arrival Abelard announced the formation of the Maquis M. with complete auxiliary services, such as Nursing, Rationing and the like. The change was not altogether welcome to the old guard, and Mulsant on his arrival in London was somewhat critical of Abelard. But it must be said in Abelard's favour that when the time did come to take to the Maquis, he took to it with effect and waged effective war in the best Maquis tradition.

232. Like Cowburn before him he carried out a most successful attack on the Troyes locomotive sheds and evidence of the effectiveness of his post-D-Day activities will be found in the list in Appendix A. Further evidence is to hand in a work, "Maquis M." written by the Abbe Bonnard, one of Abelard's more notable helpers.

233. Honore (Flight-Lieutenant Barrett) had returned to London with Mulsant, and it became necessary to supply another radio operator for the group. The choice fell on Captain Watt (Geoffroi), a diminutive person with the heart of a lion. He had already carried out one mission in Paris, where he had acted for 5 months as radio operator to Flying Officer Dericourt's circuit. In Troyes, in addition to his very capable work as wireless expert, he soon developed in his own right into a Maquis leader and Abelard's energetic and effective second-in-command. His infectious enthusiasm and gaiety were of great value to the group.

234. In view of the value of the organisation and the strategic importance of the area, it was decided in June 1944 to reinforce Abelard by sending to him three officers and a radio operator from London. This was successfully done, although the operation almost coincided with the reported arrival in Troyes of 3,000 Russians bent on wiping the group out. These Russians were real enough, but they never dared to penetrate into the woods to look for Abelard's men, believing them more powerful than they actually were.

235. The new arrivals[39] under the command of Captain Taschereau arrived in an atmosphere of Maquis skirmishes in which they took their allotted part. His rôle was that of assistant to Abelard, but in the conditions then ruling his developed into an independent command. He trained and armed a Maquis in the Foret de Soulaines, and in collaboration with another Maquis, which he also supplied with arms, carried out numerous guerrilla operations, in one of which 300 casualties were inflicted on the Germans. He worked closely (which Abelard did not) with the local F.F.I. under Commandant Montcalm, and in the later stages organised an efficient intelligence service for the Americans.

236. In the meanwhile Abelard, whose command had grown to 800 men (as compared with 400 on D-Day), had been very active. He reported that on the reception of orders for intensified guerrilla activities they occupied their sector, and put out of action 250 of the enemy and 50 vehicles. After this the Americans gave them orders to hold all bridges over the Aube until their troops had crossed. Abelard's men took up positions at 5 bridges, and despite heavy counter-attacks held them.

237. Dismissing those men who wished to return home, Abelard then formed the remainder into a French Battalion, which he placed under the orders of Colonel Diagramme. A Company was sent to Chaumont to work under Major Bodington[40]. The remainder were posted to Auxerre, and later they too went to Chalons. In due course difficulties arose concerning the command of this Battalion, and towards the end of October 1944 the Judex Mission took part in an interview, of which their Report gives the following account:

238. "The Judex party left early, having an appointment in Chalons with Abelard and the General Commanding, General Puccinelli. At this interview the General and Colonel Buckmaster exchanged courtesies, and the question then veered to the command of Abelard's F.F.I. battalion, now in barracks at Chalons.

239. At this point Abelard took charge of the interview, and in the politest and firmest manner informed the General of the conditions on which, in his view, the matter should be arranged, and finally magnanimously accepted the command, upon which the General expressed his gratification and the interview ended."

240. One thing must be added in conclusion. There have been rumours of financial malpractices and racketeering in Abelard's group, and one member, Lopez (Spaniard, Legionnaire and killer to the group), has been arrested. Nothing tangible has followed these rumours, and Abelard is now employed in one of the Ministries in Paris, but it is suggested that prior reference be made to Major Cowburn if any question should arise concerning the Troyes groups.

OTHER CIRCUITS

241. As explained in the Foreword, it has not been possible to deal with all circuits which F. Section set up in France. Opportunity is taken here to mention some of them which functioned in the Paris area.

242. The Pedlar Circuit, under Major Bodington, arrived rather late in the day, and was further hampered by a failure on the part of E.M.F.F.I. in London to give it effective liaison with the F.F.I. in its area of operations Haute Marne. It largely confined its activities to Intelligence reports, including one very valuable one on Von Kluge's newly-established headquarters near Verzy, which with R.A.F. co-operation, forced a hurried departure on the harassed general. The circuit later saw considerable action, in which Captain Peter Harratt, second-in-command, distinguished himself.

243. Captain Vallee, a Frenchman with a distinguished sabotage record in North Africa, was sent in 1943 to develop resistance in Brittany. He made rapid progress, probably in co-operation with the O.C.M. (he was in contact with General Allard), but was arrested and his circuit broken up. One of its members, Captain Hunterhue, later escaped to England and was parachuted back into Brittany as guide to the first S.A.S. party to be sent there just prior to D-Day.

244. Also in 1943 First Lieutenant Floege (Paul Fontaine), an American with a Communist background, built up a circuit on the general line Caen–Mayenne–Nantes, designed to seal off Brittany from the rest of France, when the time came, in connection with impending military operations. This circuit, too, was broken up by the Gestapo, but Floege was able to escape, with his radio operator, and worked later, as Pascal, in the Belfort area.

245. Another circuit existed in the general area Nantes–Angers–Tours at about the same time under Max (Garel) and Leopold (Rousset) as radio operator. This also came to grief at Gestapo hands.

246. No mention has been made of a number of officers, who have been sent out, but were arrested very soon after their arrival. An exception should be made for Captain Octave Simon (Badois) who was arrested at the start of his second mission. He had previously been in contact with Renaud (Antelme) and Guerin (Mulsant).

247. A very brief mention has been made of the Mitchell Circuit. Mitchell is Maitre Savy, who had been of such great assistance to Renaud and Prosper, had come to London with Renaud, and had joined de Gaulle. The Mitchell mission was really a B.C.R.A. mission, but used an F. Section radio operator and F. Section communications. It sent back a mass of extremely valuable Intelligence concerning V-1 sites and stores, and it was through it that the great dump at St. Leu d'Esserens was successfully bombed.

248. Another circuit operating under F. Section auspices was the Glover circuit led by Andre (Lieutenant Guiraud) an American officer. Andre was arrested after working for a comparatively short time, but his radio operator survived, and in co-operation with local leaders the circuit was responsible for organising the following deliveries:

1944	Operations	Containers	Packages
June	1	8	6
July	2	48	1
August	8	349	41
September	17	699	146

249. Two very efficient circuits also existed in Nievre. One of them was founded on contacts originally developed by Cesar (see Strasbourg). After Cesar's flight to Switzerland an organiser was sent from London to develop these contacts. There had been numerous arrests and conditions were difficult, but Louis (Captain Sawyer) was an efficient organiser, who already had Resistance experience in the South-West. The Gondolier Circuit was built up by him into a very efficient unit and the writer has the tribute of a French Colonel, whom he met in Lille in

November 1945, that Captain Sawyer's Maquis units were among the best armed and trained of the District.

250. Louis was ably seconded by Baptiste (Captain Mackenzie) a most capable radio operator and second-in-command. Together they ensured the following deliveries of stores to the area:

1944	Operations	Containers	Packages
May	1	12	6
June	2	24	12
July	11	270	103
August	6	235	67
September	9	423	156

251. Most regrettably Captain Sawyer was killed by a mortar explosion just before the Liberation.

252. The other Nievre circuit is the Licencee Circuit in Cosne, under Leon (Captain le Prevost). This was established on contacts provided by Virginia Hall on her second mission. When Leon arrived the local groups were complaining bitterly at being starved of stores by Central Authority in Nevers. This was soon remedied, as the figures given below demonstrate, and the group was very active, including a most efficient demolition of the St. Thibaud bridge across the Loire on the direct orders of General Patton.

1944	Operations	Containers	Packages
July	2	66	22
August	9	272	143
September	8	369	146

Appendix A:

ACTIVITIES ON AND AFTER D-DAY
OF THE BRITISH CIRCUITS IN THE PARIS REGION

This list is not exhaustive. There is on the one hand no need that it should be for the purpose in hand, and on the other no possibility that it could be really complete. The actions noted here are limited to those reported by radio to London during the heat of action itself, and for compactness sake they cover only the period 4th June–31st July, 1944.

Although this procedure is somewhat unfair as between circuits, since the actions reported depend very much on the volubility of the organiser, the capability of his wireless operator and the amount of other traffic which his communications channels had to handle, it is hoped that the attached statement will give a general view of the scope and effectiveness of the circuit's activities during the D-Day and post D-Day period, which represented the most important stage in their activities.

1. The Beggar Circuit (Senlis–Creil area)
9th June
Successful attacks on six telephone targets radiating from Creil. Successful attacks on four telephone targets radiating from Senlis. Also four of his railway targets.

30th June
Continuing action against all targets.

12th July
Continuing attacks on telephone targets.

26th July
Successful attack on small convoy on R.N.15. Switchboard at Creil station destroyed.

2. The Clergyman circuit
15th June
All traffic stopped in the Dourdan–Rambouillet area.

3. The Diplomat circuit (Troyes area)

7th June
G.M.R. (Garde Mobile de Reserve) officer and his men recruited.

15th June
In control of five villages.

19th June
Reports boundary of "Controlled Area." Has 250 men and will recruit more when he has arms. Railway sabotage on Troyes – Bar le Duc line. Road sabotage on: Arcis–Mery, Arcis–Troyes, Troyes–Brienne roads.

20th June
Whole regional H.Q. of Gendarmerie Nationale and their men have applied to join, but have had to be refused through lack of arms. Petrol train derailed on Troyes–Chalons line (four days' blockage).

21st June
Sabotage on following roads: Arcis–Mery, Arcis–Troyes, Arcis–Paris, Arcis–Brienne. Coal train derailed Troyes–Paris line.

21st June
Railway sabotage on Troyes–Chaumont line (thirty-six hours' delay). Road sabotage on: Troyes–Paris, Troyes–Sens, Troyes–Piney, Troyes–Chaumont, Troyes–Arcis roads.

22nd June
Goods train destroyed Troyes–Chalons line (twenty-four hours' delay). Road sabotage on the Troyes–Arcis, Troyes–Sens roads.

27th June
Maquis engagement.

29th June
During night successfully sabotaged telephone lines, linking 143 stations. (At least two weeks to repair.)

23rd July
Troyes–Chalons railway line cut, three locomotives across both lines.

Telephone cable on R.N. 7 cut in two places.

27th July
Explosives factory at Hery sabotaged. Paris–Troyes railway line cut.

4. *The Headmaster circuit (Le Mans area)*
13th June
All telephone lines in and out of Le Mans cut.

5. *The Hermit circuit (Blois–Vendome area)*
23rd June
Started attacks on rail and telephone targets converging on Blois and Vendome. Underground telephone cables cut Souge–Montoire. Railway line out Blois–Vendome.

26th June
Stock of Pontoons destroyed which were to replace Loire bridge at Blois.

12th July
Week's activities include: 11 Rail cuts, 7 Underground cables cut, 5 Overhead cables cut, several roads, several derailments, widespread tyre burster action.

17th July
Week's activities include: Continuous rail and telephone cuttings. Two derailments at Chapelle-Vendomoise, Chateau Renault. Continuous cutting of Underground telephone cables: Montoire–Berlin, Paris–Bordeaux, Tours–Orleans and all overhead telephone lines. High-Tension Pylons Chartres–Orleans. Widespread tyreburster action.

6. *The Historian circuit (Orleans area)*
9th June
16 attacks against Rail and Telephone targets in 48 hours. No guerrilla action yet as very little enemy traffic. Maquis being increased.

13th June
Attacks being renewed against all Rail and Telephone targets. No circulation on any of the lines round Orleans.

11th July
Bridge at Beaugency damaged beyond repair.

13th July
Continuous sabotage on roads and railway targets. Particularly Points at Vitry and Fay-aux-Loges (8 days' delay). Bridge over Orleans–Gien line at Checy. Rails at Bellegarde Station and Power distributor destroyed. Derailment at Solterres (48 hours' delay). Road bridge damaged at Beignets.

19th July
Daily sabotage on Railways Gien–Montargis, Montargis–Malesherbes. Bridge blown up 3 Kms. N.W. of Lorris on Bellegarde line. Maquis of 50 men withdraw at Suy la Chapelle without loss.

26th July
Montargis–Gien Railway line cut 4 Kms. S. of Montargis by wrecking engines in tunnel. Bridge 2 Kms. N. blown up to prevent arrival of breakdown crane.

29th July
Underground telephone cable on RN. 7 cut.

7. The Minister Circuit (Meaux-Nangis-Provins area)
9th June
Train derailed in tunnel at St. Loup de Naud on Paris–Belfort line. Train derailed at Gouaix on Flamboin–Montereau line. All telephone lines cut, including Paris–Provins–Troyes cable cut at Grand Puits. Canal lock at Bray s/Seine blown up.

13th June.
Further attacks on targets on German strategic line Montereau–Nogent s/Marne. Train derailed Verneuil L'Etang-Marles.

15th June
Two trains derailed near Nemours on Nemours–Montargis line, Report of "Controllable Area." Rozay en Brie–Nangis–Donnemarie en Montois–Vulaines en Brie–St. Juste–Corciers–Vaudon with nearly 500 men ready to defend it. Strong points at Nangis–Rozay–Jouy le Chatel, Donnemarie, Maison Rouge.

6th July
Canal Lock at Bagneaux destroyed.

19th July
Locks on Marne Canal attacked between Meaux and Esbly.

22nd July
Montargis–Melun–Paris Railway cut by destroying bridge between Souppes and Dordives.

27th July
Same line cut between Bourron and Nemours. Canal Lock at Ecueilles blown up.

8. *The Permit Circuit*
The R.A.F. having failed to destroy the viaduct at Cherisy, Permit blew up three arches on the night of 18th/19th July. Technicians considered the damage irreparable. This operation earned a special message of appreciation from S.H.A.E.F.

His group immobilised five petrol trains and ten waggons of materials and ammunition in the station at St. Sauveur by keeping up three cuts for forty-eight hours. Another part of the same convoy was immobilised at Morvilette.

Sabotage was carried out of several Tiger tanks by use of anti-tank mines, lorries of ammunition and petrol were also attacked.

On 27th July a railway bridge was blown up on the Paris-Brest line between La Coupe and Bretoncelles.

9. *The Scientist Circuit*
11th June
Reported that, apart from his own groups, all resistance groups in the area were inactive.

15th June
Paris–Granville line cut near Tessy s/Vire. Between 5th-8th June numerous objectives attacked and the Caen–Vire line cut. The beginning of an extremely valuable series of tactical Intelligence messages by Verger, Scientist's second-in-command from the Thury Harcourt area.

18th June
Reported taking command of a group of 600 men near Laval.

22nd June
Reported his Foret de Monaye Maquis re-forming in the Domfront–Mayenne–Pre en Pail triangle.

23rd June
Attempted to provide guides to assist patrols of British Airborne Troops between the Rivers Orne and Dive. This was unsuccessful.

30th June
Telephone lines and underground cables cut S. of the Cotentin Peninsula. Reported himself as able to receive paratroops on five "controllable" grounds.

30th July
Convoys blocked on roads: hundreds of lorries destroyed: infantry columns attacked: trains derailed: communications cut.

10. The Spiritualist Circuit
This circuit besides being the channel through which was received news of multiple sabotage from Lille, also transmitted at mass of information concerning V-1 sites.
Of actual sabotage in the Paris area, it reported attacks on lock gates on the canal at Sevrans, on a German electrical laboratory, on the Jaeger works (where parts for flying bombs were captured), on cables in the NE of Paris and in the Westinghouse Factory at Freinville.

Appendix B:

PROSPER CIRCUIT ORGANISATION, 1st JUNE 1943

H.Q. Prosper, Archambaud and Monique.

Area	Circuit Chief	Grounds	Stores received to date (containers)
Seine, Seine and Oise	Gaspard Armelguern[41], Paris	1	Nil
Oise (East)	Marcel Sailly, Montataire	2	Nil
Oise (West), Eure (East) Eure	George Darling[42], Triechataux	10	64
Calvados, Orne	Marcel Gouju, Evreux	1	15
	Jean Auchy[43] (Paul), Falaise	1	5
Sarthe, Mayenne, Eure and Loire	Henri Garry[44] (Cinema)	3	20
Loiret (West) Loiret (East)	Maurice Lequeux[45], Meung	1	5
Loir and Cher, Indre and Loire	Jean Baudin, Montargis	1	Nil
	P. Culioli[46] (Adolf), Mer s/Loire	13	120

N.B. In addition, the Hirson circuit (details not available) had received 25 containers. Further particulars concerning the groups under the command of Lequeux and Culioli can be found in a book, "L'Abbé Emile Pasty, Prêtre et Soldat," written in November 1945 by Paul Guillaume, "To the memory of l'Abbé Emile Pasty and his companions of 55 A" (by which name the Prosper group was locally known).

Appendix C:

ACTIVITIES OF PROSPER CIRCUIT

27th March, 1943
Twenty-four pylons destroyed and extension cables wrecked in attack on Chaigny transformer station. Electric communications stopped for one day; 40,000 litres of oil spilled.

March 1943
A train taking food-stuffs to Germany fired and destroyed as it left Paris.

March 1943
Three troop-trains derailed near Blois and 43 Germans killed, 110 wounded.

March 1943
Bombs on the Ministere de la Marine (two buildings).

March 1943
Incendiaries organised for Archives Headquarters, rue François 1.

5th April 1943
Further attack on the Chaigny transformer station; all high tension lines but one to Paris cut; extensive damage done to Chaigny–Eguzon line; three German goods trains derailed – one between Orleans and Vierzon, one between Vierzon and Tours and one between Blocs and Villefranche.

May 1943
Two grenades thrown into a charabanc of German officers, resulting in 30 or more killed.

13th May, 1943
The Sucrerie Sayat, an alcohol factory at Etrepagny (Eure), attacked and 6 million litres of alcohol destroyed.

4th June, 1943
Another alcohol distillery, the Sucrerie St. Ouen L'Aumone, attacked: the buildings damaged and 14 million litres of alcohol and the entire reserve of molasses destroyed.

Appendix D:

SABOTAGE LIST OF JEAN-MARIE CIRCUIT

August 1943
Several trains destroyed. Sabotages in Saone and Loire. 12 reapers and binders, 1 transformer, 1 German tracked vehicle, 1 Lock at Dijon, Terrot transformer works – all destroyed. 30 derailments since May, including a petrol train between Chalon-sur-Saone and Macon.

September 1943
70 reapers and binders, 6 Locks, 28 locomotives, 30 German troop trains and petrol trains destroyed.

October 1943
120 Germans killed in 15 days in the Yonne. Sabotage in proportion. 6 officers and 1 general killed. Goods train derailed in a ravine at Paray-le-Monial. Attack on an aviation depot at St.-Pierre-de-Bœuf. 1 lorry and 4 tons of clothing captured. Cellophane works at Mantes put out of action for several months. C.I.M.T. (wagon works) at Mantes out of action for several months. Compressors, electric motor, transformers, &c., destroyed. Production reduced from 40 wagons a week to 4, partial stoppage to February 1944. Munitions train destroyed at Pontigny. Powder works at le Ripault blown up. Old factory completely destroyed; important reduction in output. Barrage at Briare-le Centre.

November 1943
9 railway lines cut. 2 turntables out of action. 17 derailments, including a munitions train. 50 Germans killed. German leave train derailed (200 Germans killed). 2 50-ton cranes destroyed. 92 locomotives immobilized. Principal repair shop at Laroche immobilized by attack on machines. 4 sections of canal run dry. 15 days' stoppage of traffic. 3 Locks destroyed. 3 telephone cables cut. Many pylons destroyed. 1 coal mine stopped. 57 reapers and binders, 1 weigh-bridge, lorries for transport of aero-engines destroyed. 1 lorry stolen. Mantes-Limay cement works immobilized 2 months. Numerous vehicles sabotaged in Normandy. Grenades and petrol seized. 9 Germans and 2 collaborators killed. Many trains derailed and lorry destroyed. Soldatenheim at Lisieux burnt.

December 1943

Frouard Locks blown up. 50 barges immobilized. 5-ton lorry with French military clothing seized. Air liquide factory at Boulogne sur Seine attacked. Machines blown up, repairs impossible. 3 compressors destroyed (3000 cu. m. and 900 cu. m.). Complete sabotage of production of high altitude oxygen. Courbevoie flame-throwing factory stopped in consequence.

D-Day

Continuous harassing of the enemy on road and rail, many engagements, many hundreds of Germans killed, complete blockage in one part of the Yonne.

Chapter 2

The Bordeaux Region

BRITISH CIRCUITS IN THE BORDEAUX REGION

1. The first efforts by the British to establish a Resistance organisation in Bordeaux were made in September 1941 when Lieutenant Leroy (known as Louis) was landed by sea on the South coast of France. By October or November of that year he had made his way into Bordeaux and stayed there until January 1942 when he left for London, which he reached in May. In Bordeaux he had worked as a tractor driver for the Todt Organisation, and on ship repair work in the Docks. He had established certain contacts, which were later to prove useful and brought back some information concerning the river and docks.

2. In July 1942 steps were taken to develop the situation; Captain (later Major) Claude De Baissac, an excellent officer, was parachuted with a Radio Operator near Nimes. After a preliminary contact in Cannes his instructions were to make for Bordeaux and build up a Circuit there.

3. Unfortunately the parachutes opened badly, the Radio Operator broke his leg, and De Baissac was hurt. This meant that when the latter

did finally reach Bordeaux in September he was without direct means of communication with London. This was remedied in November by the despatch of Captain (later Major) Landes (Aristide) who was, first, radio operator to the Circuit, and later, after the departure of De Baissac, set up his own circuit.

4. Brief histories of these circuits are as follows:

Major De Baissac's Circuit.
    Operational Name of Circuit: The Scientist Circuit.
    Operational Name of Organiser: David.
    Name by which known in the Field: David or Claude.

5. David arrived in Bordeaux in September 1942 and at approximately the same time his sister Lise De Baissac (known as Lise, Irene or Odile) started work in Poitiers. They were able to render each other much mutual assistance and their organisations are considered together in what follows.

6. From very small beginnings David, by his competence and enthusiasm, built up a powerful organisation, in spite of a softness in morale in his area on which is first report lays stress.

7. In this he was greatly helped by a contact given to him by another British officer working in the Paris area. This officer (Major Anthelme, alias Renaud) had in January or February 1943 contacted the Secretary of what he describes as "a Secret Organisation, which mostly comprises legal people and which is mainly concerned with the maintenance of order when the invasion takes place, and a better orientation of the French population towards social, religious and political matters." This man told Renaud that their representative in Bordeaux had formed a strong organisation (3,000 men) and were most anxious to be connected with a serious organisation which could help them.

8. The organisation was the O.C.M. and the Bordeaux representative was Grand-Clement (known as Gerard), son of the late Admiral Grand-Clement.

9. Thereafter progress was rapid. In May 1943 David reported the following groups:

Basses Pyrenees	700 men. No arms yet received.
Landes	2,000 men. Only one reception of arms to date.
Gironde	11,000 men. Two receptions of arms to date.
Charente Maritime	500 men. No arms yet received.
Charente	1,500 men. No arms yet received.
Poitou, Vendee, Vienne, Deux Sevres	
	5,000 men. Six receptions of arms to date.

10. He estimated that if arms were sent, these troops could be armed, trained and organised militarily.

11. Grand-Clement's report, which reached us in August 1943 traces the earlier history of this organisation. Its origins were political, but from the beginning of 1941 it began to assume a para-military aspect. It had, however, no means of action, no financial resources, no contact with the French Comite d'Action or with the British. Even so, in May 1942, it had:

A nucleus in Bordeaux of 600 men.
About 1,000 men in the Gironde.
About 600 men in Charente and Vendee.

12. In May 1942 a contact was established with a national organisation deriving from the Committee in London, but material means were still almost non-existent. Nevertheless, recruitment went forward and numbers grew to 10-15,000 men.

13. Then, towards March 1943, came the contact with the W.O. (War Office) through De Baissac. Grand-Clement notes that from that moment everything changed. Recognition tests (over the B.B.C.) passed rapidly; funds became sufficient; deliveries of arms were carried out. Tasks and Missions could be undertaken in the knowledge that the means were available.

14. At the end of five months a veritable little army was ready to go into action against the enemy's rear. Its make-up was the following:

1 Commander.
1 Chief of Staff.

4 Bureaux: Personnel, Intelligence, Operations, Services.
2 Subdivisions, North and South.
1 Commanding officer per Department.
17,000 men mobilisable.
30,000 sympathisers who could be of use.

15. One-third of the effectives could be armed almost at once. If arms deliveries continued, 20,000 men could be ready to go into action by 1st September, 1943.

16. In addition there was a group in the Correze which was under prospection.

17. For David personally this represented a triumph. Since his arrival, he had gained the confidence of all the local groups and, in his own words, "had become their boss." There was one exception, Liberation, which, however, was not a military organisation.

18. It is hardly necessary to say that these reports caused considerable anxiety in London. The numbers were, of course, impressive, but large circuits of this size were the reverse of the type of organisation which the British were attempting at that time to build in France. They smacked rather more of the type of organisation in which the French specialised, and which by their very size developed weaknesses in security, which more often than not ended in disaster.

19. However, David was one of the most capable organisers we ever sent to France, segregation seemed to have been pushed to an extent which would localise any damage, and the decision was taken to support the Bordeaux organisation to the full.

20. In November 1942 David had received an assistant; Captain Charles Hayes (Yves), a specialist in electrical matters, to help him in his work. As has already been noted he had been sent his first Radio Operator Aristide in the same month; in May 1943 he was sent a second operator, Captain Defence (Dede).

21. On the material side deliveries were heavy. Between November 1942 and August 1943 no fewer than 121 successful dropping operations

were made to the Scientist circuit. In these 1,600 containers and 350 packages were delivered; these included, among other things, 18,400 lbs. of H.E., 7,500 Stens, 300 Brens, 1,500 Rifles and 17,200 Grenades. Evidently something powerful was building up.

22. On the 16th August, 1943, David returned to London for consultation. He reported that he was in a position to take the following action to prevent enemy interference with an Allied landing between the Gironde and the Spanish frontier:

(1) Deny the enemy the use of *all* railway lines south of a line Angouleme–Perigueux. The lines would be cut at pre-arranged points on a repeated plan by the cheminots.
(2) His own groups would add to such railway demolitions where necessary and increase the period of such cuttings beyond the four to seven days promised by the cheminots. He could also attack and harass enemy reinforcements proceeding by road.
(3) With his fighting guerrilla troops he could capture some aerodromes and even hold a part of the country for a limited time.

23. David and Grandclement had evidently gambled on an Allied landing in September 1943, and they might have been in a position to make a powerful contribution to its success had it taken place at that time. They also saw the dangers, and David warned London that he did not believe that his organisation could survive more than two or three months if a landing were deferred.

24. In point of fact Nemesis was already at hand. There are rumours that Grandclement had already sold out to the Gestapo in August 1943. What is incontestable is that on the 19th September he was arrested in Paris, and within a very few days was back in Bordeaux, under Gestapo patronage, busily engaged in indicating to this new masters the arms dumps which had been established so laboriously during the preceding months.

25. In a very short time the circuit as such was no more.

26. This is not the place to discuss Grandclement's motives; whether he yielded to the physical treatment which the Germans meted out to him; whether he was sincere in the belief, which he began to express, that

the basic struggle was against communism and that it was only in co-operation with the Germans that the Communist danger could be dealt with. The fact remains that in a very short time the circuit was undermined and the arms dumps betrayed. The dream had faded.

27. Not entirely, however. Aristide (Major Landes), who seems to have acted with great coolness throughout these events, did manage to preserve a part of what had been built up. Their history will be considered later.

28. David learning through Aristide of what was going on (Aristide maintained wireless contact with London throughout), was most anxious to return to Bordeaux, but London ordered otherwise, and he left later to fulfil an important mission in Normandy. He has been reproached locally with his failure to redeem his promise to return to Bordeaux; he himself would have done so, but operational necessity dictated his despatch elsewhere.

29. What had his organisation accomplished?

30. Relatively little on the material side, since David and his collaborators were all unconvinced of the value of sabotage, and concentrated their activities on the building up of a powerful organisation for para-military action at the moment of an Allied landing. Apart from a concerted attack early in 1943 upon the lines supplying the Bordeaux-Dax electric railway, followed by a carefully arranged short-circuit as soon as repairs were completed, comparatively little was done, although a number of "pills" were inserted in the distilled water destined for the batteries of submarines working out of La Pallice.

31. But one result of very great value was achieved. A mass of information began to come out of Bordeaux concerning the movements of shipping in and out of the Estuary of the Garonne. This was of such volume and of such accuracy that the Admiralty wrote in September 1943 (the following are extracts):

(1) The information ... brought by Scientist on his last visit, was the most important he has had and enabled successful measures to be taken by the Admiralty.

(2) Although air photography has contributed a little to the results, it is the ground intelligence from Bordeaux which has virtually put an end to blockade-running between Europe and the Far East this year. The stoppage of this traffic is of the highest importance as the supplies ordered are vital to the Japanese.

(3) Source has given a better intelligence service than has been available from any other enemy port.

32. David received the D.S.O. for his work in Bordeaux and Aristide the M.C.

33. The second stage consisted of the development of the Aristide Circuit out of the ruins of the David–Grand-Clement organisation.

Major Landes's Organisation.

Operational Name of Organisation: The Actor Circuit.
Operational Name of Organiser: Stanislas, later Aristide.
Name by which known in the Field: Aristide, Stanislas, Rene, Robert or Roger.

34. Throughout the above events Aristide had behaved with exemplary calm. At the time of Grand-Clément's treachery, his commanding officer David was in London, his fellow radio operator Dédé had been sent to Paris to work with the O.C.M. group there, and the only other London-sent officer remaining in the Region was Yves. Together they set about sealing off the uncontaminated portions of the circuit, a task of extraordinary difficulty since the bulk of the organisation was O.C.M. and hence liable to contamination.

35. They had one priceless ally, a police officer named Corbin (who later came to London with Aristide, was commissioned in the British Army and returned to work in the Angouleme area). Corbin undertook the extremely delicate task of remaining in contact with Grand-Clement in order to keep Aristide advised of developments.

36. In October Aristide lost Yves, who was cornered by the Gestapo in the house of M. Duboue at Lestiac, and after a very gallant three hours' fight was wounded and taken prisoner. (There were reports that in view

of his gallant behaviour in this fight he was being treated by the Germans as a P.O.W. He has not, however, returned from Germany.)

37. By the middle of November Aristide considered that he had done everything possible in the direction of establishing a new organisation, and left for London by Spain taking Corbin with him. He arrive there in January 1944, and immediately made a very strong plea to be allowed to go back to Bordeaux to build up his new organisation, which he declared to be completely sound and water-tight. His request was finally acceded to, and on the 3rd March he was dropped near Auch on the ground of another organiser, Hector. Having sprained an ankle it was not until the 14th March that he reached Bordeaux.

38. He had left behind him in Bordeaux at Madame Faget (Jacqueline) to maintain contact with 6 other persons through whom he intended to build up his organisation. On arrival he found that only one of these was still available. One had died; a second, Andre Noel, had contacted Grand-Clément and was working hand in glove with him (he had tried to trap Captain Peuleve (Jean) in the Correze); two more had made contact with Commandant Camplan in ignorance of the fact that he, too, was working with Grand-Clément and was later to be responsible for the capture and suicide of Hypothenuse, an F.F.C. agent. A fifth, Inspecteur de Police Boulliard, who had helped Aristide to leave the country in November, had had to flee to the Maquis.

39. Through the sixth contact, relations were re-established with a group in Arcachon, under Commandant de Luze (who later refused to co-operate, went over to Grand-Clément and is thought to have been the cause of a number of arrests), an organisation was formed in the Port of Bordeaux, at the Camp de Merignac, and contact was re-established with the Railwaymen.

40. Further afield Aristide endeavoured to reform the organisation in the Landes, contacting for this purpose Leonce Dussarat (Leon des Landes), then in the Maquis in Gers.

41. By the end of April the foundations of the new organisation were laid.

42. Numbers were believed to be as follows:

Group at
Arcachon	300
Merignac	20
Submarine Base	15
Lormont	40
Pessac	20
Bouscat	5
Beoles	20
Bordeaux	500
Landes	300

and three-quarters of the Railwaymen.

43. Actually these figures were illusory, Aristide having been very badly let down by his then second-in-command Luc (Pierre Chevalier) whom he later "sacked" and replaced by Lancelot (Louis Campet).

44. It is probably unnecessary to go into the details of Aristide's organisation. A statement of what they accomplished is attached at Appendix A.

45. What is of more present interest is the sequence of events which led up to Aristide's abrupt banishment from France by de Gaulle on the 16th September 1944. The account given below is taken from his own Report; the French version is already probably familiar.

46. Aristide starts by noting that London sent him to the Field with the mission of organising sabotage and guerrilla groups, these groups to be independent and completely under his control. He was informed that no other organisation existed in the Region. In particular he points out that he was ignorant of the fact that a "soi disant" État-Major de la Resistance existed in Paris, and that there were in France officers appointed by the French High Command and D.M.R.'s appointed by the representatives of de Gaulle.

47. He himself organised Resistance in the Landes, Basses Pyrenees and Gironde. There being no other organisations in the Region, he controlled all the independent Resistance groups. Certain Communist elements

tried to contact him, but he refused to see them. This point, incidentally, is not confirmed by his assistant Edouard, who reports "Aristide's circuits were helped very much by the Communists".

48. On the 6th June, 1944, only the groups which Aristide had armed went into action.

49. Shortly after D-Day Aristide received a telegram from London to the effect that all Resistance groups were merged in the F.F.I. under the orders of General Koenig. Even then, Aristide claims, nothing was done to make clear his rôle *vis-à-vis* the F.F.I. and, in the absence of any other representative, he believed himself to be the only legal representative of General Koenig. As such, he took all possible steps to secure effective action against the Germans.

50. Towards the middle of July he learned of the arrival of Triangle, D.M.R., and from that time on co-operated with him.

51. Then, in Aristide's words:

52. "At the Liberation, we passed from clandestine to open activity and, finding ourselves in a town solely occupied by F.F.I. and without special instructions, Triangle found himself in the position of having to assure all the services and take decisions in all that concerned the military organisation of the Region.

53. "There still remained innumerable Gestapo agents, Germans in plain clothes, Miliciens and Collaborators. Triangle asked me to assist him, as I had been the only organiser in the Region and the men had confidence in me.

54. "For these reasons, having no orders to reform the French Army, or to pass the F.F.I. over to the Regular Army, we continued to work on our own initiative in the interests of France.

55. "Colonel Moraglia having shown himself incapable and of doubtful loyalty ("douteux") we charged Colonel Druilhe with the task of forming a F.F.I. General Staff and directing military operations under our control.

56. "The former officers of the Armistice Army, or of 1939, presented themselves to assume the Military direction of the Region without Ordres de Mission or anything of the kind. We could not accept them, as we risked losing the confidence of the F.F.I. troops and of the population which supported us.

57. "Triangle and I considered that we were doing our duty in supporting the F.F.I. ideal against the 'arrivistes' of the 1939 Army. The Commissaire de la Republique, Monsieur Cusin, did not disapprove of our action; on the contrary, he seemed to approve and maintained close contact with Triangle.

58. "Furthermore, we kept you in touch with the situation and you replied that you were pleased with our good understanding and with the help I was giving Triangle.

59. "These facts did not seem to please the 'arrivistes' officers, and intrigues and plots began against Triangle and me.

60. "Generals Chabant-Delmas and Bertin approved of our conduct and, in the absence of special orders, we considered we were justified in continuing until none of the enemy remained, and until, on the other hand, the military organisation had been placed in the hands of those technically qualified."

61. And so on.

62. In fairness to Aristide one more extract may be given from his report:

63. "The Germans, having abandoned all the South-West of France South of Bordeaux, had retreated on Bordeaux.

64. "In agreement with the Commissaire de la Republique, M. Cusin, and with Triangle I decided to send an ultimatum to the Germans in an endeavour to save the installations of the port of Bordeaux. Our Corps Francs were positioned as follows:
   Arcachon Group at Pessac.
   Fernand Group in the Gare St. Jean, Bordeaux.
   Leon des Landes Group at Leongnan.

Georges Group at Labrede.
Dede le Basque Group at Blanque Fort and St. Andre de Cubsac.

65. "We appealed to Colonel Druilhe with 1,500 men who occupied positions between Castillon and Bordeaux.

66. "The following ultimatum was accordingly addressed to the Germans in the submarine base (Text of Ultimatum):

"Signed: The Délégué Militaire Régional.
The Commissaire de la République.
The Délégué militaire Britannique.

67. "On the 27th August the Germans replied to our ultimatum to the effect that if we abstained from all guerrilla and sabotage acts in Bordeaux they would evacuate the town without destroying any Public Works.

68. "On the 28th August we placarded throughout the town our ordre de jour No.1. "At the moment of the liberation we bring to your attention the fact that we, and only we, are authorised to receive the orders of General Koenig.

"We order all the F.F.I. not to allow premature action, complete calm must be observed. The success of our projects depends on your discipline. The regional F.F.I. chief Dufour will transmit these orders to you, counter-signed by us. Signed: TRIANGLE and ARISTIDE.

69. "In the night of the 28th/29th August the Germans evacuated Bordeaux." Thus was committed Aristide's greatest crime.

70. To finish the story, the following extracts are taken from Reports from independent sources.

71. *Extract from Report by Major Ayer. Political Situation in S.W. France*:

The case of Bordeaux is more interesting. In a previous report it was stated that with the disappearance of Triangle and Aristide, Colonel Druilhe, the Commander of the 18th Military Region, had emerged as the chief contender for power, with M. Cusin, the

Commissaire, and Colonel Martel, the F.T.P. leader, each enjoying a certain measure of authority in their own spheres. In fact, however, the situation is rather more complex. For one thing, Aristide did not disappear for good. Not long after his famous scene with De Gaulle and Diethelm he reappeared in the Landes where he held conversations with various local groups and, according to the B.C.R.A. in Bordeaux continued to receive supplies of arms and money by parachute, which he distributed to the group sympathetic to him and withheld from Colonel Druilhe. His last appearance in Bordeaux was on the 4th October, when he held a more or less secret meeting with the F.T.P. leaders. The fact that he was known as the delegate of the War Office, and that he entered the town in a car flying the British flag, naturally gave rise to the belief that he was acting upon the British Government's instructions in defiance of General de Gaulle, and aroused in some quarters a certain amount of anti-British feeling. He has now returned to London but the dissident groups remain under their various leaders, the most picturesque of whom is Leon De Landes, an ironmonger who has mysteriously become a Brigadier-General, commands perhaps a thousand followers and has set up a petty dictatorship at Dax. To him and to several others like him the unhappy Colonel Druilhe is paying "danegeld " in the form of money, arms and badges of rank, as well as to the Spanish Republicans, and the FTP. They in their turn accept the bribe and continue to go their own way. In particular, the F.T.P. has been noticeably active in the matter of requisitioning and carrying out arrests, including at one moment the arrest of members of their own Deuxieme Bureau. They were also reported on the 20th October by the B.C.R.A. to be withdrawing their men from the Atlantic front and to be concentrating a number of men, estimated at 18,000, in Bordeaux. Of all this M. Cusin remains necessarily a helpless spectator. The situation may indeed be improved by the recent appointment to command the region of Colonel Saint-Sauveur (Constant), who is a man of much stronger character than Druilhe, with a much better record in the resistance, but it is bound to remain delicate so long as the Germans occupy Point de Grave and Royan, since it is their presence that justifies the activities of the armed bands in the region, and it is from the activities of these armed bands that the most serious political difficulties result.

72. *From a source in touch with Madrid Embassy circles, dated 1st October, 1944:*

> We have no comments to make ourselves as this matter is entirely outside our sphere. In a recent conversation, however, with a member of the Madrid Embassy who has just returned to this country and who has been representing M.I.9 interests in the frontier zone, he expressed as his personal opinion that in view of the situation which had arisen he considered that the only possible course was to withdraw Aristide at the earliest opportunity. He made it clear that he held no brief whatsoever for the opposition, whom he regarded as being motivated primarily by personal interests and local politics, whereas he considered that Aristide had done an excellent job in organising the Resistance Movement whilst the opposition had done very little.

73. He also stated that the best of Aristide's men were occupied looking after the Germans in the Bordeaux area, so that they had no forces available to maintain discipline in the frontier zone.

74. We would repeat that this represents a purely personal point of view, regarding which we are not qualified to give an opinion.

75. *From a report to the British Ambassador in Madrid, dated 19th September, 1944:*

> The problem is simply one of the maintenance of public order under established authorities, and until this can be assured it will remain difficult to avoid British responsibility being involved through, for instance, agents employed in resistance activities by S.O.E. who are now, like "Aristide" at Bordeaux and "Leon des Landes" at Mont-de-Marsan, endeavouring to exercise executive powers and at the same time openly claiming to represent the War Office. There is for instance constant danger of collision between "Aristide" of Bordeaux and the Communists, while "Leon des Landes" has set himself up as a kind of dictator in an area where there is a conspicuous lack of responsible authority. All Frenchmen that I met were unanimous in urging the necessity of immediate mobilization

under a unified military control, failing which it may prove extremely difficult to curb the activities of the various groups of armed scalliwags who are at present claiming to exercise authority in such areas as this.

76. The question of Allied participation – direct or indirect – in such questions is a matter of high policy, and it may well be that it has been decided to leave such matters entirely to the French. If that is the case, it is difficult to see why deliveries of arms to Mont-de-Marsan continue and why missions such as those of "Aristide" at Bordeaux, Major Kelly at Pau and the American Colonel Fuller are not immediately terminated. On the other hand British interest in the maintenance of orderly conditions in France is undeniable and Allied responsibility for the existence of the present armed formations in the country inescapable, and it would seem desirable to put such Allied participation in French affairs on a more regular footing than that afforded by the emergence from the shadows of the German occupation of officers who though most gallant and courageous in their work of organizing resistance against the enemy (this is particularly true in the case of "Aristide," who had to build up the whole machine of resistance anew after one of the blackest acts of treachery – that of the notorious "Grandclément" – known in modern times) are probably in no way equipped to act as Allied military advisers and even as temporary administrators of places such as Bordeaux. If, therefore, Allied military missions are to be re-established in the area, the question of frontier control will be one of the questions constantly before them, and the closest liaison between them and His Majesty's Embassy in Spain and particularly the Military Attaché will be most desirable.

77. *From the same source, dated the 25th September, 1944:*

The first development was the brusque and sudden dismissal of Aristide of Bordeaux by General de Gaulle on the 17th September. The temporary authority exercised by this British agent, and by the other F.F.I. "Military Delegate," Triangle, had been recently confirmed both by S.O.E. in London and by General Koenig, and on the 14th September the latter had sent an officer of considerable prestige, Colonel Rolleau, with the mission of reorganising and encadring the French regular forces in the area, and this officer was explicitly instructed to work in co-operation with Aristide and Triangle. Yet when General de Gaulle visited Bordeaux on the 17th September he had both Aristide and Triangle summoned by his Minister of War and deprived of their functions, the former being ordered to leave the country within a few hours and the latter sent to Paris in order, it is now rumoured, to be court-martialled for the hideous crime of collaborating with the British. The political career of this rather pathetic little couple was thus cut short, and an (at least theoretical) unity of command established under Colonel Druilhe, appointed O.O.C., the 18th military region. The mission of Colonel Rolleau was also terminated, and he too was packed off to Paris.

78. It was natural that General de Gaulle's action should have considerably incensed most of the original members of the active Resistance movement in the area, since they were Aristide's associates; and it was accompanied by similar action at Cognac where the F.F.I. military delegate was also dismissed; but it also gave the local impression of a deliberately anti-British act since Aristide had (apparently with the approval of London) openly claimed to be the representative of the War Office and had travelled round, wearing a home-made "British" uniform, in a car decorated with three Union Jacks (one of them of out-size dimensions) and with the words "E.M. – War Office" painted on it. The situation thus has certain political implications (my impression is that Aristide, despite his declaration to the contrary, is loath to leave France and anxious, if possible, to make use later of his own popularity at Bordeaux and his following among the F.F.I. for whom he had himself received arms from London), and I would submit that his immediate recall to London is urgently necessary. His removal may appear tantamount to our acquiescing in a deliberate rebuff by General de Gaulle aimed against British help in any form (the General probably acted on considerably exaggerated and even deliberately misleading reports furnished by certain of his services – and in particular by the anti-British Major (now Lieutenant-Colonel) Richard who is at present in command of the whole frontier) – but the rebuff is more particularly directed at General Koenig, who had confirmed the authority of Aristide and Triangle, and is thus a typically French politico-military wrangle between the head of the provisional Government and the Commander-in-Chief of the F.F.I.

79. The incident has certainly created an atmosphere of uncertainty and unrest in Bordeaux and the Landes, and people are asking themselves why, when de Gaulle was at such pains to eliminate from political power the "Giraudist" elements – the professional soldiers – at Algiers, he now removes the original leaders of the Resistance movement in South-West France and replaces them with professional soldiers "officers of the 1939 army." The answer is probably:

(i) that the Resistance leaders are many of them incapable administrators, and
(ii) that de Gaulle is jealous by nature and unwilling to see others attaining positions of political importance especially if they are personally popular and command some local following.

80. In itself the suppression of Aristide and Triangle was probably desirable and necessary, but it was carried out in such a brusque manner as to create a most unfortunate impression.

81. *From the Report of the Judex Mission, dated the 17th December, 1944:*

"Colonel Buckmaster and Captain Dubouchage then went to see by appointment Colonel Constant, where we received the only frigid reception that we had had in France. Constant accused Actor of having returned to Bordeaux in November; he made it plain that he was not interested in any work that had been done by the British in France and he rudely refused our invitation to lunch. Since returning to London Colonel Buckmaster has written personally denying that Actor returned to France since his arrival (in England) on the 8th October, and asking that sanctions may be taken against the person who started this rumour."

82. The same rumour obtained currency once again in January. There were still apparently influences at work anxious to cause friction between the French and ourselves. This rumour, of course, was as false as the previous one.

83. It is difficult to form a complete judgment on the Aristide affair. It is the opinion of the writer that Aristide acted honestly and capably according to his lights, and there is no doubt that, so long as only

Germans were against them, Aristide and his men did extremely well. Later things became much more complicated; Battle gave way to Intrigue, Plot and Counter-Plot almost over-night (little more than a fortnight elapsed between the liberation of Bordeaux and Aristide's dismissal by de Gaulle). And, as Aristide records, no help in solving the local confusion was available from Higher Authority, where the situation was not much clearer.

84. Aristide's groups are reproached with a great deal of "bumping off" of rivals, with embezzlement and most of the other crimes in the Calendar. As to the first of these it is necessary to bear in mind the circumstances in which the circuit was built up: any contact of Grandclement's – and there had been upwards of 30,000 of them as has been seen – was a potential worker with the Gestapo and a (real or imaginary) traitor. Hence, accusations were bound to be rife, more particularly as – incredible though it may seem – not all are convinced even yet of Grandclement's treachery. The writer was approached in Bordeaux as recently as the 21st January, 1946, by a man who had known Grandclement well, and who asked if it was really believed that he had been a traitor.

85. As to the other accusations, Aristide states in his Report that, at least in the early stages, he refused to work with the Communists. He also observes under date of the 14th September: "The situation is becoming critical in Bordeaux. The F.T.P. are arriving from everywhere, they are requisitioning (it is more like pillage) and arresting people whom they call collaborators, but who are really those who will not co-operate with the F.T.P. They have their prison, their courts and carry out summary executions. They claim to be F.F.I. but do not take orders from the F.F.I. Staff. Order reigned in Bordeaux before their arrival."

86. Aristide reports that the day after this event, Monsieur Cusin, Commissaire de la Republique (of whom the Judex Mission formed a very high opinion when they saw him in December) gave a dinner in honour of Triangle and Aristide. He is said to have borne tribute to the correctness of their actions and to have told Aristide that the contretemps in his case doubtless arose from a heated discussion, which de Gaulle had had with Aristide's colleague Hilaire (Lieutenant-Colonel Starr) in Toulouse. De Gaulle, in fact, was doing a great deal of this kind of thing at this time.

87. An abbreviated account of the activities of the Aristide groups will be found at Appendix A.

Appendix A:

SABOTAGE AND GUERRILLA ACTIVITIES OF THE ARISTIDE CIRCUIT

The original report on the activities of the Actor circuit covers twenty pages of foolscap. What follows is merely a summary listing the main events.

April 1944
Corps Franc Pierre de Merignac
Various telephone lines cut including those of German A.A. batteries. The Bordeaux–Lacaneau railway and lines connecting Peugeot factory at Merignac and the various German command posts.

May 1944
Railway Team
Sabotage of sixteen electric locomotives out of eighteen at Morcenx Station.

Corps Franc Pierre de Merignac
Continuation of telephone cutting operations.

June 1944
Corps Franc Pierre de Merignac
Continuation of cutting German lines. Sabotage of nine electric locomotives and two electric Michelines near Pessac Station.

Corps Franc Dede le Basque
Attack on motorised column leaving Bordeaux by route nationale 137. Destruction of fourteen lorries, sixty-two Germans killed, eighty-two wounded, remainder of column retired to Bordeaux.

Corps Franc Leon des Landes
Dax–Bayonne. 60,000-volt line cut at four points. Railway 10,000-volt line cut at three points. Dax–Bayonne underground cable cut, trees felled on Dax–Bayonne road. All telephone and telegraph lines on Dax–Bayonne and secondary roads cut. German telephone lines cut. Four pylons down on 150,000 volt line at Nanosse. 150,000, 60,000 and 10,000-

volt lines cut in six places between Dax and Bordeaux. Underground cable Bordeaux–Dax–Toulouse cut. Numerous other cuts on H.T. lines. Forty-two Germans killed in combat. Underground cable Dax–Bordeaux blown between Dax and Castets–interruption of several days. Underground cable Dax–Bordeaux, Dax–Pau and Toulouse interrupting communications between Dax–Bordeaux, Spain and Portugal.

Corps Franc Arcachon
Pylons and telephones sabotaged.

Corps Franc Fernand
Destruction of 33-ton crane and locomotive.

Corps Franc Georges
Multiple attacks on H.T. lines, telephones and telegraphs. Attacks against railway lines, points, signals, &c., including signalling system at Bordeaux-St. Jean. Destruction of four bridges.

Corps Franc Dede le Basque
Sundry attacks on German telephone communications. Attack on Kommandatur at Bordeaux. Material damaged. German losses unknown. Railway sabotaged, three German trains derailed near Jonzac, one near Pons, goods train near Fleac, munitions train near Jonzac. German express derailed following sabotage to petrol train north of Bordeaux.

July 1944
Corps Franc Fernand
Multiple attacks against pylons.

Corps Franc Pierre de Merignac
Multiple attacks against German telegraph and telephone communications and electrical supplies to railways.

Roland Group Port of Bordeaux
This group cut all the electric cables supplying the installations for the mining of the right bank of the Garonne. The electric cables were then made up again in order that the damage should be difficult to trace. A similar operation on the left bank was unsuccessful but the third

operation on the electric cables supplying installations for the mining of the stone bridge at La Bastide was successful.

Corps Franc Georges

Attack on St. Medard powder works (out of action 15 days), Four bridges destroyed.

Corps Franc Dede le Basque

Attack's against railways, destruction of Pacific type locomotive, derailment of munition trains. Attacks against the cellulose works at Facture. Destruction of munition depot at Jonzac. On RN. 137, blockage of road by felling of trees, complete destruction of bridge at Bougneau. Destruction of two proto-types of "V.4" weapon in the Latécoère Works at Toulouse.

Corps Franc Fernand

Attacks on railways and sabotage of transformers in repair shops at Bordeaux-St. Jean.

Corps Franc Leon des Landes

All railway, telephone, telegraph and power lines cut on lines round Mont de Marsan. Attacks on German trains on Dax–Bayonne, Dax–Bordeaux, Dax–Pau and Dax–Mont de Marsan lines. Complete interruption of traffic. Important attacks on underground cables Bordeaux–Dax and Dax–Toulouse. Complete destruction of petrol depot at St. Paul les Dax. 436,000 litres of petrol burnt and 200,000 litres of oil. Operation carried out in broad daylight.

Multiple attacks on H.T. lines, telephones and railways in general. In the station of Laluque an entire train of munitions on its way to Normandy was blown up. Twenty-two waggons loaded with shells and munitions of all sorts were destroyed. First explosion occurred at 2030 hours and explosions went on all night. In addition, forty-seven waggons loaded with material exclusively for German use were destroyed. Complete stoppage of traffic between Bordeaux–Hendaye.

August 1944
Corps Franc Dede le Basque

Multiple attacks on R.N. 137 and R.N. 730 and various other roads in the district. Multiple attacks on railway, telegraph, and power lines. Occupation of the town of Montandre and capture of ammunition lorry. Capture of 27 Germans fleeing into the forests of Bussac, Bedenac and Chatenet. German passenger train and ammunition train derailed at Mosnac.

On the 23rd August, Dede le Basque (real name Andre Bouillard) with 18 men attacked a German column composed of armoured cars, vehicles and lorries – strength 435 men near Montandre. The fight lasted four hours, 2 armoured cars and 16 lorries were destroyed and the Germans lost more than 16 men in the battle. Andre Bouillard was killed and 3 of his men were wounded.

Corps Franc Georges
Multiple attacks on pylons, including 16 pylons and H.T. lines north and south of Bordeaux. Multiple attacks on German isolated transport. *Corps Franc Arcachon* Various attacks on railways.

Corps Franc Leon des Landes
Multiple attacks on H.T. pylons, under-ground cables. Attack on train carrying heavy guns at Buglose and Tarnos and on military train at Caudos.

"All the HT. lines are blown up from Pays-Basque (Mauleon) to the Bearn (Sauveterre), passing by the Landes, Dax, Mont de Marsan, Morcenx, Labouheyre and the region of Bayonne. There is no longer any electrical power in these lines, cuts are maintained permanently and traffic is forced to use steam.

"Our men derail all the trains which attempt to pass, thus realising complete stoppage of traffic which I have sworn to obtain. The German troops, which had received an order to evacuate, are blocked in all directions. They requisition bicycles, horse-drawn vehicles, farm carts and lorries in their attempts to flee. It is easy to see the nervousness of their troops and their officers and the greatest confusion reigns."

Bayonne–Dax
Attack on train pulling 50-ton crane intended to clear the wreckage of

a supply train destroyed previously. The crane fell over the permanent-way and was completely out of service.

On the 20th August the plans for the total occupation of Landes Department were put into action with 700 men and the German garrison of Mont de Marsan was attacked. Seeing the attack in force, the enemy abandoned the town without carrying out their plan of destruction and abandoning much material, including a large quantity of petrol. In the afternoon of the 21st August, a strong German column of 35 lorries approached Mont de Marsan and with 1,000 men attempted to pass at all costs. The battle lasted 7 hours and the enemy was forced to retire, abandoning 2 guns, 10 cars, a petrol lorry with 36,000 litres of oil, and a field work-shop. On the 23rd August, attack on the town of Dax; the capture of Mont de Marsan and Dax put to rout the Germans in Bayonne, Hendaye and St. Jean de Luz, and thus prevented the destruction of permanent works in those towns.

Corps Franc Dédé-le-Basque
170 Germans killed in a brush With Pauillac Maquis.

Corps Franc d'Arcachon
On the 25th August an attack on the Arcachon garrison with 300 men against 1,500 Germans. The Germans abandoned Arcachon and made for Bordeaux.

All Actor Groups
The Germans abandoned all the South-West of France, South of Bordeaux, and retreated on Bordeaux. The events subsequent to this are treated in the main report on the Actor circuit.

Chapter 3

The Lille Region

BRITISH CIRCUIT ACTIVITIES IN THE LILLE REGION

1. In November 1942 a parachute operation was carried out South-West of Paris in which three British officers were dropped, two organisers. Captain Trotobas and Major Bieler, and Captain Trotobas's Wireless Operator, Lieutenant Staggs.

2. F Section of S.O.E. had at that time no contacts of their own in the Nord and Pas-de-Calais, but such was the importance of the area from the military point of view that two of the best officers ever to be sent out by the Section were chosen and entrusted with the mission of organising sabotage there. Major Bieler was given contacts with another organisation (the Carte organisation) which was said to be active, but Captain Trotobas had to start from scratch.

3. In spite of a serious injury to his back on landing Major Bieler insisted on carrying on with his mission. He spent the first few months in Paris,

where he acted as liaison between Captain Trotobas, who had gone on to Lille, and the Prosper (Major Suttill's) organisation in Paris. Lieutenant Staggs, Captain Trotobas's W/T operator, having proved incapable, all communications with London at this stage were passed by Prosper.

4. The Carte contact proved unsatisfactory (there were many arrests and great confusion within that organisation), and it was not until the end of March 1943 that Major Bieler managed to establish his own contacts and get to work in the Valenciennes–St. Quentin area.

Major Bieler's Organisation.

Operational name of organisation: The Musician Circuit.
Operational name of organiser: Blanc and, later, Tell.
Name by which known in the Field: Guy.

5. Major Bieler (Guy) arrived in the St. Quentin area in March 1943 and began the slow process of building up his organisation. An extremely thorough and conscientious worker, he was handicapped by the injury to his back (bicycling was impossible), but by the end of May he was able to report that he had organised his primary targets, 13 cuts in the Railway lines in the vicinity of Douai, Cambrai, Busigny, Laon, Aulnoye and Valenciennes. He was in contact by this time with a number of Gaullist organisations and notably with Resistance circles in the S.N.C.F., with Liberation and with organisations of the Far Left. To all these he contributed the benefit of his experience, of his training, and of the possibilities which he represented of communication with, and supply from, London.

6. This question of communications was for most of the period a difficult one. As already mentioned, in the early stages the only means of direct W/T communication was through the Prosper Group in Paris. With the dissolution of this group by the Gestapo in June 1943 the only route was through an even more distant operator, Hercule, in the Tours area. In September 1943, however, a Radio Operator was sent to the Field by Lysander, made her way to St. Quentin from the other side of Paris, Wireless Set in hand, and started operating in November 1943. This operator was a woman, Section Officer Unternahrer, W.A.A.F., known in the Field as Yvonne.

7. Major Bieler's organisation survived the disasters in the Prosper circuit and was apparently unaffected by the death of Captain Trotobas in Lille on the 27th November. 1943. But in January 1944 he and his W/T operator were arrested together with 45 other persons.[47]

8. One of the major objectives given to Major Bieler for attack was the St. Quentin Canal and in January 1944, only a day or two before the arrests, an assistant, Lieutenant Tessier (Christophe), was sent to him specially briefed in this objective.

9. Records available in London do not carry the history of the Musician Circuit beyond the arrest of its leader. More up-to-date information can be obtained from the persons mentioned below, at Appendix C.

10. Quite recently a memorial plaque in honour of Major Guy (Major Bieler) was unveiled in Fonsomme (Aisne).

Captain Trotobas's Organisation.
Operational name of organisation: The Farmer Circuit.
Operational name of organiser: Sylvestre.
Name by which known in the Field: Michel.

11. Whereas Major Bieler remained, under orders from London, in Paris for some months after his arrival in the Field, Captain Trotobas made his way to the Lille area shortly after his arrival in November 1942. He already knew the area, and hoped to make his own contacts there. In this, however, he was disappointed and immediately found himself in the unenviable position of being alone in the street with a small sum of money, a pistol and nowhere to lodge himself in a city over-run with Germans.

12. The notes that follow give a summary of the development and achievements of the Circuit, which he founded. They come not so much from official records in London as from information gathered in Lille subsequent to the Liberation, since, unlike Major Bieler, Captain Trotobas never sent us written reports. On the other hand, the organisation of which he so painfully established the foundations in December 1942 did not die with him, but on the contrary, developed into the W.O. Organisation which is said at the present time to number upwards of 10,000 members.

13. The possessor of a flair for choosing men, Captain Michel (to adopt the name by which he is universally known in the Lille area) was soon able to make for himself the necessary contacts from which an organisation could begin to take shape. But the circles in which he was able to move at this period were not impressive. In May 1943 Prosper reported that Captain Michel "is known to move in a very tough circuit of *maquereaux* and race-horse gangs; apparently he fits into this crowd, and is doing very good work."

14. The work *was* good; in the same month Captain Michel was able to report that all his material had been distributed in Lille, Roubaix, Armentières and St. Pol and that he was limiting numbers to 200. In early June plans for the destruction of all German and S.N.C.F. lines in and out of Lille were reported as nearing completion.

15. At least three of those who worked with him at this time are alive and still in the Lille region. Arthur (Arthur Malfait, of whom more anon), Jacky (Julian Gerskens) and Mado (Madeleine Thirou). Arthur and Jacky were his lieutenants in sabotage operations, while Mado, proprietress of a small café, gave him shelter, and her café served as H.Q.

16. It must have been at about this time, or shortly after, that a change came over the character of the organisation. This followed upon Captain Michel's being put in contact with an indigenous group led by Commandant Bayart (R.10) and Commandant Pierre Seailles (P.S.). It is a further tribute to Captain Michel's qualities that he was equally able to impress these new contacts with the seriousness of his mission and his own ideals and qualities as an organiser. With this acquisition new avenues of recruitment were opened and the organisation took on a much more serious character.

17. It also assumed the intensely British character, which it never subsequently lost, and which is now such a feature of the W.O. Organisation.

18. Although this was the organisational period it was not in Captain Michel's nature to confine his activities to pure organisation, and indeed the best and only way to the establishment of mutual confidence and

respect lies in action against the enemy. This was not lacking. Later in these notes will be found a list of the operations undertaken by the Farmer circuit; it is only proposed to include here an account of one of them in order to show the type of man that Captain Michel was and the type of operation which his organisation was capable of carrying out.

Attack on the Fives-Lille Works. June 1943.
19. (Report based on interrogation carried out on the spot in 1945.) At midnight on the 27th June, a party of 25 men, some of them dressed in French police uniform, others in German uniform and a few in civilian clothes, entered the factory. One of the "civilians," speaking only German through an interpreter, gave the factory guards to understand that he was a member of the Gestapo and that he had come with large forces to protect the factory, as Allied parachutist saboteurs were believed to have been dropped in the vicinity to attack the transformers.

20. He then gave orders to disperse his forces as guards, and ordered the factory electrician to come with him and a few assistants to the Transformer Station. This, and the secondary Transformer Station were thoroughly searched and the whole party left the plant. While they were at the entrance some explosions occurred. The man who was posing as a member of the Gestapo immediately stated that he must go and fetch reinforcements, and the whole party left in a hurry.

21. While pretending to search the transformer stations charges had been placed on the three 600 KVA transformers. Similarly, at the secondary transformer station a charge had been placed on the small transformer and on one oil-bath switch.

22. The three 600 KVA transformers were completely destroyed, and fire ensued destroying the switch gear and control panels and the transformer building. At the secondary transformer building the transformer and switch gear were also destroyed.

23. During all this time the organisation operated under two crippling disadvantages. The first lay in the fact that the R.A.F. route from England to Lille passed by Cabourg and south of Paris (after D-Day it was even longer) and the R.A.F. were furthermore most unwilling to fly to the area at all, owing to the prevalence of flak; in the early (1943) days

a certain number of direct deliveries were made, but in 1944 the only materials, which the group received, were run by lorry from the Paris area.

24. The second difficulty was communications. Up to June 1943, as has been noted, there was a possibility of communication through Prosper in Paris. After that date any message to London had to take the long road to Tours (Indre-et-Loire). On the 4th November Major Bieler's new Radio Operator (Yvonne) started working, and a more direct line of communication might have been established, but on the 28th November Captain Michel was killed by the Gestapo. At 7 o'clock in the morning the street was cordoned off, and an officer (stated to be the "Grand Chef") and four men went to the house where Captain Michel was lodging. In the ensuing struggle Captain Michel killed the officer and two of his men, but was himself killed, as was also a young woman (Denise), a member of the group, who was also in the house.

25. These events followed within a few hours of the arrest in Arras of a British officer, Lieutenant Reeves (Olivier), who had been sent out in 1943, as assistant to Captain Michel, had not seen eye to eye with him, and had finally been given a relatively independent command in Arras. He is strongly suspected locally of having betrayed his commanding officer, although he has been officially cleared in England of the charge of having wilfully done so. He is reproached with being an empty boaster (he habitually carried 3 revolvers, but did not use them on the occasion of his arrest) and with being the only one of the group leaders who, when faced with arrest, did not die in action or in silence at the hands of the Gestapo.

26. Accounts of the above happenings were given to us by Major Bieler, but, with his disappearance in January 1944, silence descended on the Lille–St. Quentin area.

27. On the 10th February, 1944, however, a message arrived in London from Berne signed by R.10 (Commandant Bayart) and P.S. (Pierre Séailles) (Commandant Bayart was later killed by the Gestapo, but Commandant Séailles survives), bringing the welcome news that the circuit was far from dead, although it lacked money, materials and communications. In April working contact was established through

another organiser, Commandant Dumont-Guillemet (Armand, but known in the Lille region as Hercule), working from Paris. He was able to supply them with money and a certain amount of materials, by lorry, from Paris.

28. Records are available which show that in November 1943, at the time of Captain Michel's death, there were 1,200 members of the group. In April 1944 when contact was established with Commandant Dumont-Guillemet, numbers had grown to 2,000. On D-Day (6th June) further progress had been made to 5,000 and at the moment of the Insurrection in the Nord and Pas-de-Calais the organisation numbered no less than 8,000 men. Of these approximately half were well organised and sufficiently armed. The remainder served as Reserve.

   The Casualties have been:
   Shot by the Germans: 50.
   Fallen in battle: 200.
   Deported and assumed dead: 85.

29. It remains to add that the W.O. (or O.F.A.C.M.) Organisation has gone from strength to strength and, as already noted, is said now to have some 10,000 members. Its intensely pro-British spirit and its high degree of *esprit de corps* are an object of jealous dislike by the Communists, and are also an embarrassment to the central "Amicale" in Paris, which is endeavouring to come to an arrangement with the French "Action" Section of the D.G.E.R. Relations between Paris and Lille, which wishes to remain obstinately British, are somewhat strained.

30. The following Appendices are attached:

Appendix A: Report of the Judex Mission on its visit to Lille, 3rd-6th October, 1944.
Appendix B: Summary of activities of the Farmer Circuit.

Appendix A:

REPORT OF JUDEX MISSION

We arrived at about five o'clock on the evening of Monday, the 3rd October, 1944, at H.Q., 129 Boulevard de la Liberté, Lille. This building, next door to F.F.I. H.Q., at No. 127, was decorated with a large sign bearing the legend O.F.A.C.M. – Organisation Franco-Anglaise du Capitaine Michel. On our entry the party, consisting of the Colonel, Captain Francis, myself, Captain Prévost and Spiritualist, was received by a group of approximately 15 Senior Officers. After the customary valedictory speech by the Colonel, their leader, Pierrot (Commandant Pierre Seailles), began an account of their preoccupations.

In the first place they were intensely proud of the fact that they had always been free from politics and had worked under the War Office (we found later that all their banners bore the letters W.O. prominently displayed, their cars bore W.O. numbers, their shoulder flashes were W.O. – some of them specially made in metal in a Tourcoing factory – and W.O. was completely uppermost in all their thoughts and actions). Captain Michel – Farmer – had promised them that they could consider themselves as soldiers of the British Army with corresponding rights and responsibilities. It is evident that Spiritualist had carried out an extremely tactful and efficient job in persuading them that the rôle of the War Office had ceased with the driving of the Germans out of France, and that the surviving members must make their arrangements for "becoming French." This was, of course, a very obvious disappointment to them, but one which they were persuaded to accept.

The real problem lay in those of their numbers who had been killed, confident in the fact that their dependants would receive pensions from the British Government on the British scale.

The other grave problem was the lack of funds. In view of their intense pride it was perhaps natural that the W.O. Organisation had been left to stand on its own feet. They had been affiliated for military purposes, but not for civil purposes, with the F.F.I., and were drawing rations like the other organisations: but they had no money and were completely at the end of their funds.

These, and other problems less grave, were discussed, more particularly with Captain Prévost, and it was agreed that the first necessity lay in completing the affiliation with the F.F.I. After this meeting we all went with Captain Prévost to try and find Colonel Bastien, Regional Chief of the F.F.I. He was not there, and a tentative rendezvous was fixed for next morning.

In résumé, a number of problems had been unearthed, most of them somewhat tricky, but none of them as serious as the problem with which we had believed we were to be faced, of 2,500 men determined through thick and thin to remain defiantly under the W.O. banner.

Wednesday, the 4th October, was devoted to a tour of inspection of the various groups, and a very surprising day it proved.

Our first rendezvous was at 129 Rue de la Liberté, where a procession of 3 cars and a motorcyclist had been formed. (The motorcyclist had a chequered career – at first his engine gave trouble and he fell behind. Later, attempting to make up time, he charged a motor car at 50 m.p.h. and had to be taken off to hospital).

The procession left at breakneck speed for the first group to be visited at Auchel. Here some 20 men sprang smartly to attention on our arrival, the sentry and the guard of honour (of 7 or 8 men) presented arms, and an inspection was made of the men's quarters and of their Field kitchen.

The same general procedure was followed at all the barracks we visited, varying in simplicity and elaborateness with the size and importance of the detachment visited.

Thus at Aire-sur-la-Lys, which we visited next, the drill was the same with the exception that here some 300-400 men were on parade, their quarters being an old convent which had been used by the Germans as an H.Q.

At Bailleul the scale was again small, but at Lille, which was next visited, we had a reception which will always remain memorable.

This was the detachment which under the command of Lieutenant-Colonel Herry had been incorporated as a Company in the Premier Bataillon de Sécurité. After having been received by the Colonel and a number of high police dignitaries, we found the men drawn up in a hollow square, impeccably equipped with uniform, greatcoats and helmets. To the strains of "God Save The King," extremely well, if a little fancifully, rendered by the Band, the twin flags – sewn together – of France and England were solemnly raised to the top of the flagpole. Then the Marseillaise, followed by a withdrawal to a short flight of steps behind the house, which served as dais for the March Past, the Colonel taking the salute, and the troops, with their colours, marching past with great efficiency.

Then a great lunch, with speeches before and after, and the party was on its way again, somewhat behind schedule.

Further detachments were visited at Phalempin, Cysoing and Roubaix. By this time a graceful little speech on Anglo-French co-operation, and on the necessity for the extermination of the Germans, had crept into the proceedings. Local members were presented, and congratulated, including one "Tarzan" who had strangled a German Officer with his own hands. By a delightful coincidence he himself was apparently suffering from sore throat, as his neck was swathed in bandages.

The second great moment of the day came with the inspection of the Roubaix Sector. This was under the command of Captain "Arthur," one of the most active saboteurs, and an old associate of Captain Michel's. Three companies were drawn up on three sides of a square in front of their chateau H.Q.; there was a colour party in the middle and a rank of about 30 officers and men on the fourth side awaiting presentation to the Colonel.

After the usual ceremonies, the party left amid fervent cries of "Vive l'Angleterre!" from a crowd which had gathered outside the gate to watch the proceedings.

That evening we dined at the Officers' Mess – a building captured from the Germans, who had used it for the same purpose – with Lieutenant-Colonel Herry, Commandant Séailles, Captain Jacky, an one or two others. The gravest of the problems calling for comment was the method of incorporation into the Police Forces. The leaders of our own organisation were intensely anxious that the spirit of enthusiasm and comradeship, of which we had been witnesses, should not be lost; whereas the Army authorities were said to be unwilling to allow existing units to preserve their corporate existence and insisted on a complete admixture of the various organisations, right down to platoon level.

There was apparently also a notable lack of sympathy and tact on the side of the military in the person of the General commanding the region, with whom Lieutenant-Colonel Herry had already had an unsatisfactory interview. Nevertheless, he agreed to approach him again in an endeavour to secure the formation of another W.O. Company as part of a second battalion of Security Police then in course of formation.

Outstanding in all our contacts with the various groups was the evidence of a fervent admiration, amounting almost to worship, of

Captain Michel (Farmer), of a burning desire to continue to rank as part of a British War Office organisation, and of the development of an *esprit de corps* which was remarkable. It was in its way a tragedy that part of our mission was to declare the British connection officially ended, though there is no doubt whatever that unofficially it will continue to exist for a very long time to come.

On the practical side, the much deferred meeting between the Colonel, Captain Prévost and the local W.O. and F.F.I. leaders duly took place. It was suggested that the question of British pensions might be met by a one-time payment in the neighbourhood of Frs. 100,000, in which case the French were prepared to pay this sum. They would provide Frs. 200,000 for necessitous cases where immediate assistance was necessary. Arrangements for complete affiliation would be proceeded with.

In conclusion note should perhaps be made of a meeting between Captain Hazeldine and myself and a number of the leading saboteurs of the organisation. They numbered six or seven, and had all been leading figures in *coup de main* tasks carried out against the enemy. Two of them, Arthur and Jacky, had been original associates of Captain Michel's. This talk was at once inspiring and disappointing; inspiring in the actions they had carried out whenever they had materials with which to work, and disappointing in the realisation of the immense amount of work which might have been done by our group in the Lille area, if we had only been able to send the supplies which they so richly deserved.

Appendix B:

SUMMARY OF ACTIVITIES OF THE FARMER CIRCUIT

1. Sabotage.

(*a*) Up to the 6th June, 1944:

Railway.   Railway Cuts:
17, of which 1 interrupted traffic for 8 days; 1 interrupted traffic for 5 days.
Derailments:
8, causing the derailment of
52 Wagons.
10 Tank Wagons.
3 Tenders.
2 Locomotives.
Material: Sabotage of
52 Locomotives (some out of action for 6 months).
12 Machine Tools (of which 9 completely destroyed).
3 Compressor Stations.
2 Cranes.
2 Electric Sub-Stations.
1 Signal Box.
1 Compressor.
Burning of:
152 Wagons of Straw, &c.
44 Wagons of Ammunition.
22 Tank Wagons of Petrol.
3 Tank Wagons of Oil.

Electricity.   Sabotage of:
2 H.T. Lines (Current cut off for 15 days in the Région Boulonnaise).
2 Mine Power Plants (Current cut off for 48 hours in 5 Mine Shafts).
1 Sub-Station.
5 45,000-volt Transformers.
3 Pylons.
1 Switching Station.

Canals.   Sabotage of:

2 Locks (Canal stopped 4 months).
1 Bridge (stoppage 2 months).
6 Tractors (of which 4 destroyed).
3 Barges sunk (740 tons of Maizena).

Factories, &c.   Distilleries:
Allennes-les-Marais 1,800,000 litres of Spirit burnt.
Ascq 600,000 litres of Spirit poured away.
Tressin 500,000 litres of Spirit burnt.
2,900,000
Ets. Desmet at Ronchin Destruction of Machine Tools and of Radar sets for German
A.A. Works stopped 3-4 months.
Sté. des Produits du Maïs at Haubourdin: 23 Oil Tanks pierced, 1 Elevator damaged (stoppage 4 weeks).
Fives-Lille 22 Transformers, 8 Switches destroyed.
S.N.C.F. Depot at Tourcoing: 400 litres oil, 1,600 litres petrol seized.
German Garage, Tourcoing: 17 lorries, 116 cars destroyed, oil and petrol stocks burnt.
La Dray Works, Cysoing.
Office of Inspecteur du Travail en Allemagne in Lille Station burnt.

Sundry.   15 Concrete Mixers.
10 Tracked Vehicles and Tanks.
2 Trainer Aircraft.
1 Crane.
1 A.A. Gun.
Various crop fires.

(*b*) After the 6th June, 1944:

Railway.   Railway Cuts: 31, of which 1 interrupted traffic for 3 days; 11 interrupted traffic for more than 30 hours.
Derailments: 8, causing the derailment of
14 Wagons.
5 Locomotives.
1 Tender.
1 Train of V.I.'s.

Bridges: 8, of which 1 interrupted traffic for 8 days: 1 interrupted traffic for 3 days.

Tracks ploughed up: (By a special attachment to locomotives, which the circuit itself invented and manufactured, on the lines of the German track-destroying apparatus used in Italy)

Lille-Armentières, over 1 km.

Houpline-Armentières, over 1 km.

Wavrin-Armentières, over 2 km.

Material: Sabotage of

16 Locomotives.

45 Wagons.

7 Compressed Air Pumps.

3 Signal Boxes.

3 Water Towers.

1 Reservoir.

1 Wheel Pit.

Burning of:

1 Train of Ammunition.

4 Wagons of Straw.

Telegraph and Telephone. Cutting of:

28 Cables, wherefrom 1 interruption of 10 days, 1 interruption of 3-4 days.

67 German Telephone Lines.

170 French Telephone Lines.

Sabotage of:

18 Section Boxes.

1 Relay Cabin.

Canals. Sabotage of:

4 Locks.

3 Syphons.

3 Bridges.

1 Culvert.

Sinking of 1 Barge (Coal).

Factories, &c. Sté. de Produits du Maïs at Haubourdin: 5 motors (loss of 8 weeks' production).

S.T.O. Offices, Lille: Files burnt.

Sundry. German Barracks burnt.

300,000 kgs. of hay and straw burn

About 1,500 German Vehicles immobilised by punctures caused by "Starfish" Nails.
15 German horses injured by same means.
Suppression and Tarring of Sign Posts.

2. Executions.

16 Members of German C.E. Services executed, most of them Sectional Heads.

3. False Papers.

An effective service. The Germans, having committed the error of having established a large number of different types of papers, were unable (in barrages, controls, &c.) to distinguish real from false. 4,500 workers helped with false papers to avoid work in Germany. At the Liberation the False Paper Section of the O.F.A.C.M. had issued more than 150 different types of papers and possessed 124 stamps and photographs.

4. Aid to Allied Troops.

Gave shelter to 120 persons, including 30 British airmen, 2 Canadian airmen, 65 American airmen. Set up a service for passing the Spanish Frontier. Helped numerous British troops cut off in 1940 and some 20 other persons of various types, escaping through the area from the Gestapo.

5. Intelligence.

Sent a mass of Intelligence to London, notably concerning V-1 Launching sites. As to these 75 Maps were sent to Hercule's Paris group for transmission to London giving the exact emplacement of V-1 sites in the Pas-de-Calais.

6. Combat.

Considerable activity in support of British armour, clearing-up operations, guarding of bridges, &c.

Chapter 4

The Rouen Region

BRITISH CIRCUITS IN THE ROUEN REGION

1. There has only been one British Circuit working in the Rouen area.

2. In April 1943 two officers were landed by Lysander near Tours, their mission being to make their way to Rouen and establish a circuit there and in Le Havre. The leader was Major (then Captain) Staunton (real name Philippe Liewer), his helper was Lieutenant Chartrand (known in the field as Dieudonne). Together they founded the Salesman Circuit.

Major Staunton's Circuit.
    Operational name of circuit: The Salesman Circuit.
    Operational name of organiser: Clément.
    Name by which known in the field: Charles, Albert or Clément.

3. After a number of false starts, contact with Rouen was established towards the end of May 1943, through a Mme. Micheline who had a dress shop in Paris with a branch in Rouen. Through her Rouen manager, Jean Sueur, Major Staunton managed to build up his whole organisation.

4. In July a W/T Operator, Captain Newman (known as Pepe or Pierre) was sent to the field, and started transmitting at the end of that month. In August Dieudonne was replaced by Lieutenant Mortier (known as Paco or Robert: real name Maloubier).

5. The programme given by London for the circuit was an active one, and it was well carried out. By the middle of August combat groups numbered 80 in Rouen and 40 in Le Havre. By February 1944 the numbers had grown to 350 thoroughly reliable men. Major Staunton was an extremely competent organiser and the security of the circuit was very much above the average. It was also Major Staunton's policy never to risk a person's safety without warning him of what was being done; anyone housing a W/T operator, or transporting arms, &c., was told the truth. As a result the Clément group had an amazing reputation for fairness. As an example, when members of the Front National tried to claim credit for the blowing up of the Compagnie Française des Métaux at Déville, the general answer was "Don't boast. You couldn't have done it so fairly and with so little loss of life. Of course it was the Clément group."

6. But no circuit is proof against accident. Trouble began with the arrest on the 15th February of the leader of the Serquigny Group. The trouble spread, and ten days later Major Staunton's second in command for the Rouen area (Cicero, Claude Malraux) was arrested as was also the radio operator, and by the middle of March 1944 the circuit was liquidated. On the 12th March 98 members of the Rouen and Le Havre organisations left Rouen under guard, for Compiègne and later for Germany.

7. By a stroke of good fortune, Clément (Major Staunton) was in England during these events. Had the weather been fine on the day on which he was due to return to the field, he would have been dropped straight to the Gestapo. Providentially the weather was bad, a warning message from the South of France[48] was received the next day, and his departure was cancelled. At the beginning of April he returned to France to ascertain if any of the broken threads could be picked up, but finding this impossible, returned to England at the end of the same month.[49]

8. During the course of its existence the Circuit had an impressive record of successful sabotage, all personally organised by Clément and generally under the personal command of Paco.

9. (1) The sinking of a German Minesweeper at Rouen. September 1943. This epic story is worth recounting in detail.

10. A 900-ton Minesweeper had been damaged by Typhoons in the Channel and was brought to Rouen for repairs. The repairs finished, acceptance trials took place in the Seine. These were satisfactory, the German Admiralty representatives were pleased, champagne flowed and a cheque for Frs. 5,000,000 was handed over to the French repairers.

11. The crew then came aboard, loaded Frs. 12,000,000 worth of Asdic equipment, 20 tons of ammunition and supplies for three months. At 9 p.m. they returned to barracks, sailing time to be 4 o'clock next morning.

12. Meanwhile, one of Clément's men had managed to get aboard and place an explosive charge on the inside of the hull. In due course this went off and the ship sank in six minutes.

13. The Gestapo quickly decided that this was an inside job, but the German Admiralty, sending down a diver, concluded that it had been done from without. Their view was held to prevail and, logically enough, the German sentry, who had been patrolling the quay, was shot!

14. In addition, the crew, arriving at what should have been the ship's side at 2 a.m. and finding no ship, had been overjoyed – and showed it. One of their number was shot as an example, and the remainder sent as soldiers to the Russian front!

15. (The name of the man who actually placed the charge is Hugues Paccaud, rue Louis-Pasteur, Grand Quevilly. It is not known whether he has survived.)

16. (2) Attack on Cie. Française des Métaux at Déville. October 1943.

17. This factory was making aluminium alloy on urgent orders for the Luftwaffe and steel tubes for bicycles.

18. On the 3rd October 8 men under the command of Cicero, and including Paco, entered the factory, and rounded up the guards and night workers. The object of the attack was to destroy the pumps

supplying pressure for the operating presses and hammers in the machine shops and also a 1,200-h.p. motor. Four out of the six pumps were put completely out of action and a fifth subsequently broke down under the increased pressure.

19. The factory was completely stopped for 15 days and production was reduced to 50 per cent. for over 6 months.

20. (3) Electrical Sub-stations at Yainville and Dieppedalle. October 1943.

21. These attacks were to have been carried out in co-operation with the R.A.F., but unfortunately the arrangements for air cover fell through. Yainville was so heavily guarded that, failing this cover, the attack had to be called off. At Dieppedalle, however, it was possible to carry on.

22. The attack was carried out by a party of 6 under Paco. The guards and workers on duty were locked up and charges were placed on the transformers and switches. As a result of the attack one transformer was completely destroyed and the other so heavily damaged that it had not yet been repaired in May 1945. Two switches were destroyed and one damaged. The sub-station was completely out of action for 6 months, after which time it was able to work at reduced capacity with a substitute transformer.

23. In November 1943 a German leave train was derailed. Reports stated that 196 Germans were killed and several hundreds wounded.

24. Not less important than these activities was a mass of information concerning German dispositions in the port of Le Havre which were supplied to the British Admiralty. The majority of this came through M. Peeters, one of the chief engineers of the Port Autonome (it is not known here if he has survived). Plans were afoot for preventing enemy demolitions and for making Le Havre pilots available to the Royal Navy. Clément was in consultation with Admiralty representatives on these matters in London in February 1944. Unfortunately the collapse of the circuit prevented anything being done.

25. Clément and Paco returned together to England in February 1944, Paco to receive medical attention. He had had a brush with a

Feldgendarmerie patrol and one of their bullets had passed through the base of a lung and his liver and lodged against his spine. In spite of this he ran 500 yards and out into the open country, concealed himself in a marsh all night and in the morning covered 9 Kms. back to Rouen before he could get medical attention.

Chapter 5

The Strasbourg Region

BRITISH CIRCUITS IN THE STRASBOURG REGION

1. British circuit activities in this region have not been very considerable. As far as Alsace and Lorraine are concerned this is understandable enough when the attempted Germanisation of this area is borne in mind.

2. As to the rest, an organisation existed in the second half of 1941 under the leadership of Baron Jean de Vomecourt (known as Constantin), brother of Pierre, who (as noted under Paris) was building up a large and important organisation covering the whole of the Occupied Zone. Constantin had many contacts in Railway circles, and had organised teams among the railwaymen for the purpose of cutting all communications between Germany and France when the moment came. Unfortunately, the moment was not destined to come for nearly three years; in the meanwhile, Pierre's organisation broke up in early 1942, Constantin was arrested with the rest and died in Germany.

3. Thereafter the British organisation was without a representative in the region until May 1943, when Captain Harry Ree (pronounced to rhyme with Hay) arrived in Montbéliard.

Captain Ree's Organisation: The Stockbroker Circuit.
Operational name of organisation: The Stockbroker Circuit.
Operational name of organiser: César.
Name by which known in the Field: Henri.

4. Henri had been dropped on the 15th April, 1943, as assistant to Captain Rafferty (Dominique), who, after the arrest of his head organiser, Captain Hudson, was in charge of a circuit in Clermont-Ferrand. In the course of his work he had picked up contacts in Dijon and in the Jura and Doubs, and it was to the development of these that Henri was to devote himself.

5. In May 1943 he came for the first time to Montbéliard. His mission here was to make contact with André[50], a lieutenant in the French Army with a group at Valentigney.

6. After carrying out a successful reception of stores for him, Henri returned to Lons-le-Saunier, where he heard of the arrest of Dominique and of the arrival in Dijon of Bob and Gabriel (Captain J.A.R. Starr and Young, radio operator). The next step was to install these two by making over to them the joints of the organisational work already carried out in that town. Henri then proceeded to the Belfort region in order to establish a line for communication to London through Switzerland.

7. This done, he returned to Montbéliard just in time for the first R.A.F. raid on the Peugeot works at Sochaux. (Before dealing with the effect of this raid on Henri's work it may be advantageous to digress a little in order to clear the stage of the affairs of Bob and Gabriel. In June Henri was in the Dijon region for the purpose of organising receptions of materials there, and on the 14th July he had a rendezvous with Bob, which the latter did not keep. On the 19th Henri learned of Bob's arrest, having been betrayed by a double-agent, by the name of Pierre Martin. On the 23rd Pedro (Lieutenant Cauchy) arrived, parachuted to assist Gabriel. With him Henri made plans for the liquidation of Pierre Martin.

8. The next stage was to find safe quarters for Gabriel whose bad French made such dispositions necessary. This was done, and he and his courier Paulette were accommodated at M. Poly's sawmill at Clairvaux (Jura). There all went well with Gabriel transmitting messages quite normally until he and Paulette were arrested in mysterious circumstances connected with the arrival of Lieutenant Maugenet, whom London had sent out, by Lysander, to act as his assistant.

9. The R.A.F. raid mentioned above was a tragic affair. The factory was untouched, and the bombs fell wide, causing very heavy casualties in the neighbouring village.

10. In early July 1943 Henri had made his first contact with the Peugeot management in the person of Paul Sire, Director of Co-ordination for all Peugeot factories, who proved very helpful indeed. Much to his interest Henri found that the Peugeot people themselves were toying with the idea of sabotaging their own factory, in order to stop production and thereby prevent a repetition of the disastrous bombardment by the R.A.F. Nothing could have been more convenient from Henri's point of view. Through Roger Fouillette, an Alsatian Artillery Captain, he made the acquaintance of Pierre Lucas, chief electrician of Peugeot, who became wildly enthusiastic, when Henri was able to point out to him the practicability of putting the factory out of action by sabotage. Delighted with the possibility of avoiding further loss of life through R.A.F. action, he showed Henri all over the factory and machinery.

11. (The treatment applied to Peugeot became the prototype for operations at other factories. It was evidently not absolutely necessary for the management to be spontaneous co-operators, since the menace of R.A.F. action was frequently sufficient to "persuade" the most recalcitrant of managements.)

12. In the meanwhile Henri had advised London of what was going on and London had obtained a grudging – and conditional – agreement from the R.A.F. to postpone further efforts against what was rapidly becoming their favourite target.

13. The condition, reasonably enough, was that really effective action should be taken from the ground.

14. 3rd November, 1943, was therefore, a rather important date, for on that night a party of six workmen, under the leadership of André, entered the works to make the first attack. They had been carefully coached by Henri in what to do and they carefully placed their charges on transformers and compressors, made their way out, and sat back in pleased anticipation, to await the expected results. Alas! Nothing happened, and subsequent examination revealed that, despite the careful coaching, the detonators had been put in the wrong way round!

15. On the 5th November (Guy Fawkes no doubt providing the inspiration) the attack was repeated, this time with success.

16. Thereafter many successful attacks were made on Peugeot and similar works in the district. These attacks were carefully analysed in London, and although it was often touch and go, the R.A.F. were successfully dissuaded from making another attack.

17. Henri himself had not participated personally in these attacks, and this proved to be as well, since his own personal contact with the district was some-what brutally cut short on 27th November when the Peugeot plan was still in its infancy. On that day he was calling at the house of M. Hauger, schoolmaster in Sochaux, and on the door being opened was greeted by a Feldgendarme who pointed a pistol at him in an unfriendly manner, and told him to come inside. It appeared that arms had been found in the house and that Henri would have to remain with his host until 6 p.m. when they would both repair to the Police Station.

18. Making the best of a bad job, Henri suggested to his captor that a drink would not come amiss, and a bottle and glasses were produced. During the next half-hour conversation proceeded on the war and other general matters, while Henri contemplated the skull before him with a view to deciding where its softer spots might be. Unfortunately the theoretical was not borne out by the practical, as the application of the bottle to the chosen target was almost entirely unproductive. Indeed, the result on balance must be accounted negative, since in reply the German fired on him at point-blank range, and although Henri felt nothing at the time, he afterwards found that he had been shot right through the chest.

19. Thereupon ensued a desperate hand-to-hand struggle, each of them employing all the methods he knew. For fully half an hour the fight swayed, in and out of the rooms and up and down the stairs. At the end, each of them leaned fainting against a wall. Henri, recovering first, was about to rush at his opponent again, when the German shouted "*Sortez*" and remained propping up the wall. Henri staggered out of the house, and in spite of his punctured condition, made his way across the garden, over the wall, across a field, over a small stream and to a house 3 kms. away where he was taken in and bound up. As soon as he was able he crossed over into Switzerland.

20. A statement is attached (Appendix A) of the various sabotage actions carried out by Henri's circuit mainly against Peugeot and similar works in the neighbourhood. One thing, however, was never attacked, and this the most important of all, the Peugeot Main Transformer. This was, of course, well guarded and was surrounded by blast walls, but it appeared feasible to attack it by Mortar fire from the window of a neighbouring workers' hostel. After many delays the necessary weapon and ammunition were delivered.

21. Unfortunately, Henri's departure for Switzerland had occurred shortly before, and none of the members of his circuit knew how the weapon worked. Worse still, a successor[51] sent from London on 14th April, 1944, and specially trained in its use was killed by the Gestapo immediately on arrival. In May 1944 he was succeeded in his turn by another American officer,[5] but it transpired later that he was no more familiar with the weapon than the local members of the circuit. So the main transformers survived, which was in the end a good thing, since the Peugeot production was already so reduced as to be of little value to the Germans, who in fact began removing the machinery from the factory into Germany.

22. Under Pascal's leadership the circuit played an effective part in the closing stages, although severely hampered, as was everyone in this part of the world, by a lack of arms and ammunition. Pascal, a capable, rugged individualist, apparently managed to disagree profoundly with local F.F.I. Commanders, but there is no doubt that his groups were well in evidence in action against the enemy.

The Chancellor Circuit.

23. Three other British circuits were also active at about this time near the South-Western limits of the Strasbourg area. Two of them, under the command of Scholar (Baron de St. Génies) and Treasurer (Comte Maze-Sencier de Brouville) had their centre of gravity in Jura and will be dealt with under that heading. The third, the Chancellor circuit under Captain George Millar,[53] has been vividly and accurately described in George Millar's book "Maquis," to which the reader in search of further information is referred.

24. This operated in the Northern Doubs, Millar's own personal headquarters being in the village of Vieilley, North-East of Besançon, and from there was able to organise an almost complete hold-up on the important railway line running to Vesoul and Belfort.

The Pedagogue Circuit.

25. The British circuits had never been able to establish a group in Meurthe-et-Moselle, until right at the end, when two organisers made their way into the area.

26. One of them, Captain Pearson (Philippe), accompanied by a radio operator, Lieut. Breen (Bruno), arrived at the beginning of August 1944 with the intention of building up a circuit[5] with contacts supplied to him by Major Cowburn. The first of these was M. Adrien Schmidt, a prominent industrialist: he unfortunately had to leave for Paris and was unable to return till after the Liberation, but his chauffeur, M. Georges Dubois, proved very capable and helpful. The other prominent helper was M.L. Sutty, head of the Chèques Postaux department of the P.T.T. in Nancy.

27. During the early settling-in period, and more as an experiment than anything else, Philippe sent to London information that 110 new fighter planes had landed on the airfield at Essey-les-Nancy. Much to his gratification and to the huge delight of the entire population of Nancy, several formations of Lightnings arrived 24 hours later and liquidated all the enemy planes.

28. The most useful contact made during this period from the practical point of view was undoubtedly Noel (M. Frédéric Remelius) of

Blainville, who led a large and excellently disciplined Marquis in the Forêt de Charmes. To him Philippe gave details of the two grounds he had reconnoitred and Noel was able to provide the man-power necessary for the reception of material on them.

29. Another contact made at this time was M. Larivière, said to be "head of all the Resistance in Nancy." Philippe reports that he was scared stiff all the time, but did render him one or two services, including "putting me in touch with Planète[55] (if this can indeed be termed a service)." He goes on:

30. "I noticed very early on that these gentlemen of the Central Resistance committee were embarrassed by my presence among them, and mainly pursued at policy of non-co-operation: there is no doubt that they imagined that I was out to steal all the credit for their liberation from them, and on two occasions they sent me messages stating that the Gestapo were on my heels, and that I must get out of town as rapidly as possible – in neither case was this true, and the messages were only sent with a view to hindering my work. Of course, I disregarded all this.

31. "My collaboration with Planète was a rather one-sided affair. I have no doubt that he worked excellently in other parts of his region, but my impression of him was that he was vain, plausible, rather frightened and meddlesome. As I had instructions to regard myself as under his orders, I could hardly refuse his request to send messages by my radio, although this put a very severe strain on the already over-wrought Lieut. Breen, besides doubling his risk of being caught. I took the liberty of cutting out altogether what messages I considered not of primary urgency (which annoyed Planète intensely when Lieut. Breen had the impudence to tell him), since Planète had a habit of writing his messages in rolling Macauleyan periods, and at that time there were matters of more urgency than footling administrative gossip."[56]

32. Then came the closing phase, the last ten days of August until the Liberation of Nancy on the 15th September.

33. Towards the end of August M. Sutty produced his trump card, M. Lacier (M. Michel Groenner), a prominent member of General Koenig's information service: he had a first-class intelligence service and also dabbled in resistance work of an operational order. Philippe

immediately took control of this. It consisted mainly of groups coming under the ægis of the Mouvement National des Prisonniers de Guerre et Déportés, who did splendid work.

34. Philippe reports that during this time he and Lacier were "in contact and on agreeable terms with" Planète and Larivière.

35. On the 1st September the Germans left Nancy in a panic, but returned on the 2nd (the Americans having run out of petrol) and remained till the 15th. During this time Philippe controlled extensive telephone cable-cutting operations by the Mouvement des Prisonniers. They also took all the information collected about the exact positions of German batteries, units, mines, stores, &c., and got through the lines to the Americans, with pages of such information. The direct result of this was that, instead of being massacred on their way through the Forêt de Haye into Nancy, the 3rd Army came through without the loss of one man and saw nothing but dead Germans, 7,000 of them.

36. On the 15th September Philippe himself made contact with the Americans and returned to Nancy with Col. Hoyne of the 35th Division. 37. As to Maquis activity, the following is taken from the report of the Judex Mission, which visited the area in October:

38. "Next morning, the 21st October, we motored to Blainville. The first intention had been that we – or at least the Colonel – should attend a memorial service being held that day, but we were not in time for this.

39. We lunched at the house of Commandant Noël, the officer commanding, the company including Pedagogue and Denning. Conversation ranged from the early days when Pedagogue's arrival saved the maquis from extinction for lack of arms, material and money, through the Resistance period when obviously the group had been extremely active, to the final phase, when the maquis had held the local Germans in complete terror.

40. Of the intermediate period we learnt of one saboteur who, in one night at Blainville station, placed no less than fifty charges. Of the final stage the following episode demonstrates most clearly the respect in which the German L. of C. troops held the men of Commandant Noël's maquis.

115

41. It was the custom – and of course the necessity – of the maquis to send a daily convoy of three or four lorries from their quarters in the woods down to neighbouring farms for supplies. The regular route for these convoys lay across a railway line where the level crossing was guarded by German troops. Such, however, was the ascendancy of the maquis over their adversaries that each day the Germans were forced to open the gates to them in both their outward and their inward journeys; and this without a shot being fired; the threat of action was sufficient.

42. Once more there was every evidence that our officers enjoyed a very fine reputation with those whom they had helped with advice and with materials. An application had, in fact, been made for Major Denning to remain, but as he told us that the Americans already suspected him, as a Britisher, of spying on their activities, it was decided that he must return home forthwith. He and Pedagogue were each given a week in which to settle up their affairs, after which they were to report to London.

43. After lunch Commandant Noël's troops were inspected and addressed by the Colonel. Their discipline on parade and their March Past were of a very high order. It was, I think, the first time that we had seen a Red Cross detachment on parade.

44. Also on parade was a priest, another member of the Church Militant, who had wielded his carbine against the foe, and had provided the maquis with an extremely valuable information service; he had been in charge of a hospital, and much of the information came through the nurses from German officers themselves.

45. We left Blainville with regret – regret for these men who had been so magnificent in action, but who were now destined to feel, more bitterly perhaps than most, the formalities and obstructions of the period of reorganisation, in which they were being called upon to play their part."

46. Capt. Pearson and Lieut. Breen were both awarded the M.B.E.

The Woodcutter Circuit.

47. On the night of 17th/18th July another officer, Lieut. A. Woerther (Justin), accompanied by his radio operator, was parachuted to the Field near Mâcon. His mission was to obtain from the Donkeyman (Major

Frager) organisation in Yonne the necessary contacts in the Nancy neighbourhood to enable him to develop an Alsatian group which Major Frager reported to exist in the neighbourhood of Metz.

48. There were difficulties in making contact with the Donkeyman organisation, and indeed in this matter of contact-making Justin may be said to have been in almost constant touch with the Gestapo. He first found that they were in occupation of the safe-house to which he should have gone on first landing. In Paris he was taken in hand by Roger (second-in-command to Frager and now under suspicion of having worked earlier with the Gestapo), who gave him the name of another Roger of the Sté. Lorema whom he was to see in Nancy. This man turned out to be a Gestapo agent. Then, to crown everything, soon after his arrival in Nancy a certain Jean, who had been the previous leader of the group, came out of prison. He gave Justin a rendezvous in Metz at which he only just escaped being arrested, since Jean was in league with the Gestapo.

49. Justin did contact M. Marcel Perrin, a grocer and wine merchant of Maxeville who put him in touch with the F.F.I., but here the reception was unfriendly and they declared (untruthfully) that they had at their disposal all the arms and material necessary, and refused to work with the British services.

50. Through a M. Traber garage-keeper, Justin did, however, make contact with a group of 50 men and worked with them. But time was now too short, and although some stores were received by parachute, the American advance cut the circuit in two almost immediately after, and prevented their effective use.

51. This comparative lack of activity in no wise diminishes the pro-British feelings of the members of the group, and their reception of the second Judex Mission in February 1945 was memorable. So memorable indeed that Planète sent for Justin immediately afterwards and "sacked" him!

52. Justin was awarded the MC. for his work in France.

Appendix A:

SABOTAGE BY STOCKBROKER CIRCUIT

Sawmill at Maîche set on fire. (Out of action for a month.) September 1943.

6 Locomotive cylinders blown between Dijon and Dôle.

Train derailed at Voujeaucourt (15th July).

Destruction of 6,030 lorry tyres in tyre-dump.

Train derailed at Luzy. October 1943.

2 Locomotives and 2 trains destroyed in Dôle station. November 1943.

Peugeot: Compressors, Electric Motors and Gas Producer Plant successfully attacked the 5th November, 1943.

Leroy Foundries, Ste.-Suzanne, attacked the 4th November, 1943. Both 550Kw. transformers blown up. (One completely destroyed, other 3 months to repair.)

Marty Piston Factory, Sochaux, attacked the 6th November, 1943. Two transformers (500 and 100 Kw.) and 3 electric motors destroyed. 1,500 litres of oil lost, 3 electric motors, a switchboard and 2 batteries of accumulators smashed.

Seven derailments at Monchanin, Millay and Luzy. November 1943.

Peugeot: Letter from Elmag works, Mulhouse, states that repairs to turbo-compressor (attacked the 5th November) would take 10-12 months.

L'Epée Machine Tool shop at Ste.-Suzanne attacked.

Maillard works, Montbéliard. Transformer attacked and out of action for 1 month. December 1943.

Wittmer Works, Seloncourt. Similar damage the 27th January, 1944. Almost total stoppage.

Train burnt out at Chagny.

Leave train derailed at Millay. 37 dead.

Goods train derailed at Monchanin.

Peugeot: Tank chain production held up since November 1943 for lack of special springs, which arrived the 8th December, 1943. Delivery was intercepted and they were dumped in the canal. Stoppage prolonged till the 5th January, 1944. Following machines put out of action January 1944;
1. Milling machines for tank track teeth.
2. Krauss boring and homing machine. 160 chassis held up. Cylinder production stopped indefinitely.
3. High precision Churchill rectifying machine.
4. Special tank lathe for Focke-Wulf wing parts. (2, 3 and 4 the only machines of their kind in area and irreplaceable.)

Japy Works, Beaucourt. 4 turret lathes, due to go into production the 15th December, 1943, on fuze screws (90,000 per month) for Schuster works in Vienne was destroyed the 13th December, 1943. These American machines cannot be replaced.

Koechlin Works. Belfort. Shed containing 800 tyres, 7 lorries and fuel and paint store destroyed by fire the 18th December, 1943.

At Gy aerodrome hangars containing all German army fodder were destroyed by fire. Damage several million francs.

Peugeot. 12th January, 1944, transformers in coach building plant destroyed.

Belfort. 8 locomotives damaged by placing scrap iron in cylinders. Locomotive Hydraulic Jack destroyed. Cannot be repaired or replaced, hence replacement of axles at Belfort is paralysed and locomotives have to be sent elsewhere.

Peugeot. 10th February, 1944, a new compressor arriving from Germany was destroyed before it was even installed. 10th February, 1944, 2 Turret lathes just arrived from Germany for Focke-Wulf part production were destroyed before they were installed.

Derailment the 10th January, 1944, at Dampierre destroyed German Army material and caused a 72-hour blockage.

Derailment the 20th January, 1944, at Voujeaucourt destroved locomotive and 4 wagons, causing 4-day stoppage.

Derailment 20th February, 1944, between Besançon and Montbéliard destroyed 7 trucks of war material.

21st February, 1944, Loading crane Montbéliard Canal destroyed.

March 1944. 11 H.T. Pylons destroyed, cutting electricity supply to Peugeot.

Peugeot: Electrically treated oven for aircraft parts for which Germans had been waiting 3 months, destroyed the 15th March, 1944, within half an hour of arrival from Fallersleben. Same treatment applied to a Hartz hydraulic press for Focke-Wulf engine cowling which it had just taken 3 weeks to install and adjust. Focke-Wulf order on Peugeot reduced by 60 per cent. Peugeot workers went on strike from evening of the 22nd March, 1944, owing to German anti-sabotage measures and threats.

22nd April, 1944. Steel railway bridge over Haute-Saône Canal destroyed 1 Km. South of Bavilliers.

16th May, 1914. Train stopped in broad daylight and then sent at full speed into empty train 500 yards South of Montbéliard. Line blocked.[57]

Chapter 6

The Indre, Vienne, Deux-Sèvres, Charente Area

1. This rather curious area does not fit in of itself with any Consular region, and it also lies partly on one side, partly on the other, of the old line of Demarcation. To those, therefore, to whom it may seem curious that it should be treated as a single unit, the explanation is the simple one that it "happened like that." These Departments, in fact, represent the remarkable organisational feat of one man Samuel, originally Hector's radio operator, then his second-in- command and, finally, his successor.

Major S. Maingard's Organisation.
Operational name of organisation: The Shipwright Circuit.
Operational name of organiser: Samuel.
Name by which known in the Field: Samuel.

2. Samuel joined Hector (see under Châteauroux–Limoges) in April 1943 as radio operator, and in six months sent over 200 messages, an extraordinary record and obviously a great contribution to the success of the circuit. As an operator Samuel did not spare himself, but the strain was beginning to tell and early in 1944 Hector was planning to make Samuel his second-in-

command, a process made easier by the fact that Samuel had himself trained two local recruits, who had been accepted as operators by London.

3. At the beginning of May 1944 Hector was arrested and Samuel took over his circuit, or rather part of it, as London split off that portion South of and including Limoges and sent out Hamlet to administer it.

4. Samuel had already, under Hector, been in contact with F.F.I. groups in Indre numbering some 2,000 men, both personally and through Marie (F/O Pearl Witherington, W.A.A.F.), who acted as courier and *agent de liaison*.

5. Shortly after D-Day two Jedburgh teams were sent to Samuel in Indre, and by the 15th June he had arranged with the F.F.I. chief to divide the Department into three sectors, the South-Eastern and South-Western, each being in the charge of one of these teams, and the Northern, being allocated to Marie. This Northern sector included the important Railway targets at Vierzon, which had formed one of the circuit's main objectives ever since the early Valérien days in 1942 (see Châteauroux–Limoges).

6. Samuel himself moved off into Vienne. Here, surprisingly enough, nothing appears to have been done by the French services (there had been no British Circuit working in this area), and Samuel reported in August 1944: "We are the only service to have armed the Vienne, and resistance there only exists through us, as the D.M.R. only contacted them with my help at the beginning of August." Samuel had also been entirely responsible for their finance up to this time. He was having some trouble with the F.T.P., who, since they had received arms, were attempting to group themselves independently. He reported, however that he would be able to deal with the situation.

7. Similarly, for Charente, where no effective Resistance organisation appeared to exist.[58] Samuel had been sent a Jedburgh team to help him in Vienne: he sent this team (Ian) to Charente, where it did extremely well and was in action almost continuously against the Germans.

8. Deux–Sèvres, where equally nothing effective existed, was not contacted by Samuel until the beginning of July, but by the 15th of that month stores were already being received.

Above: A member of the Resistance is photographed whilst laying explosive charges on a section of track near Roanne railway station.

Below: A derailment of a train in the Jura area – where George Millar was in command. A section of the rail was removed with the results shown.

Above: The aftermath of a Resistance attack on three propeller blade copying machines at the Ratier works at Figeac, France, on 19 January 1944. A 3lb charge was used for each machine, being placed on the main casting which, as can be seen from the photograph, was completely shattered. The photograph was taken during December 1944, twelve months later.

Below: The wreckage of two trains, one a bauxite train, which were derailed by the Resistance near Polignac in South Jura, can be seen on the left. The culvert marked with the arrow was blown up and two trains standing on either side of it were started up by the members of the FFI and run into the crater. In this photograph the lines have been repaired but the wreckage is still there.

Above: Allied troops mingle with members of the Resistance in the village of Couterne, roughly half-way between Caen and Le Mans, during its liberation on 14 August 1944. Some of the men in the background are freed prisoners of war. The resistor seen here centre-left, with the glasses and beret, is named as Jacques Morel. (Conseil Regional de Basse-Normandie/US National Archives)

Above: Members of the French Forces of the Interior in La Trésorerie near Boulogne during September 1944. (Library and Archives Canada, PA-166396)

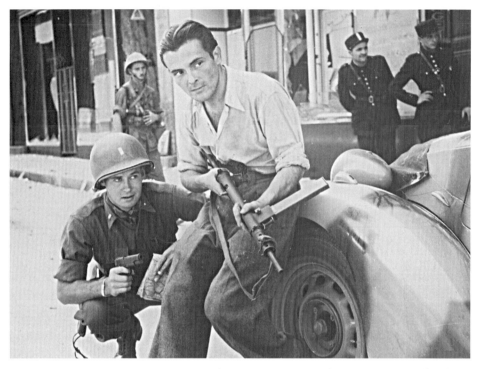

Above: An American officer and a French partisan armed with a Sten gun crouch behind a car during a street fight in a French city in the summer of 1944. (NARA)

Below: Residents celebrate with members of the French Forces of the Interior after the liberation of the town of Écouché in north-western France. Note the weapons resting on the table. (Conseil Regional de Basse-Normandie/US National Archives)

Right: A member the French Forces of the Interior in the Chartres area, 18-year-old Simone Segouin, poses for the camera with a captured German MP 40 submachine-gun. Also known by her *nom de guerre* of Nicole Minet, Segouin was also involved in the liberation of Paris. She was promoted to lieutenant and awarded the *Croix de Guerre*. A street in Courville-sur-Eure was named after her. (NARA)

Above: Members of the Resistance in the area of Huelgoat in Brittany pose for the camera. (Courtesy of Henri Moreau)

Above: Members of the Resistance undergoing training on the Vercors Plateau. Straddling the départements of Isère and Drôme in the French Prealps, the Vercors Plateau was a natural limestone fortress regarded as a 'national redoubt' for France's growing resistance movement. The high plateau with its woods and mountain ridges provided the ideal terrain for a gathering point and training area for the Maquis. The clandestine army was mobilised on 7 June 1944, transforming the Vercors into the first area of Free France, with tricolours flying in all its towns and villages. The Germans crushed the rebellion. (Historic Military Press)

Above: Members of the French Forces of the Interior march through the streets of Vannes while civilians cheer from the sidewalks and balconies as the French seaport celebrates its liberation. (Historic Military Press)

Above: A Resistance guard of honour at the funeral for forty-two members of the French Forces of the Interior who died during the liberation of Chartres, a cathedral a city in north-central France southwest of Paris. Chartres was liberated by American and French forces on 17 August 1944. (Historic Military Press)

Below: Another view of members of the Resistance in the city of Chartres after its liberation by American and French forces on 17 August 1944. (Historic Military Press)

Above: One of many who gave their lives in the name of France. This picture shows the funeral of Special Operations Executive agent Francisque Eugene Bec at Le Mans West Cemetery. Second Lieutenant Bec, whose coffin can be seen in the centre, was killed on 16 June 1944 in the Forêt de Charnie. A holder of dual British and French nationality, Bec had joined the SOE on 20 February 1944. (Historic Military Press)

Left: The unveiling of the SOE and Resistance memorial in the village of Beleymas in the Dordogne. Note the parachute and container carvings on the memorial. The inscription reads: 'At this place was made the first parachute drop of personnel and equipment for the resistance in France by the British War Office. The execution of this operation and the reception on the ground were arranged by Max Hymans, J. Pierre-Bloch, Georges Begue, Edouard Dupuy, Albert Rigoulet dit "Le Frise". On 10 October 1941 they received four British officers: Marc Jumeau (died during deportation), Jack Hayes, Jean Le Harivel, Daniel Turberville.' As it says, the memorial commemorates Operation *Corsican*, the first simultaneous drop of men and weapons (which were in two containers) in France. (Courtesy of Mark Hillier)

9. In all this Samuel had worked in the closest co-operation with the D.M.R. Ellipse, and, indeed, Samuel's great claim to distinction is that he was able to integrate his own "British" circuit into the overall "French" picture with so little friction and such effectiveness.

10. As to the effectiveness, the record of the delivery of stores to Samuel's organisation is probably the best tribute, bearing always in mind that these figures do not, of course, include the quite considerable deliveries to the Jedburgh teams, which he had received and installed.

11. From the date of Hector's arrest, the 1st May, the figures of deliveries are:

Date. 1944.	Operations.	Containers.	Packages.
May	19	296	85
June	50	1,137	376
July	36	1,077	342
August	20	726	206

N.B. From the end of June onwards these figures are exclusive of deliveries made to Hamlet in the Southern half of Hector's old circuit.

12. In July Samuel paid a fleeting visit to London, and was decorated by General Koenig with the Croix de Guerre avec Palmes. From the British he has received the D.S.O.

13. In the meanwhile Marie had been busy in Northern Indre.

F/O Witherington's Organisation.
Operational name of organisation: The Wrestler Circuit.
Operational name of organiser: Marie.
Name by which known in the Field: Marie.

14. Marie arrived in the Field in September 1943 to act as courier to Hector's circuit. In this capacity she was responsible for some important contacts, notably with the Gaspard organisation, this being of particular interest as it was through them that an attempt was to be made to sabotage the Michelin works, the production of which was of such vital importance to the enemy's war effort.

15. On Hector's arrest, Marie, like the other members of the circuit, had a great deal of travelling to do in order to warn the various parts of this wide-spread circuit of what had happened. Finally, after escaping through a cordon of French and German troops encircling Montluçon, she and Henri Cornioley (who is now her husband) arrived at the Château des Souches in Northern Indre, which had been assigned to her by Samuel as her area.

16. There the resistance situation was chaotic, following on the arrest of M. Mardon, the local resistance head. He had not nominated a successor, and apart from a few odd arms, there was no equipment to speak of. Apparently 80 per cent. of the arms which Mardon had received had gone to the F.T.P. His arrest took place on the 1st June, and, on the refusal of the A.S. to accept a M. Briand of the F.T.P. as successor, Marie took charge, and on receipt of the action messages, the D-Day programme was put into effect. Railways and Telephones were cut and roads blocked.

17. Marie herself formed a small Maquis of about 40 men at the Château des Souches and on the 11th June they were attacked by 7,000 Germans! A neighbouring F.T.P. Maquis from Dun-le-Poêlier came to their assistance and 120 men which they were able together to muster fought the enemy from 10 in the morning till 11 at night. The Maquis lost 20, and the Germans (who had thought they were dealing with 3,000 Maquisards) lost 86 dead and nearly 200 wounded.

18. Marie and her men had fought like lions, but after the action the Maquis was compleletly disorganished; the next day the Germans came back, burnt the Château and blew up the Maquis arms dumps at Souches and Dun-le-Poêlier.

19. The work of reorganisation was hampered by the temporary absence of Marie's radio operator (Tutur), but she managed to contact Antoine (Major de Vomecourt) and a delivery of stores was successfully received on the 24th June and did much to relieve the situation.

20. The great difficulty in the way of reorganisation was to lay hands on a military chief, who had to be French. This was successfully accomplished through the C.D.L. at Châteauroux, who dispatched to

Marie a Commandant, Francis, and his Deputy, Capitaine Bourguignon. These two officers took over the organisation of the Maquisards, who numbered at that time (the 27th July) 1,500. Marie reports that both of these officers were excellent and that the three of them worked in complete harmony.

21. By the end of September effectives amounted to 2,600 men grouped in four sub-sectors.

22. For them Marie received 23 parachute operations.

23. From the beginning of July there were constant engagements against the enemy, including many successful attacks on convoys, noteworthy among which is one attack against an S.S. convoy on R.N.20, where the Germans admitted to losses of 76 killed and 125 wounded, Maquis losses being 5 wounded. Maquis morale was evidently high, for on the 21st August one sub-sector, consisting of 800 men under Capitaine Comte, being encircled by 4,000 Germans at Valençay and 6,000 at Saint-Aignan with tanks and artillery, engaged them. The battle was violent, the Maquis lost 21 killed and German losses were estimated at 180 dead and 300 wounded.

24. During the whole five months it is estimated that the Germans lost 1,000 men killed and thousands wounded.

25. Marie's organisation, like others, had rendered further valuable services, having been instrumental in bringing the R.A.F. into action against numerous targets, notably 60 petrol wagons on the Tours–Vierzon line and 4 munitions trains. They received the congratulations of the Supreme Commander for the intelligence they provided concerning 60 armoured trains which arrived from Strasbourg on their way to Normandy at the time of the landing.

26. Marie ends her Report with mention of one matter, concerning which Antoine was also very vocal at the time, the negotiations between General Macon, United States Army, and General Elster covering the surrender of the latter's forces. General Macon was apparently completely ignorant of the fact that the capitulation of the Germans was due to the F.F.I., and they were excluded from the negotiations. This,

she points out, "was a heavy blow to F.F.I. pride, and totally undeserved, when it is considered that no Americans were anywhere near our circuit or further South."

27. Marie has been awarded the Croix de Guerre and the M.B.E. (Civil). The latter honour she has declined on the grounds that her work had been purely military and merited a military decoration, and, on the above record, one sympathises with her.

Notes to Part I

1. Lieutenant R. Cottin (also known as Cotton-Burnett).
2. Lieutenant N.F.R. Burdeyron (also known as Burley).
3. Lieutenant M. Fincken.
4. Lieutenant A.G. Bloch (also known as Boyd).
5. Major B.H. Cowburn.
6. Flying-Officer E.M. Wilkinson, known as Alexandre.
7. Captain Grover-Williams, known as Sebastien.
8. Lieutenant Dowlen, known as Achille.
9. Captain (later Lieutenant-Colonel) Heslop, known as Fabien and later as Xavier.
10. Lieutenant Clech, known as "Georges 60" and Andre.
11. Flying-Officer R. Flower, known as Gaspard.
12. Known in the Field as Monique or Denise.
13. Flight-Lieutenant Agazarian (Marcel) who was accompanied by his wife, known as Marguerite.
14. Not to be confused with the Gaspard (Flying-Officer Flower) already mentioned.
15. Lieutenant Marcel Fox.
16. Lieutenant Jean Worms.
17. See below at para. 59.
18. Known as Cinema and as Phono.
19. Flight-Lieutenant D.J. Barrett, known as Honore.
20. Captain S.C. Jones, R.E., known as Felix or Elie.
21. On the 23rd April, 1946, Henri Dericourt, French Air Line pilot, was fined £500 for attempted smuggling of gold and platinum out of Croydon to France. He was ordered to be held in custody until the fine was paid, and was recommended for deportation.
22. Known originally as Mickey, but later as Conte or Armand.
23. Squadron Leader M. Southgate, known as Philippe or Hector and now resident in Paris (see Chateauroux-Limoges, Appendix A).
24. Lieutenant Henquet and Lieutenant Bassett were Americans, trained in America and in England, and under F. Section "management" in the Field.
25. Arrested in July 1944 together with his radio operator Flight-Lieutenant Barrett. In August Lieutenant Veillard (Vulcain) was sent from London to take over what was left of his circuit.
26. Lieutenant Henquet and Lieutenant Bassett were Americans, trained in America and in England, and under F. Section "management" in the Field.
27. A Frenchman in the United States Army named Baron.
28. Lieutenant E. Levene.

127

[29] Lieutenant Diacono, M.B.E., known as Blaise.

[30] Although in the taut atmosphere of the clandestine period various organisers, including Prosper, were prepared to maintain that Frager was a double-agent. This was mere supposition, however.

[31] Captain G.D. Jones, M.C., Croix de Guerre (avec Palme), known as Gaston or Isidore.

[32] Lieutenant R.P. Glaesner, D.S.O., known as Aleide; Lieutenant F.E. Bec (killed in action, buried in Le mans Cemetry), known as Hugues, Mentioned in Despatches; A.S.O. S.E.F. Butt, W.A.A.F., M.B.E., known as Blanche.

[33] Commandant Pierre Charie.

[34] After the liberation he remained in command of a Battalion formed from the raw levies of the Maquis. The writer of these notes visited him and his Battalion in the late summer of 1945 when they were mounting guard over 16,000 German prisoners just outside Chartres. The demeanour of the Guard Company, both on parade and in the march past, was worthy of the best infantry in any army.

[35] Délégué Militaire Régional.

[36] Lieutenant M.L.M.A. Larcher, posthumously mentioned in despatches 21st June, 1945.

[37] Captain Basset, Lieutenant Beugnon and lieutenant Morange, who set up the Beggar Circuit round Creil and Senlis.

[38] Bernard Bemberg, cousin of De Ganay and a prominent helper.

[39] Captain L.J. Taschereau, M.C., Canadian Army, Lieutenant G. Duclos, M.C., Lieutenant P. Thibeault, Canadian Army, Lieutenant Le Riche (wireless operator).

[40] It was also to a reception organised by Abelard that in there arrived Major Bodington and his party on their way to the Marne Department. Owing to a breakdown in liaison arrangements Major Bodington remained for some time with the Troyes group before moving on to the Haute Marne where he finally set up his own organisation.

[41] Was at one time suspected of having caused the arrests in the circuit. Came to Great Britain in May 1944, and officially cleared.

[42] Reported killed at Triechateaux end June 1943. Leaves a widow.

[43] "Paul of Falaise," reported as being a traitor in Gestapo employ. Report received from another circuit in October 1943, that he been arrested with his wife, taken to Caen and shot.

[44] Arrested October 1943. Leaves a widow.

[45] Has recently (approximately October 1945) been given a long term of imprisonment by the French for having betrayed his associates. Claimed, as his defence, that all the betraying had been done by Archambaud.

[46] Has returned from Germany to his home in Mer. Acts as local "liquidateur": unpopular locally.

[47] Accounts of his arrest and subsequent fate vary. The above is given by Lieutenant Staveley, R.N.V.R., who, having been shot down, stayed in a house in St. Quentin which had been occupied by Major Bieler's second-in-command. He last saw Major Bieler on the 12th January, 1944, two days before his arrest.

[48] Where Claude Malraux's brother, André, was working with another British officer.

[49] He later distinguished himself in the carrying out of a difficult mission in the Limoges area.

[50] André van der Straeten, foreman in the Peugeot works, and prime mover in the sabotage which went on there.

[51] Lieutenant Ullmann (known as Alceste).

[52] 1st Lieutenant E.F. Floege (known as Paul Fontaine and as Pascal).

[53] Captain Millar, who already held the M.C., was awarded the D.S.O. for his work in France.

[54] Known as the Pedagogue circuit.

[55] Colonel Grandval.

[56] Eight or nine radio operators were arrested on almost the same day and Lieutenant Breen

was the only one left. The writer was in London when these telegrams came rolling in. Their volume was such that they might at any moment have entailed his arrest also.

⁵⁷ Under the leadership of Henri's successor Pascal.

⁵⁸ Although, presumably unknown to Samuel, there did exist a small British circuit under Allyre (Captain Carton, M.C.), in the Angoulême-Cognac area. In August Allyre was joined by Gustave (Captain Sirois), radio operator to Julien's (Captain Rechenman) Circuit. Julien himself had been arrested, but Gustave had been able to carry on. Taking Julien, Gustave and Carver together, 24 operations had been carried out comprising 379 Containers and 125 Packages.

Part II

The Old Unoccupied Zone

Chapter 7

A General Account of the Unoccupied Zone

ORIGINS OF THE "BRITISH" CIRCUITS IN FRANCE

1. The whole British organisation in France started on the 5th May, 1941, with the dropping by parachute in the neighbourhood of Châteauroux (Valençay to be exact) of a radio operator, known throughout his long career as George Noble. His real name is Georges Begue, and he left the British Army in November 1944 to become Commandant Georges Begue of the French army.

2. That his name is a household word in F. Section is due as much to his personal character as to the character of his mission. The mission was difficult enough; in addition to being the first man to be parachuted by F. Section, he was to act as the lynch-pin to the whole organisation which the British were trying at this time to set up in France (the Free French organisation in London was not yet on its feet). His instructions were to establish himself as inconspicuously as possible in or near Châteauroux and to send back to London as soon as possible a contact address, to which messages could be sent by other organisers standing by in England to leave for the Field.

3. It is at once pathetic and impressive to consider the slenderness of the foundation on which was built the system which on D-Day went into action with such devastating effect. It started with one man on the 5th May, 1941, a little more than three years before the landing in Normandy.

4. Technically George Noble was superb. Arriving in the small hours of the morning of the 6th, he was taken into Châteauroux on the 8th, recruited his "letter-box" the same evening, and on the 9th had communicated it to London. The link was forged.

5. The name of the man who received Noble on the morning after his arrival is worthy of record. He is Max Hymans, a former Under-Secretary of State. The address through which other organisers were to communicate with him was that of a chemist, M. Renan [from] Châteauroux, and this was later changed to M. Fleuret, keeper of a garage.

6. By the end of June Noble had contacted Lucas (Pierre de Vomecourt), sent from London to organise in the Occupied Zone, and his brother, Philippe de Vomecourt, recruited by Lucas and known as Lionel. Albert (Lieutenant Cottin) another London-sent officer had got in touch with him from Brittany. Wireless traffic grew rapidly.

7. In mid-June took place the first parachuting of stores to the Field, arranged through Noble, for delivery to Lionel. This operation was a land-mark, both on its own account, and because Noble found that communication, between himself at his wireless set and Lionel in the fields awaiting the aircraft, was too slow, and resulted in the unfortunate Lionel spending two nights uselessly in the open air, when London had already sent a message to say that the aircraft could not fly owing to bad weather.

8. This led Noble in his next message to suggest the use of a B.B.C. message, to notify teams on the ground of impending operations: thus was born the system of "messages personnels" which has meant so much to the course of the war.

9. In the ensuing months approximately a dozen agents were sent into Unoccupied France, a few of them for circuits in the Occupied Zone, to which direct access was difficult, but most of them to groups which

were building up in the Unoccupied Zone, more particularly in the neighbourhoods of Lyon, Marseille and Toulouse. For those arriving by air, reception arrangements were generally in the hands of Max Hymans or George Noble, and the latter had on one occasion to dive fully clothed into a lake to rescue one new arrival, who had dropped rather wide.

10. But the distinction of being the only clandestine radio in France, while full of honour, was not without its disadvantages. Radio detection soon established the fact that an alien note was sounding in the Vichy air, and the hunt for the "radio de Châteauroux" became a prime objective.

11. Noble, of course, was aware of this and took the usual precautions, but little by little the net closed in, Fleuret was arrested and it became evident that continued operation in Châteauroux was becoming impossible. Limoges was visited, but conditions there proved no better, and although Noble transmitted for a time from the house of Madame Sevenet[1] at Château Dubrueil, near Loches, it was evidently only a question of time before this, too, would be pin-pointed by the Vichy police. Radio detection cars were already in evidence when Noble left for Marseille to consult another organiser, Christophe (Captain Turck), who had established himself in that town.

12. Christophe had arrived in August 1941 in the company of Captain (later Major) J.V. de Guelis (Jacques). They had been dropped "blind" and a long way from the place chosen for their descent. Jacques had dropped in rough ground, but, although severely cut and bruised, was not gravely injured: Christophe was more unlucky, as he was dropped into a quarry and completely knocked out. Jacques, despite his own injuries, spent the rest of the night in a fruitless search for his companion, but with day-break was obliged to suspend the search and continue on his mission. Christophe was picked up still unconscious by the French police, and the next news which London had of him was that he had installed himself, or been installed, in a villa (the Villa des Bois) near Marseille, where he was working in harmonious relations with the French Deuxième Bureau.

13. Jacques' mission was a roving one. He was to investigate the affairs of the circuits in Unoccupied France, make recommendations for their further development, arrange for the infiltration of agents by sea on the

south coast, do some recruiting on his own account and return to London approximately a month later. He carried out this mission with distinction, had meetings with George Noble, with Lucas from the Occupied Zone, and with Lionel, interviewed a number of the leaders of the indigenous Resistance movements which were beginning to crystallise, and recruited three men who were, later on, to play a considerable part in F. Section history, Philippe Liewer, who carried out two missions with great success in Rouen and in Limoges, Francis Garel, who built up a circuit in Brittany, and Robert Lyon, who was active in the final liberation of the region of Roanne.

14. Jacques's return to England was not without drama. He was to travel by Lysander aircraft and had installed himself in a hotel conveniently near the selected ground, when on the night of the operation the police arrived and proceeded to check the papers of everyone there. None could leave until the process was complete, and Jacques was forced to see the precious minutes fleeting away, while preserving an impression of complete calm. As soon as the police had departed he leapt on his bicycle and began a mad rush through the night, arriving at the ground just as the noise of the approaching aircraft's engine was beginning to make itself heard. Rapidly laying out the lights, he guided the aircraft in[2] and was soon on his way to London, where he presented an extremely valuable report.

15. The new arrival, Gerry Morel (later Major), for whom Jacques had left his bicycle, missed him in the confusion and was forced to make his way on foot.

16. Between them they had taken part in the first Lysander operation to Occupied Europe.

17. Gerry's mission unfortunately proved unsuccessful. He was denounced, probably by one of the people he had been sent to contact, was arrested and imprisoned in Limoges. Here he became acutely ill, underwent a severe operation and, to the stupefaction of everybody, a few days later walked out of hospital, took the train to the Spanish frontier and walked across the Pyrenees. In due course he reached London, where he continued to render the most exceptional services until he returned again to the Field as a member of the Étoile mission in September 1944.

18. In the meanwhile curious things had been going on in Marseille, and in October 1941 the police of that town, using Christophe's villa as a trap, made an almost clear sweep of the British organisers in the Unoccupied Zone. They had obtained the address of the villa from a man who had been arrested at Fleuret's garage, where they had also been keeping watch. Their haul was a considerable one, since a number of the newcomers had contacts to make with Christophe. Unfortunately George Noble was one of them.

19. A list of those involved appears at Appendix A.

20. That the sweep was not complete was due in no small measure to the inspired activities of an American lady with a wooden leg, working in Lyon. Virginia Hall (Marie) was sent to the Field from London in September 1941 to work under journalistic cover in Lyon and Vichy. In this she was amazingly successful, almost embarrassingly so, since Major Cowburn complained on is return to England from his second mission that one had only to sit for long enough in the kitchen of Marie's flat, to see every British organiser in France. Be this as it may, there is no doubt that without her the progress which was in fact made would have been impossible. She was guide, philosopher and friend to a large number of organisers, helping them with Papers, with Finance, with Advice, with Wireless sets and even on occasions obtaining police uniforms for them and endeavouring to get them out of gaol. In all this she enjoyed the advantages of American citizenship at this time, but even so her work was quite outstanding and in February 1942 by one action alone she probably saved the whole set-up in Unoccupied France from premature extinction. A radio operator had been dropped near Vaas (Sarthe), where he was to be received by Lucas (Paris area). He was, however, dropped well away (35 kms.) from the proper spot, and after a good deal of wandering was at Marseille trying to get out of the country, when Virginia grabbed him, sent him to Châteauroux to collect a set which George Noble had left behind him and brought him to Lyon, thus re-establishing wireless communication with London.

21. In November 1942 she left France, luckily just before the German occupation of the Southern zone, she and Cuthbert (the name by which her wooden leg was affectionately known in F. Section) accomplishing a crossing of the Pyrenees in winter, which must surely constitute a

record all by itself! She returned to France in March 1944 when she further distinguished herself in organising guerrilla activities in Nièvre and Haute-Loire.

22. Although quite obviously the work of George Noble and of Marie had a local habitat, it would have been inappropriate to have given it local treatment in view of its universal character. The other circuits, with one exception, are susceptible of being treated regionally and are divided into the following areas:-
    1. Châteauroux–Limoges.
    2. Corrèze–Dordogne.
    3. Toulouse and the South-West.
    4. Marseille.
    5. Lyon.

23. The exception to this treatment is the Pimento circuit under Lieutenant (later Major) A. Brooks (Alphonse). This young man of 20, after a completely normal training, was given half an hour's talk by a Trades Union Representative in London and incontinently parachuted to the Field. He was to make contact with a mysterious gentleman named Charles (and later Robert), a prominent Trade Unionist, who was reputed to have action groups among French railway-men throughout France, and who required an officer from London to minister to their material wants, to bring them directives and to co-ordinate their activities. Alphonse, in spite of his youth, was able to gain their confidence and respect, and for close on three years his railway teams put together a truly astonishing record of activity against German communications. Alphonse himself remained constantly in the Field from July 1942 to the Liberation, with one short break for consultation in London. His groups were continuously operative over a wide area, their principal axis of activity being along a line Bourg-en-Bresse, Lyon, Aix-en-Provence, Montauban, with a very important spur running out on the strategically valuable line to Italy via Culoz. Their basic long-term activity was the "grease gun" attack, by which abrasives were introduced into the bearings of rolling-stock. This was reinforced by line-cutting, sabotage by explosives and derailments, and in the later stages, when railway traffic had been brought to a standstill, by attacks on road transport and guerrilla action.

24. A detailed report of the impressive activities of this circuit is at Appendix B.

25. Before the German occupation in 1942, working conditions were naturally easier in the Unoccupied than in the Occupied Zone. This was fortunate as it enabled the Southern Zone to be used as a stepping-stone for work in the North, and full advantage was taken of this fact, an appreciable number of organisers being parachuted into the Unoccupied Zone or landed on its Southern coast from surface craft or submarine with instructions to cross the Demarcation Line into German-occupied territory.

26. With German occupation of the whole country conditions tended to equality in both zones. Some circuits were unable to stand the change in atmosphere, and it is from this time that the big names begin to appear, Squadron Leader Southgate in Châteauroux and Limoges, Lieutenant-Colonel Starr in the South-West, Lieutenant-Colonel Cammaerts in the South-East, Lieutenant-Colonel Heslop in the Ain Department. Major Brooks was also continuing on his destructive way and Captain Joseph Marchand crowned a long history with Resistance, beginning in 1941, by reappearing in St.-Étienne.

27. All these officers were awarded the D.S.O. for truly outstanding services.

Appendix A:

LIST OF THOSE INVOLVED IN THE ARRESTS OF OCTOBER 1941

1. George Noble (Fr.)
W/T operator and organiser at Châteauroux. Arrested at Christophe's villa.

2. Pierre Bloch (Fr.)
Socialist Deputy and organiser of Reception Committee to receive Jumeau, Turberville and Hayes.

3. Gerry Morel (Fr.)
Engaged on independent mission. Arrived by Lysander 1941.

4. Lieut. Clement Jumeau (Br.)
Lieutenant. Travelling to Marseille circuit to act as technical adviser to M. Bardanne. Arrested at Christophe's villa.

5. Lieut. Jack Hayes (Br.)
Travelling to Dordogne to act as technical adviser to Pierre Bloch. Arrested at Christophe's villa.

6. Lieut. Daniel Turberville (Br.)
Travelling to Antibes to act as assistant to Mantout. Arrested owing to bad dropping.

7. Lieut. Jean Philippe Le Harivel (Br.)
Travelling to Lyon to act as W /T operator. Arrested following visit to Christophe's villa.

8. Lieut. Bruce Cadogan (Fr.)
Landed by sea September 1941; travelling to the Landes on a sabotage mission. Arrested at Christophe's villa.

9. Lieut. George Langelaan (Br.)
Parachuted in September 1941 on a propaganda mission. Châteauroux trying to contact Noble.

10. Lieut. Michael Trotobas (Br.)
Travelling to Marseille. Arrested in Châteauroux in identity check-up.

11. Francis Garel (Fr.)
Locally recruited. Arrested at Fleuret Garage.

12. Philippe Liewer (Fr.)
Locally recruited by De Guelis. Arrested in Antibes as a result of arrest of Langelaan.

13. Marcel Fleuret (Fr.)
Locally recruited. His name was found on an arrested agent.

Appendix B:

ACTIVITIES OF THE PIMENTO CIRCUIT

August 1942
Experiments with abrasive grease on German railway waggon bearings. These were successful and the formation of grease-gun crews was started; crews recruited in Toulouse, Tarbes and Sète.

September 1942
Crews recruited in Montauban, Agen, Capdenac, Ambérieu, St.-Étienne, Valence, Mâcon, Lyon-Vaise, Bourg, Lons-le-Saunier.

October 1942
Contacted 5 C.G.T. leaders, who put Alphonse in touch with police, fonctionnaires and railwaymen and extended parachute teams in Bourg area. Grease-gun crews extended to Belgarde, Culoz, Chambéry, Aix-les-Bains, Annemasse, Modane, Grenoble, Chasse, Givors, Oullins, Roanne, St.-Germain-des-Fosses, Périgueux, Brive, La Joliette, Nîmes, Blancarde.

November 1942
Began recruiting railway cutting crews. Very difficult, as most members were railwaymen who had an inherent dislike of killing their fellow workers. Liaison with Berne secured after German occupation.

December 1942
All work slowed down to improve security. Circuit divided into groups, group leaders only in contact with Alphonse through cut-outs:
    Area 1 – Lyon, Mâcon, Chalon, Lons-le-Saunier, Ambérieu.
    Area 2 – Bellegarde, Culoz, Chambéry, Thonon.
    Area 3 – Marseille, Avignon, Nîmes.
    Area 4 – Grenoble, Valence, Modane.
    Area 5 – Sète, Toulouse, Tarbes.
    Area 6 – Montauban, Capdenac, Brive, Périgueux.

January 1943
Established system for distributing stores by engine tenders to all areas. First derailment near Mâcon for training purposes.

February 1943
Rail cutting crews on Modane line extended to St.-Jean-de-Maurienne and Montmélian. New group in Limoges area, grease-gun crews at Limoges, Montluçon and Figeac. Derailment S. of Toulouse and pylon cutting Le Portet St.-Simon-Pyrenees as training exercise. Also Grenoble–Montmélian line.

March 1943
Head of Area 1 arrested. Contact lost, but damage localised. Series of attacks on petrol trains going south between Mâcon and Lyon. Very successful. Railway cutting crews recruited at Chalon and Lozanne. Wheel balancing lathe successfully attacked at Oullins.

April 1943
Training derailment near Nîmes. Grease-gun crews set up at Narbonne, Perpignan, Castelnaudary, Béziers. Five successful parachute operations in Area 1. Engine driver group contacted in Lyon, La Mouche.

May 1943
Explosives supplied La Mouche for engine sabotage. Contact nearly fully re-established with Area 1.

June 1943
Toulouse–Capdenac Railway cut for training purposes. Two steam engines attacked at Montauban.

July 1943
At London's special request made several attacks on Italian supply route between Mâcon, Bourg, Ambérieu, Culoz, Montmélian, Modane as well as Lyon–Ambérieu and Lyon–Grenoble–Montmélian. All highly successful.

August 1943
Various arrests and security measures. Eight successful parachute operations in Area 1. Alphonse leaves for London.

September 1943
Two successful parachute operations in Jura.

October 1943
Attacks on Montmélian–Modane Railway continue.

November 1943
Railway cutting crews set up on Toulouse–Sète line.

December 1943
Contact with Oullins lost after several arrests in P.L.M. workshops. Link with London via Berne cut owing to German measures against Savoie Maquis. Alphonse returns to Field.

January 1944
Railway cutting crews set up on following lines: Lyon–Mâcon, Lyon–Bourg, Lyon–Ambérieu, Lyon–Vienne, Lyon–Grenoble, Givors–Nîmes, Villefranche–Lozanne, Toulouse–Tarbes, Toulouse–Lavaur, Toulouse–Montauban, Montauban–Cahors, Montauban–Agen.

February 1944
Received radio operator. Head of Area 4 killed.

March 1944
Checked and retrained all railway cutting crews on lines Bourg–Lyon, Bourg–Mâcon, Bourg–St.-Amour, Bourg–Ambérieu, Ambérieu–Culoz, Chambéry–Montmélian, St.-Germain-des-Fosses–Gannat, Figeac–Capdenac, Valence–Avignon, Lyon–Chasse. Re-established contact with Oullins workshops, supplied explosive to La Mouche, Toulouse. Montauban running sheds.

April 1944
Began setting up road blocking crews in Toulouse–Montauban area. Completed railway cutting system by crews on Cahors–Figeac, Cahors–Villeneuve, Agen–Villeneuve, Pau–Tarbes, Béziers–Bédarieux, Béziers–Sète, St.-Étienne–Roanne lines. Attacked seven steam engines at La Mouche, six successfully. Attacked supply trains on Modane line between Ambérieu and Chambéry. Attacked ammunition trains in Vavrette siding S. of Bourg. Attacked two Midi transformers at Cazères. Attacked eighty-two bogied tank-carrying trucks belonging to Das Reich, Deutschland and Der Fuehrer Divisions in Montauban marshalling yards with grease-guns.

May 1944

Prepared special area H.Q.s with internal couriers, with leaders fully briefed for D-Day. Attacked pylons parallel to Montauban–Cahors line, also leading from Pyrenees to Le Portet St.-Simon, Verlaghuet–Colaynac, Verlaghuet–Le Viviez, Le Viviez–La Môle. This compelled steam working of Montauban–Brive line for a week. Fourteen parachute operations successful in Area 1. Attacks on supply trains on Mâcon–Lyon, Mâcon–Bourg–Ambérieu lines. Attacked pylons St.-Fons–Oullins, turn-table at La Mouche, petrol barge at Castel Sarrasin. Grease-gunned forty Berliet lorries destined for Germany.

June 1944

Action messages passed. Following results: Permanent railway cut Montauban–Cahors. Intermittent cuts Montauban–Agen, Agen–Villeneuve, Cahors–Capdenac, Cahors–Villeneuve, Montauban–Lexos, Capenac–Brive, Toulouse–Montauban, Toulouse–Tarbes, Sète–Béziers, Valence–Vienne, Le Teil–Givors, Lyon–Bourgoin, Lyon–Mâcon, Mâcon–Bourg, Bourg–St. Amour, St. Germain–Lozanne, Roanne–St. Étienne, Poligny–Lons-le-Saunier, St. Jean de Maurienne–Modane, Grenoble–Voiron, St. Sulpice–Capdenac, Toulouse–St. Sulpice, Lavaur–Castres, Toulouse–Castelnaudary. Destroyed seventy-eight steam engines and twenty-nine electric engines. Agen and Ambérieu break-down cranes heavily damaged; Montauban and Bourg slightly. Two turn-tables at Lyon damaged. Bourg signal box completely destroyed. Road convoys attacked near Bourg.

July 1944

Continued railway cuts and attacks on petrol trains. Maquis armed in Area 5. Arms being brought into suburbs of Lyon.

August 1944

Attacks on railways continued. Maquis fighting begins in Area 1. Lavaur, St.-Sulpice-la-Pointe, St. Pol and Girousens liberated, and move towards Toulouse. St. Gaudens, St. Croix, Cazères and Tarbes partly liberated. Toulouse–Narbonne and Montauban–Castel Sarrasin lines continuously cut. Road blocks on all major roads where military conditions permit. Toulouse finally liberated, Gilbert (Alphonse's commander there) occupies Prefecture, later to hand over to Hilaire (Lt.-Colonel Starr). All troops who wished to remain armed and fight joined regular F.F.I. forces: others (the majority) returned to their normal work. On Southern D-Day railway cutting was increased in the Rhone valley and on the lines from Lyon to Bourg and Mâcon. Outstanding results were: Blocking of Givors tunnel and then derailment of Givors breakdown crane, cutting of Lyon–Givors, Lyon–Vienne, Lyon–Bourgoin, Grenoble–Montmélian, Culoz–Ambérieu, Bourg–Lyon, Mâcon–Chalon, Mâcon–Bourg, Villefranche–Lyon, Villefrance–Mâcon, Lyon–Ambérieu, Nîmes–Tarascon, Nîmes–Remoulins, Nîmes–Montpellier lines. Groups co-operated in fighting in Ain and Jura. Alphonse personally led several attacks on German road convoys south of Lyon on the Vienne road and north of Crépieux-la-Pape.

As 7th Army approached Lyon all attacks on German transport were intensified. Railways at a complete standstill, all efforts were diverted to road blocks. Culverts blown where possible, and trees felled south of Lyon and on the Lyon-Mâcon and Lyon-Bourg roads. Telephone wires systematically cut round Lyon and Bourg. Attempt (unsuccessful) to save road bridges over the Rhone at Lyon. Alphonse personally led the first American tank patrol into Lyon.

Chapter 8

The Bordeaux Region,
Châteauroux–Limoges

1. The first circuit indigenous to this area was that of Baron Philippe de Vomecourt (Gauthier). As already mentioned, he had been recruited by his brother Pierre in May 1941, been put in touch with George Noble, and in June 1941 had received near Limoges the first operation ever carried out for the parachuting of stores into France.[3]

2. But fortunately he was not involved in the arrests of October 1941, although he had had contacts with both George Noble and Christophe. He was, however, deprived by these arrests of all radio connection with London, and his only means of communication was through Virginia Hall in Lyon. This state of affairs was not completely remedied till September 1942 when he received his own radio operator. In the meanwhile, communication through Virginia Hall had been speeded up by her own acquisition of a wireless operator in February 1942. Stores deliveries began again in June 1942, there being one operation that month, five in July, six in August, one in September, and two in October. They were not large operations, and they were widely scattered.

3. It was never quite clear just where Gauthier's groups operated, nor how effective they were. The scatter in the parachute operations (one was as far afield as Lons-le-Saunier) indicates that they were widespread, and it is known that Gauthier was endeavouring to build up in the Unoccupied Zone the parallel to his brother's organisation the other side of the line, and his brother's group numbered many thousands.

4. He was evidently making progress, for in September 1942 he proposed to divide his organisation into three autonomous groups with himself as co-ordinator. One was to be commanded by Henri Sevenet, another by Joseph Aron (an important man in Citroën) and the third by "Adolphe" (Piercy).

5. Finally, on the disappearance of his brother in April 1942, Gauthier got into touch with various groups in the Occupied Zone. Knowing his character, his enthusiasm and his capacity for hard work, it is certain that Gauthier's organisation was on a large scale.

6. As to their effectiveness, Virginia Hall commented in September 1942: "Am forwarding plans drawn up by Gauthier and Joseph for the division of Z.N.O. in three districts – 'all Gaul' ... You might tell them to make less vast plans and concentrate on a little petty but practical work ... There is too much stress on grandiloquent plans, too many words and far too little grubbing." A sane comment on a rather too French method of circuit building.

7. Whatever the merits of the respective methods, however, the question became academic on the 12th November, 1942, when Gauthier was arrested. (Over a year later he escaped, came to England, and returned to France on a second mission in April 1944.)

8. In the meanwhile, without fanfares and without fuss, Captain (later Major) Cowburn (Valérien) had appeared in the area. A highly skilled petroleum engineer, he had first been parachuted to the Field in September 1941 to occupy himself specially with Petrol targets. He had got into contact with Lucas (Pierre de Vomecourt), and in February 1942 he left France by Spain with a report for London on the affairs of the Lucas circuit. In May 1942 he was back with a double mission, firstly to launch another officer in Paris, and secondly, to organise on his own

account by using certain contacts which he had made on his first mission. His circuit when established was to take care of a limited number of targets, notable among them being the Railway junction at Vierzon. He had expressly requested that this, his second, mission, should not last more than three months, since he was already well known to the gestapo, and it would not be advisable to stay longer.

9. The first part of the mission – the Paris part – took longer than had been anticipated, since the radio operator who was to have met them in Paris did not materialise, and Valérien and his companion Alexandre[4] had to return to Lyon to find out what had happened. By the time that they had found another operator, much valuable time had elapsed, but in August 1942 Alexandre and his new radio operator Justin (Lieutenant Rake), accompanied by Fabien (Captain, later Lieutenant-Colonel Heslop) started on their journey to Paris. They had got as far as Limoges when they were all arrested in the Hôtel du Faisan while waiting for their train. They were held by the French police until November 1942, when with the German occupation of the Southern Zone, they were released.

10. In the meanwhile, Valérien, of course, had proceeded on the second part of his mission. His work was characterised by extreme efficiency, a very high degree of security and was altogether first-class. He laboured under the handicap of having to communicate with London through a wireless set situated in Lyon, but in spite of this disadvantage he competently completed what he had set out to do.

11. His first contact was with M. Chantraine (known as Octave), President of the Fédération Paysnnne of the Indre and the possessor of a farm 15 kiloms. south of Châteauroux[5] and a house at Tendu. Two receptions of material were made to this farm, the first a few hundred yards away, the second, to avoid difficulties of carriage, in a field near the house. All this material was safely distributed and stowed away.

12. Valérien's other important contact was Julien (Charles Rechenmann) an ex-army officer from Lorraine. Belonging to a firm of electrical instrument manufacturers, he was able to travel all over Unoccupied France on business. He lived, and had a small group, at Tarbes, but visited Lyon and Châteauroux fairly regularly.

13. Valérien had three targets, the Railway junction at Vierzon, the Aircraft Factory at Châteauroux, and the Transformer Station at Éguzon. On his return to England in October 1942 he reported that everything was ready for an attack on Vierzon when required (no one was to know that it would not be required for well over eighteen months), that the aircraft factory was inactive and that his men had made an attack on the Power lines leading out of Éguzon on the 1st October. This was one of the first multiple attacks on High Tension lines and it demonstrated the fact that (at least at this period) repairs could be carried out very rapidly. Another of his groups had attacked, with abrasives, the Debard factory at Châteauroux, making pistons for engines.

14. All this is doubtless somewhat small beer in relation to later happenings. But it has an importance all its own. In addition to being a pioneer effort, which achieved something definite, at a time when this was the exception rather than the rule, Valérien's organisation had another supremely useful feature. He left it (as he was to do with another organisation which he later built up at Troyes) as a going concern, with the necessary stores tucked away, with enough money to last it out the winter and all ready, in fact, for his successor to take up where he had left off.

15. His successor was Flight-Lieutenant (Later Squadron-Leader) M. Southgate who reached the Field in January 1943.

Squadron-Leader Southgate's Organisation.
Operational name of organisation: The Stationer Circuit.
Operational name of organiser: Hector.
Name by which known in the Field: Hector, Maurice and Philippe.

16. His mission was to contact Octave and Julien and through them to develop the circuit which he had inherited from Valérien. He was given a somewhat ample list of targets and his brief called for more action than had that of his predecessor.

17. He arrived in the Field accompanied by a courier Jacqueline Néarne, and was received near Clermont-Ferrand by Captain Jones (Isidore) radio operator and sole survivor of a party of three organisers who had been sent there in September 1942.

18. Contact with Octave and Julien was soon made, and development began. Octave and Julien were incorporated in Hector's organisation as the heads of the Northern and Southern portions respectively.

19. At the outset Hector was instructed to use Isidore for communicating with London, but on the 23rd May, 1943, Isidore in his turn was arrested, and Hector, like so many others, suffered all the disadvantages, delays and disappointments which lack of communications engenders. In April 1943 he was at last relieved of his immediate anxieties by the arrival of Samuel (Captain Maingard) his own radio operator, and deliveries of stores began in April 1943.

20. But Hector was a man of action, and the absence of stores from England had not prevented him from starting operations in the meanwhile. In April 1943 he and his men broke into a local quarry, stole 250lbs. of Dynamite and with it blew up the water tower at Ussel station. This supplied water for all the locomotives in the district, and its destruction interfered greatly with traffic for five weeks.

21. Hector had need of all his energy and activity, for his area was a quite impossible one. He reported, rather ruefully, that his circuit stretched from Châteauroux to Tarbes, and included Vierzon, Villefranche s/Cher, Limoges, Tarbes and Pau. He was, of course, greatly helped by his two chiefs:

Octave with groups in: Vierzon, Beauge, Villefranche s/Cher, Éguzon, La Souterraine, Argenton s/Creuse, Dun-le-Poellier.
Julien with groups in Pau, Tarbes, Lannemezan, Sarrancolin.

22. Octave had twenty good men in each of the places mentioned, and 400 in La Souterraine, who, however, were still without arms when Hector returned to London to report. Julien's groups numbered between 50 and 100 all told. Octave's men were almost entirely Communist, while Julien's were recruited almost exclusively from P.O.W.s escaped from Germany. Octave had been working in Resistance for 2½ years and Julien for 18 months.

23. The communications side of the organisation had been strengthened by this time, Samuel having trained a local radio operator, Pierre Hirsch

(Popaul), who had been accepted by London. Popaul transmitted at this time from Montluçon, while Samuel's beat covered the entire circuit.

24. By October 1943, when Hector reached London, he was able to report that a considerable amount of sabotage had been accomplished, mostly against communications, trains had been derailed (one of them at La Souterraine contained five waggons of wine, and after it Gendarmes, Gardes Mobiles and cheminots could be seen lying along the line sunk in a deep and contented slumber), pylons and transformers attacked.

25. The most notable single act of sabotage was probably that at Lannemezan, where the electric current supplying the important aluminium plant there was cut off, the aluminium set solid in the kilns and the works were completely out of action for some weeks. Others included the successful sabotage by abrasives of a large aero engine under test (the Germans were so puzzled that they sent it to Berlin, for verification of the quality of the steel!), and attacks by explosives on German aircraft.

26. Hector tells the story of two peasants in a field when a German aircraft flew over from Châteauroux. "If only that ————'s wing would drop off," says one, and at that moment it *did* drop off with a flash, a bang and a puff of smoke. One of Hector's charges had exploded.

27. Particular mention should be made of a reinforcement which the circuit had received in September 1943 in the person of Marie (F/O Pearl Witherington, W.A.A.F.) to act as additional courier to Jacqueline. She was used principally to the North of the circuit, and in particular was in contact with a group of the Armee Secrete in Clermont-Ferrand. This group had previously been in contact with, and supplied by, Dominique (Captain Rafferty) of the same party as Isidore, who had been arrested. With his arrest supplies from F. Section stopped, but the French supply organisation worked most inefficiently, and no stores were obtainable that way, and Hector was approached. The connection was a valuable one, in particular as it was the means of setting fire to 40,000 tyres at the Michelin stores in Clermont-Ferrand. Efforts were made to develop this contact for the purpose of large-scale sabotage at the Michelin works, but without success.

28. This was to have been another of what became known as "Blackmail" sabotage operations, *i.e.*, factory sabotage with the co-operation of the management, but in the present case the management refused to co-operate.

29. In January 1944 Hector returned to France and set to work with redoubled vigour. There was much to do: he had been away three months, and during that time Octave had been arrested. There was also a new stage, the Maquis stage, of activity to be organised. So Samuel ceased to act as radio operator and became Hector's A.D.C. (the circuit was by now well provided with wireless operators).

30. At the beginning of April 1944 small Maquis groups were reported in Cher and Loir-et-Cher near Vierzon and Romorantin, and German transport was being constantly slowed down in the neighbourhood of Villefranche s/Cher. Similar small Maquis groups existed in Indre and Hautes-Pyrénées. At Châteauneuf S.E. of Limoges a Maquis of 350 men had grown up. There were also 2,000 men available in Indre, who could not take to the Maquis as the country was not suitable.

31. At Terrasson in Dordogne there was also a Maquis of 50 men. But this had been the object of a German punitive expedition and had been in action for two days, killing or wounding 80 Germans. In reprisal the Germans had shot 40 hostages in Terrasson and burnt a number of houses.

32. In addition to all the internal organisation which this represented, the high quality of Hector's circuit led him to be called upon to undertake increased tasks for the Organisation as a whole.

33. During this period he was sent two Lysander experts, one of whom successfully arranged two operations, on one of which the wife of General Cochet was exfiltrated. In addition, the circuit was called upon to man two radio-navigational-beacons which the R.A.F. wished to install as an aid to the navigation of their aircraft. Finally, in April 1944 he was required by London to organise the reception of no less than sixteen organisers, radio operators. &c., who had urgently to be got to the Field in order to build up those new circuits behind the Normandy battle line, which played such a great part after D-Day.

34. Among them were Major de Vomecourt on his way to Loir-et-Cher, Major Hudson making for Sarthe, Captain Wilkinson going to Loiret, Louis to build up a group in Tours, Captain Corbin bound for Angoulême and Lise de Baissac, destined for the Pimento circuit in Lyon, but who finally joined her brother in Normandy.

35. As if this was not enough, Hector was approached "on bended knees," as he put it, by Gaspard (of Clermont-Ferrand), who now commanded an important French group covering a wide area in Puy-de-Dôme, Loire, Haute-Loire and Cantal. In his case also the French supply services had broken down and Hector was appealed to, to put him in effective touch with London. This he did, and London sent two British officers and a radio operator to work with Gaspard. Their reception was also carried out by Hector's circuit.

36. And all this was in addition to the normal programme of stores delivery which, as the following statement shows, had also grown considerably.

37. Stationer Circuit Stores Operations.

Date.	Operations.	Containers.	Packages.
1943.			
April	2	4	2
May	2	10	2
July	2	15	3
August	5	30	9
September	2	30	5
October	2	21	5
November	1	3	1
1944.			
January	1	15	6
February	2	1	9
March	7	85	12
April	18	252	103
May	19	296	85
June	50	1,137	376

38. But Hector himself never saw the figures for May and June. Tired out as the result of the arduous and nerve-wracking life he had led since January, he went on the 1st May, 1944, to Montluçon, to the house where his new radio operator Aimé was living, and knocked at the door without taking those security precautions which he would normally have taken. The door was opened to him by the Gestapo and all was over.[6]

39. But his work went on. The basis of his circuit was sound, and Samuel was able to take over; the component parts of the circuit, under new leaders, were able to take part, and take part effectively, in the liberation of the country.

40. The sub-division of Hector's circuit had already been discussed with him in London, and in point of fact a good deal of insulation already existed. With his arrest and Samuel's succession, London seized the opportunity of still further division.

41. Firstly, Tarbes was separated off and left to its own devices. Next, in the centre, Haute-Vienne was divided into two, and the Southern part, and such elements in Dordogne as might still be attached to the circuit allocated to an officer who was parachuted to the Field on the 7th June, 1944. (This was Hamlet, Major Staunton, who had already carried out one very successful mission in Rouen.) The Northern part of Haute-Vienne and Indre was allocated to Samuel, assisted by Marie. Samuel accepted this amputation of his kingdom with good grace, and the stage was set for the next and final stage. Gaspard, as already noted, had received an organiser, courier and radio operator and was already independent.

42. Before finally leaving the Hector circuit, as such, a list is appended of the sabotage it carried out:
  Aluminium works, Lannemezan: 50 per cent. "Destroyed" the 12th September, 1943.
  Hispano-Suiza, Tarbes: 3 Transformers destroyed 24th August 1943. Transformers attacked again the 25th March, 1944. Models and Moulds destroyed 24th April, 1944. Production 25 per cent only; repairs 3 months, important damage.

Reyrode Works: Attacked September 1943.

S.N.C.A. Châteauroux: 5 Aircraft destroyed with explosives the 1st April, 1944.

Marignane: Aircraft damaged with abrasives.

Gnome-et-Rhône, Limoges: Partial stoppage, end June 1943.

Chartoir works, Clermont-Ferrand: 2 Transformers and Drawing office destroyed the 22nd January, 1944.

Bersac: Sub-station destroyed, end June 1943.

Dun-le-Poellier: Two pylons destroyed.

Vierzon – Pau: Several pylons destroyed, July 1943.

Éguzon: Barrage attacked, "encouraging results."

Tulle Arsenal: Power Plant blown up. Arms works stopped August 1943.

Tarbes Arsenal: Electric Distribution Board in Construction. Workshop blown up the

23rd September, 1943. Several weeks' stoppage.

Ussel: Water tower destroyed the 4th April. 1943.

Ancizes: Steel works stopped 3 months, the 5th December, 1943, by fire and destruction of pumps.

Bersac: 27 lorries burnt June 1943.

Brive: Breakdown crane destroyed September 1943.

Tulle: Breakdown crane destroyed October 1943. Turntable attacked August 1943.

Massiac: Liquid oxygen works attacked, Transformers, Distributor and 2

Compressors destroyed the 20th January, 1944.

Clermont-Ferrand: Stock of 40,000 tyres burnt at Michelin store December 1943.

Saignes: 30,000 litres of petrol captured December 1943.

In addition, over 100 locomotives were put out of action and a German patent Reaper and Binder destroyed.

43. The "team" which secured these results was:
Officers from London.
Hector: S/Ldr. M. Southgate. D.S.O., Légion d'Honneur.
Samuel: Major René Maingard, D.S.O., Croix de Guerre.
Jacqueline: Ensign Jacqueline Néarne (F.A.N.Y.), M.B.E.
Marie: F/O Pearl Witherington, M.B.E.
Olive: (Lysander Expert): Lieut. A.P. Shaw.[7]

Gaétan: (Lysander Expert): Lieut. Pierre Mattei. Arrested February 1944.

Aimé: (Radio Operator): Roger Milhaud. (American.)

Aided by various local recruits including two radio operators trained by Samuel.

44. The subsequent course of events was briefly this:

45. Hamlet in June 1944 took over in Southern Haute-Vienne and in a short time became responsible for the whole Department.

46. Samuel concentrated on Indre, which he divided into three and entrusted to Marie and to two Jedburgh teams, Hugh and Hamish: himself proceeded into Vienne where no organisation existed and which he armed. In early July he managed to establish contact with Deux-Sèvres where equally no Resistance existed, and despatched Jedburgh team Ian to Charente.

Major Staunton's Organisation.

Operational name of organisation: The Salesman Circuit.

Operational name of organiser: Hamlet.

Name by which known in the Field: Hamlet.

47. Hamlet reached the Field for this, his third mission, on the night of the 7th June, 1944. He was accompanied by Clotaire (Captain Maloubier), who had already worked with him in Rouen (q.v.), and Mrs. Szabo (Louise) as courier. The latter was, unluckily, arrested by the Germans after a sten-gun battle and was last heard of at Limoges prison, on the 12th August.

48. Extracts from Hamlet's report give a good idea of progress made and the problems which had to be face.

49. When I left I was given to understand that I would find on arrival a well-organised Maquis, devoid of political intrigues, which would constitute a good basis for extending a circuit throughout the area.

50. On arrival I did find a Maquis, roughly 600 strong, plus 200 gendarmes who joined up on D-Day; but these men were commanded by the most incapable people I have ever met.

51. The chief of this Maquis, who calls himself Colonel Charles, was a soldat 2eme classe, with no war experience. He had been for Hector, Samuel and Anastasie their only contact with the Maquis, which neither of them had ever really visited,[8] relying on Charles for their information.

52. The story in short is that Charles had been acting as decoy for George Guingoin, the local F.T.P. leader. My opportunity to extend my grip on Charles and get troops in Haute-Vienne was to get Guingoin under moral control, and to get the C.F.L. contact as well. This last contact I never managed to get, either through failure of the proper people to appear, or through the fact that whenever I struck on an A.S. Maquis, clamouring for arms, they each time admitted having already received a few deliveries. I was therefore in the position, if I started arming them, of appearing to play a dirty game behind somebody else's back, pinching his troops, or reporting him to London as not doing his work properly. On the other hand, the F.T.P.s in Haute-Vienne were numerous enough to provide me with the necessary troops to attend to my targets.

53. When I finally met Guingoin after the first day operation on the 25th June, he was very outspoken, in his desire to collaborate with me on condition that I had no political motive; I was just as bold, and stated that I was only interested in winning the war, and that providing he undertook to attend to all targets which I might designate, I would arm his troops to the best of our ability.

54. After some arguing he accepted the agreement, and from that day he has *never* failed to execute immediately all orders from London, as well as to attend to all targets.

Formation of the Haute-Vienne E.M.F.F.I.

55. From the end of June I lived in daily contact with Guingoin, and constantly kept his mind aimed at the goal of unification under the F.F.I. banner. The Department of Haute-Vienne held a large majority of F.T.P. Maquis; therefore the point of view of the F.T.P. leaders was that, whereas in other Departments such as Creuse, where F.T.P.s are a minority, the F.F.I. chief belongs to the A.S. and the F.T.P.s have accepted the work under his command, in Haute-Vienne the command should he

given to them. Late in July this point of view was adopted as well by Colonel Rivier, Chef d'État Major, Région Cinq.

56. In the meanwhile, the D.M.R. Ellipse, whom I had not been able to contact, was following another line of thought, and was trying to nominate as F.F.I. chief an officer from another Department belonging to the O.R.A. orgainsation. This solution, had it been carried out, would have provoked the nastiest mess, as the F.T.P.s, supported by their own national headquarters in this matter, would never have accepted that unity of command. Fortunately I managed to secure on the 10th August an interview with Ellipse, and found, to my relief, that, acting on better information, he had changed his ideas and was working on a new plan of organising the Haute-Vienne F.F.I.s under two co-chiefs, Guingoin and Commandant Huard, of the A.S. Ellipse furthermore admitted handsomely to me that he made a blunder in advocating the O.R.A. officer, and asked me to use whatever influence I had with Guingoin to bring him to accept the new set-up. This I managed to do, and the arrangement was sealed on the 15th August.

57. I would like to point out that whatever aims the F.T.P.s have for the future, they have for the last three months constantly played the game. I may point out, for instance, that during the last week in August, when Haute-Vienne, as well as Creuse and Corrèze were entirely liberated, while both Creuse and Corrèze were sending out about 700 men each to fight in other Departments, Haute-Vienne was sending out at the same time over 3,500.

Main Operations since D-Day in Haute-Vienne.

Railways.
58. Not a single convoy has been able to go by any of the railways through Haute-Vienne, which is the main Paris–Toulouse and the main Bordeaux–Lyon routes.

59. During June we constantly blew up small bridges, then by the end of June, under the German menace of the shooting of hostages if this destruction of bridges was carried on, we piled up in a deep cutting two km. north of Salon-la-Tour two successive passenger trains, which we had allowed to resume service between Limoges and Brive. Of course,

the trains were both stopped one km. before the demolition, and the passengers were ordered out. This produced an effective block for six weeks, the Germans being short of heavy cranes.

60. Later on, in early August, the Germans finally managed to rebuild a single line in between the wreckage, and tried to get three convoys through, protected by an armoured train. At the same time another armoured train was coming up from Brive to meet the convoy. I attacked this armoured train with my O.G. and S.A.S. groups[9], with the result that the three convoys returned to Limoges. At the same time my Garage Maquis in Corrèze piled several hundreds of tons of rock on the line between Uzerche and Brive, effectively stopping the other armoured train.

Roads.
61. From the end of June onwards all main roads in the Department were constantly ambushed, and from the date when the all-out order came, permanent heavily-mined road blocks were established on these same roads, particularly on the Route Nationale No.10 between Masseret and Magnac; on the Angoulême–Limoges road a few miles West of Chavagnac, and on the Angoulême–Confolens–Bellac road at Confolens itself. Furthermore, two strong attempts by Germans in July to use the Angoulême–Limoges road were repulsed after several hours' heavy fighting on the crossings of the Vienne at Confolens and Chabanais.

Telephones.
62. It is impossible to state the number of cuts made in telephone lines, both aerial and underground, all over the Department.

Guerrilla.
63. During the period from the 16th July to the 28th July, when we were attacked in the Châteauneuf area by 1,800 S.S., 700 German infantry and 500 milices, our losses totalled 32 men killed. Known losses inflicted on the enemy 250, including 12 officers. It is, as usual, impossible to know the exact total of losses inflicted.

64. Apart from that action, and that in the North of the Department, on which I sent a report by W/T, the enemy abandoned any idea he might have had to use the roads in that Department. Nevertheless,

immediately after the fall of Limoges, Haute-Vienne Maquis were sent out first to the Angoulême–Ruffec district, where they actually took Angoulême by following up the enemy inside the town after a sortie, and later on in the Vienne, where they partook in the fighting between Civray and Montmorillon.

65. Between the 25th June (from which date separate records were kept in London of deliveries to Hamlet as distinct from the former Stationer Circuit as a whole) till the 17th September, the stores delivered to Hamlet's group were:-

1944.	Operations.	Containers.	Packages.
June	1	83	9[10]
July	48	2,093[11]	361
August	24	691	147
September	3	72	54

66. Hamlet's claim to fame rests also on two other achievements. He was responsible for the reception of two daylight dropping operations on the 25th June and the 14th July, on which 839 and 409 containers of stores were dropped respectively. These massive operations were carried out by the American Air Force and were completely successful. Their tonic effect, particularly that of the 14th July, can well be imagined.

67. His other great distinction is that he was leader of the Allied Delegation which negotiated the surrender of Limoges with General Gleiniger. After prolonged discussion, under the auspices of M. d'Albis, Correspondent of the Swiss Legation, between Hamlet and the General, the latter agreed to the Allied terms. The Allied delegation consisted of:-

G.M. Staunton,[12] Major, British Army, representative in Haute-Vienne of the
Allied High Command.
J. Guéry, Captain, F.F.I.
M. Viguier, Captain, F.F.I.
Ch. A. Brown, Captain, U.S.A.

68. (Samuel's and Marie's subsequent movements, which took them into Indre, Vienne, &c., will be dealt with in the appropriate place.)

69. Before leaving the Limoges region, mention must be made of one other circuit.

70. During the course of the above events another circuit had been building up in the same neighbourhood.

71. In October 1943 Captain Peuleve (Jean), who had been working in the Corrèze on contacts which had originally been given him by Major de Baissac from Bordeaux, reported that he was in contact with a certain Colonel Veni. This Colonel had been a member of the Conseil Central de la Résistance, but (to cut a long story short) had left this Council and prepared to throw in his lot with the British. Captain Peuleve asked that a British officer be sent to assure the liaison.

72. The officer selected for this somewhat tricky assignment was Captain (later Major) Hiller (whose group will be considered later) and he in his turn reported that Colonel Veni had groups in and around Limoges to which an officer should be sent, London's design, of course, being to split the group up, in the interests of security and practical working.

73. On the 7th March, therefore, Major Percy Mayer (Edouard) and his brother, Lieutenant (later Captain) E.R. Mayer (Maurice), were dropped near St.-Céré (Lot) to undertake this mission. On the 23rd they were joined by their radio operator, Miss M.P. O'Sullivan, and later they were reinforced, on the 1st July, by the dropping of Lieutenant A. Campbell and, on the 3rd August, by Lieutenant A. Cameron.

Major P. Mayer's Organisation.
  Operational name of organisation: The Fireman Circuit.
  Operational name of organiser: Barthélemy.
  Name by which known in the Field: Édouard.

74. After first contacts with Major Hiller and Colonel Veni, Édouard and Maurice set to work on the organisation of the Veni groups in the Limoges area. As time passed, however, it became ever more clear (to use Édouard's own words) that the Veni organisation was "more a theoretical conception than a practical reality."

75. The nominal head of Limoges was a M. Tavet, both he and his right-hand man, M. Pariset, being in the Intendance Militaire at Limoges. Their wives also took an active part in the organisation.

76. Édouard describes Tavet as "honest, straightforward, courageous, hard-working, trying his best to serve his country, and, as far as I can see, having no personal ambition." Pariset, on the other hand, appears as "weak, chicken-hearted, dragged into the Résistance movement by his entourage and not through personal inclination and sense of duty. In due course he proved worthless."

77. Tavet had belonged to the Communist party, but had severed the connection: but the wives, Mesdames Tavet and Pariset, had been active and open Communists before the war and still were.

78. Tavet had many contacts with Résistance, particularly with the F.T.P. He was anxious to obtain support and material for all resistance groups, without worrying about the affiliations of these groups with existing organisations, such as F.T.P., M.U.R., A.S., &c. There was therefore never, in fact, an allegiance to the Veni group, as such, and with Tavet's arrest in May 1944, the "Veni groups" in the Limoges area vanished into thin air.

79. It had been at trying period for the Mayers. At the end of March the Gestapo got on their tracks and they had to leave Limoges for Argenton. At the end of April they had to move again, Maurice to Chaillac, then St.-Gaultier and finally Prissac, Édouard to "Le Pin" and then Fresselines.

80. And in the meanwhile nothing had been accomplished.

81. Édouard, of course, had kept London advised of what was going on and about mid-May was authorised to work with groups other than Veni.

82. Late in April he had quite accidentally contacted a resistance group which Tavet had said belonged to Veni, but which turned out to be purely and simply F.T.P. It wanted arms, but was not prepared to accept any directives. As, however, it was actively engaged in the sabotage of the Paris-Toulouse railway, Édouard asked H.Q. for authority to supply

it. It became known as Robert group, after its leader Robert Delfait (killed the 9th June).

83. Through Robert, Édouard was put in contact with the head of the F.T.P. in Indre. He too needed arms badly, but he was not prepared to accept the directives of the Allied High Command and Édouard refused to supply him.

84. At the end of May he also met Commandant Maldant in North Creuse, a member of the M.U.R. under Colonel François. He was perfectly willing to follow Édouard's directives, but François refused to allow him to accept arms from the British, saying that he would supply them himself in due course.

85. So, by D-Day there was no working arrangement with Resistance groups.

86. After D-Day things became easier. Contact had been established (Maurice handled practically all the F.T.P. contacts) with Roland, head of the F.T.P. in Southern Indre, he had finally agreed to accept the Allied High Command directives and the first delivery took place on the 12th June. Later Roland became F.T.P. chief for the whole of Indre and Édouard continued to supply him with arms for the Southern portion.

87. At the end of June Édouard made the acquaintance of Colonel François, who asked for the arming of all his groups in North Creuse, particularly that of Commandant Moisson.

88. In the early days of August Colonel François, commander of all the F.F.I. forces in Creuse, asked Édouard to take direct command of all fighting forces in Northern Creuse, both M.U.R. and F.T.P. This Édouard hesitated to do, as it was not in the terms of his mission, but as the order came from the D.M.R., he complied. In late August, when the German columns began retreating through the Châteauroux area, Colonel François put several extra Companies from South Creuse at his disposal. The Creuse units under Édouard's command were active in harassing these German columns, co-operating in this task with Colonel Robert commanding M.U.R. fighting units in East Indre.

89. Édouard's report observes that the main sabotage which they carried out was that of Masonry bridges. The results of guerrilla activities were surprisingly good in North Creuse, where they attacked the enemy every time they had the chance and killed some 250 without a single casualty on their own side. In South Indre results were also very good, but some casualties were incurred.

90. So ended a mission which concluded very successfully in spite of the disappointing and difficult start. That it was appreciated is shown by a letter which Colonel François wrote on the 22nd September, 1944, from Guéret to Major Édouard:

"Dear Major, I have just learnt that you are going back to England. I trust you will let me tell you how grateful I am for the actions which you have carried out in the North of our Department. We owe to you the Military organisation of this sector, we owe to you the not inconsiderable results which have been achieved there. I congratulate you on the decoration which was given to you at Limoges last Sunday, I wish I could have been there in order to mark by my presence how much I approved the symbolical gesture which this presentation implied both as regards yourself and your comrades of the Inter-Allied Mission. I shall never forget what the Creuse owes to you. I hope always to keep your friendship and I hope to be able to go one day to prove to you in your own country that the French are not ungrateful."

91. As to politics it may still be of interest to quote Édouard's observations:

92. "We of course were not in any way interested in political questions of any sort and I always took good care to make that quite clear. As a result, we never got involved, however remotely, in that delicate matter. I must say that I was greatly surprised what little place political matters ever had with the various groups with whom we worked, whether F.T.P. or C.F.L.

93. In the Indre Department we only worked with the F.T.P., except for one small independent group led by Commandant Moret. I know that the F.T.P. groups had strict orders from their head of department

(D.M.R.) Roland never to discuss political matters in camp. Lieutenant Mayer, who was directly in charge of these groups, confirms that he never heard of any political issues raised or discussed amongst the F.T.P. in his area. In the beginning there seemed to be a slight mistrust shown by Roland on our behalf. He did not seem to like the idea of Lieutenant Mayer visiting all the F.T.P. camps regularly to insure that all the men were quite familiar with all our weapons and knew my ideas about the type of guerrilla warfare which I advocated. I took the matter up very frankly with Roland and he declared that it was a general measure applied throughout the F.T.P. organisation that no strangers to the organisation could visit the camps without first obtaining the D.M.R.'s authority. He explained that they had had trouble with persons penetrating their camps to spy on their organisation and report it to the A.S., &c. He thanked me very sincerely for having never interfered in political matters, but said that this had not always been the case with all British officers and made some vague remarks about trouble in the north of the department. After a very frank discussion, the matter was cleared up and we never again had the slightest difficulty on that score. Lieutenant Mayer was after that always genuinely welcomed in all the camps, and I myself was several times invited by Roland to inspect his camps and talk to his men on military matters.

94. In Northern Creuse the work was not quite so simple. When I started working there both the M.U.R. and F.T.P. organisation existed only on paper. I started to equip them at the same time, each organisation having its own grounds. At first I had some slight trouble, each party accusing me of favouring the other. This trouble was soon cleared up as they realised and became convinced that I had no special interest to favour the one or the other. Complete harmony was soon established between the two organisations and they really worked hand in hand. I did my best to ensure an equitable distribution of arms and stores between the two organisations and everything worked really smoothly. Whenever I visited an F.T.P. camp I was asked to take some of my M.U.R. officer friends with me and *vice versa*. After I had been given the direct military command of all the fighting units in Northern Creuse the understanding between the F.T.P. and M.U.R. was so complete that I was sometimes embarrassed, as some F.T.P. groups would insist on working on the same jobs as their M.U.R. friends and side by side. As an instance of the harmony that reigned between the two organisations

I shall mention a luncheon farewell party that I gave at Fresselines to all company commanders that had been under my orders. Speeches were made by Commandant Maldart, M.U.R., and Commandant Melon, F.T.P., and both spoke, in very moving terms, of the perfect understanding that had existed between the two organisations in Northern Creuse and claimed, rightly or wrongly, that I was the main factor that had contributed to it. I have annexed to this report, as a matter of interest, copies of letters that I received from Colonel François and a few company commanders before I left France.

95. One of my first jobs in Northern Creuse was to equip an independent group known as Groupes Marquis. The head of that group, Roger Pesault, insisted in remaining independent of all political ties and I, of course, had nothing to say about that. Some internal trouble later developed in that group and I took that opportunity to use my influence to make them join up with some recognised organisation. That group was eventually absorbed by Commandant Maldart's M.U.R. organisation, and all worked satisfactorily thereafter.

96. Some time in July I finally discovered a group in Haute-Vienne that had been in contact with Tavet for the supply of arms. That group, nominally about five hundred strong, was nothing more nor less than a M.U.R. group. As they could not be supplied by their own organisation I submitted the case to H.Q., who accepted to serve them. This was done and they received in all five 'planes. Some trouble developed with that group as they wanted to break away from the M.U.R. organisation, and remain independent, as the M.U.R. had not been able to equip them. The D.M.R. presumably intervened and ordered that about half the equipment received by this group must he handed over to some neighbouring M.U.R. organisation. They appealed to me, and I referred the matter back to London for a decision. On receiving H.Q.'s orders that the D.M.R,'s decision in the matter had to be followed I gave instructions accordingly. As the position was getting involved I broke off all connections with this group and asked them to follow the D.M.R.'s orders.

97. For his work during this Mission Major Mayer (who had received the O.B.E. for his work in Madagascar) was awarded the M.C. Lieutenant Mayer and Miss O'Sullivan received the M.B.E.

Chapter 9

The Bordeaux Region, Corrèze–Dordogne

1. Another circuit, which merits separate study, has its origins in David's work in Bordeaux in late 1942 and early 1943. David had established a loose contact with Corrèze and these appeared of sufficient importance to warrant the sending of a separate organiser to develop them.
On the 18th September, 1943, this organiser, Jean, arrived in France.

Major H. Peuleve's organisation.
   Operational name of organisation: The Author circuit.
   Operational name of organisation: Jean.
   Name by which known in the Field: Jean and Henri.

2. Jean arrived at an inauspicious moment, since, as already reported, the Grandclément bubble burst on the 19th September and within a very short time the Bordeaux circuit had virtually disappeared. Aristide still remained, and Jean made contact with him, but obviously he was unable to help and Jean had to make his own way into the Corrèze.

3. This he successfully did and left Bordeaux for his own district in mid-October. On the 31st October he made his first contact with London (he was his own radio operator). At this period his main contacts were with the F.T.P. and he continued working with them until his arrest in March

1944. His most important contact was André Malraux, whose name had been given to him from London.

4. By the beginning of March 1944 he was able to report that he had 2,500 men under his control in Corrèze and Dordogne, two-thirds of them in the Maquis. In addition, he was in contact with 1,500 F.T.P., whom he armed and directed. He had established a striking force, which he himself led in attacks on enemy communications. Early in March one of his guerrilla groups was attacked by Germans and Miliciens and killed fifty-one of the enemy.

5. Jean was responsible for the organisation of twenty-four successful stores deliveries by parachute.

6. On the 21st March, 1943, Jean was arrested by the Gestapo. With him was taken a locally-recruited wireless operator, Berthou, Roland Malraux, and an ex-Vichy commissaire de police working with him, called Delsanti. The Germans also found a number of codes and papers.

7. Jean has been suspected of having sold out to the Gestapo after his capture, and a "document" was found in the Gestapo archives at Limoges which seemed to confirm this. Jean was shown this on his return from Buchenwald in April 1945 and has pointed out that the "document" is a mixture of mis-statements and of facts which were already known to the Gestapo before his arrest. Nestor, also, has confirmed that no arrests took place in the circuit after Jean's capture.

8. Nestor had joined Jean at the end of January as his lieutenant, and was luckily away at the moment of Jean's arrest. He was warned of what had happened, and was able to take over the circuit without accident.

9. In April he was sent Casimir (Captain Beauclerc), radio operator, and Basil (Captain P.I. Lake) as lieutenant and instructor.

10. Nestor apparently had found it almost impossible to take in hand the remnants of Jean's circuit, and had in consequence addressed himself to new groupings in an endeavour to set his organisation on foot.

11. The contact with André Malraux was unbroken, and from this London knew that Nestor was continuing to work with the F.T.P. Another influential contact, of which London was ignorant, was Commandant Gisèle, head of the C.F.L. in Dordogne, and Martial, the F.F.I. chief with whom he worked in complete accord. This same Martial has evoked very unflattering references from Philibert, Hilaire's lieutenant for the Dordogne, and Philibert and Nestor were evidently very much crossing wires in this region.

12. The whole situation in this part of the world, indeed, was very confused. Quite apart from whatever purely French organisation might be working in the region, F. Section alone had the Northern part of Hilaire and the Southern part of Hector both overlapping with Nestor, notably in Dordogne. Furthermore, the only thing that London really knew about Nestor was the F.T.P. contact, and so when in the May moon Nestor put up some fifty grounds for stores deliveries in six or seven Départements, it was felt that the time had come to call for a restriction.

13. What Nestor never did, and indeed refused to, explain was that he had also made contact with a Commandant Robert, head of a widespread Intelligence circuit in the region. This Commandant had expressed a desire to meet Nestor, a meeting had been arranged, and they had found that they were father and son!

14. Nestor was, therefore, in fact working with groups of all complexions and not at all entirely Communist. He had groups working with him throughout Dordogne, Corrèze and Lot, amounting to some 10,000 men.

15. The high lights of their activities are the delay, claimed to be as long as seven days, which they imposed on the Das Reich Armoured Division, which was endeavouring to make its way to the front in Normandy, and in which Basil particularly distinguished himself by blowing up several bridges in the Périgueux neighbourhood, and the surrender of the German garrison at Brive, Nestor having the satisfaction of being one of the four signatories of the surrender terms on the French side.

16. Nestor's was a surprisingly successful mission, more particularly as he was not a man of whom a great deal was expected. He was awarded the D.S.O. for his activities and Basil received the M.C.

17. The record of stores delivered to Nestor is as follows (the figures for Jean are not available):-

Date. 1944	Operations.	Containers.	Packages.
May	11	149	40
June	4	54	30
July	43	1,085[13]	227
August	2	48	18

Chapter 10

The Bordeaux Region, Toulouse and the South-West

GENERAL

1. British activities in this area have their roots in the work done by three men, Lieutenant Pertschuk (Eugène),[14] Captain (later Lieutenant-Colonel) G.R. Starr (Hilaire) sent from London, and Baron Philippe de Vomecourt (Gauthier) recruited locally and commissioned into the British Army.

2. Gauthier, whose connection with the British organisation dates from 1941, had his base at Limoges and his own activities are dealt with under the heading "Châteauroux–Limoges" area at paragraphs 1-7. Subsequent events, and the manner in which Hilaire became the heir to the South-Western part of his area, are related below. Meanwhile, a word must be said as to Eugène's appearance in the Field and subsequent activities. Eugène unfortunately never returned from

Germany and the elements of his story have been in the main obtained from Philippe de Gunzbourg (Philibert), who worked with him.

Lieutenant Pertschuk's Organisation.

Operational name of organisation: The Prunus circuit.
Operational name of organiser: Eugène.
Name by which known in the Field: Eugène.

3. Eugène was a delicate, highly-strung, extremely intelligent, very young man who arrived in the Field in May 1942. Obviously neither his youth nor his lack of robustness made of him the ideal leader of a sabotage group. He was, in fact, intended to carry out a propaganda mission for another Department. F. Section of S.O.E. being responsible only for the physical arrangements for his upkeep and supply while in the Field.

4. But the dividing line between sabotage by the written or spoken word and sabotage by more direct means is a narrow one, and one fine day Eugène reported back to London that he was in contact with a very powerful action group in the Toulouse area, with numerous possibilities for the disruption of rail and telephone communications, and capable, as one particular instance, of dealing with the Toulouse telephone exchange itself. It did not take London long to decide to acquiesce in this modification of Eugène's original mission, and for F. Section to begin to take a direct interest in his activities.

5. Eugène had with him a radio operator, Lieutenant Marcus Bloom (Urbain), to provide him with the necessary means of direct communication with Headquarters. He also possessed indirect means of communication through another circuit working the Riviera.

6. Philibert reports that Eugène's circuit extended over Haute-Garonne, Gers, Tarn et Garonne, Lot-et-Garonne, Lot and, later, Southern Dordogne. In Gers his work was based on Vic-Fezensac and Auch; he was very active in the region of Montrejeau in Haute-Garonne, at Soturac and Tauriac in Lot and at Agen and Mézin in Lot-en-Garonne. He had the basis of an important organisation in Toulouse, centred round the École Vétérinaire and its director Petit. He had strong

connections with the Deuxième Bureau and contact with Vichy, where he was on good terms, directly or indirectly with one of Pétain's Ministers.

7. Philibert, who had organised a small group of his own, worked under Eugène, but for security reasons was kept apart from the main stream of Eugène's activities.

8. (This may explain why Philibert was unable to speak with any precision as to the *origins* of Eugène's group. The writer is not certain whether it was ever established what exactly this group was. But there is a strong probability that it was an offshoot of the ubiquitous Carte[15] group, and a possibility that the subsequent arrest of Eugène and Urbain may have been due to that sinister character Roger Bardet.[16])

9. This separation of Philibert's activities from those of the rest of the group was fortunate for him, since in March and April 1943 a wide series of arrests took place; on the 23rd April Eugène and Urbain were themselves arrested and the circuit, to all intents and purposes, ceased to exist. Philibert and his own group, however, were not affected and they were able to pass over to Hilaire's command without incident.

10. Eugène's organisation had been full of promise, but it was probably already insecure when he first came into contact with it.

11.What emerges is the extent to which Eugène, in spite of his youth and his lack of physical toughness, had been able to acquire the devotion and co-operation of men much older and more experienced than himself.

Lieutenant-Colonel G.R. Starr's Organisation.
Operational name of organisation: The Wheelwright circuit.
Operational name of organiser: Hilaire.
Names by which known in the Field: Hilaire and Gaston.

12. Towards the end of October 1942 Hilaire set out from Liverpool on the mission which culminated in his building up one of the biggest circuits which the British ever had in France, and ended, in September 1944, in verbal fireworks with General de Gaulle, when the latter

endeavoured to apply to Hilaire his (at the time) usual technique of ordering all British officers out of France instanter as having no interest in the liberation of the country from the German invader.

13. The rôle which London proposed for him was to act as assistant and technical adviser to Rodolphe (Henri Sevenet), who had just been appointed by Gauthier (Baron Philippe de Vomecourt) to command one of the three parts into which the latter had divided his organisation.[17] Hilaire, who was mining engineer of some repute, was an ideal man for any organiser to have working for him.

14. On arrival in the South of France towards the end of November 1942, Hilaire did not go direct to his contact address in Lyon, but waited in Marseille for some things to be forwarded to him. This was extremely fortunate, since it was while he was in Marseille that he learned of the arrests of Gauthier and others of his circuit, including the contacts in Lyon to whom he was going.

15. In due course, however, he made contact with Rodolphe, whom he found endeavouring to take over the command of the whole of Gauthier's organisation, but endangering everybody by his imprudences, which attracted the attention of the Gestapo. So much so, that Hilaire besought him to leave the country;[18] this he refused to do.

16. The position seems to have settled down into Hilaire successfully reorganising the South-West (Lot-et-Garonne, Gironde, Dordogne, Gers, Landes, Basses- and Hautes-Pyrénées), while Rodolphe was reputed to be himself reorganising Gauthier's groups in Lyon, Le Puy and Clermont-Ferrand. But even here his lack of capacity was evident, and Hilaire was forced to investigate. To his relief he found that Lyon was in a sound condition under Étienne's[19] leadership.

17. He could therefore decide to concentrate on his own sector.

18. Here it was inevitable that Hilaire should have come into contact with Eugène's organisation and it was indeed extremely fortunate that he did so, since he was able to establish direct communication with London through Eugène's radio operator and to organise, through him, the first two deliveries of stores for his own circuit. And as luck would

have it, one of these deliveries included the S. phone which, as will be related later, played such a crucial part in the affairs of the whole South Western area.[20]

19. With the arrest of Eugène and Urbain, Hilaire found himself with the remnants of two powerful organisations, Gauthier's and Eugène's on his hands and no means of direct communication with Headquarters. He had, it is true, developed lines of communication through Madrid and Berne, but these channels were so laborious and slow as to be almost useless for operational purposes.

20. The position was so serious that on the 2nd May Hilaire sent two of his helpers, Mlle. Denise Bloch[21] and Sgt. Dupont[22] out through Spain with a report for London. This report was unfortunately lost, but the picture they brought was of a circuit well organised, with Hilaire's own position sound,[23] but with everything held up for lack of arms, munitions and money (although Hilaire had been able to borrow some money locally, and communicate the details to London through Berne).

21. It was already clear that Hilaire's circuit was an important and widespread one (although details did not become available in London till August, when Hilaire reported through Berne that his group was divided into ten districts, each with its own chief and its own Headquarters for D-Day).

22. At about the same time a message reached London viâ Berne, in which Hilaire asked that an officer from Headquarters might be sent in an aircraft equipped with S. phone apparatus, in order that he might report progress and that arrangements might be made for the stores deliveries necessary to put the group on its feet. This conversation took place on the 22nd July, 1943.

23. There may have been more epoch-making telephone conversations, but it is certain that the effect of this one on the whole course of the war in the South-West was remarkable. This is most graphically shown by the following table of successful dropping operations carried out to the Wheelwright Circuit (and bearing in mind that the disappointingly small figures for October 1943-January 1944 are a reflection of the weather and not of the group's capacity to receive stores).

24. Stores delivered to Wheelwright Circuit:

Date.	No. of Operations.	No. of Containers.	No. of Packages.
1943			
April	2	9	2
July	3	20	5
August	12	102	8
October	7	87	2
November	7	104	19
1944			
January	5	66	10
February	23	364	31
March	26	375	24
April	17	237	86
May	34	390	108
June	2	47	65
July	7	148	149
August	3	117	39
September	1	12	7

25. To give credit where credit is due, an appreciable share of this success is due to a lady, S/O Yvonne Cormeau (Annette), who was sent to Hilaire as his first wireless operator in August 1943. She worked untiringly and well right up to the Liberation, in spite of a period of illness and in spite, on one occasion, of being woken up at dead of night by the Gestapo and having to take to the fields in her nightgown, pursued by German bullets. It is recorded that two of these bullets pierced her night-attire but, luckily for Annette and for the Circuit, in one of the spots where Annette wasn't! During her time in the Field S/O Cormeau transmitted 400 messages, an outstanding record, which fully merited the Croix de Guerre, which she received in December 1944.

26. Hilaire was supplied with three other helpers from London during the course of his mission. In January 1944 he was joined by Lieut. Arrachart (Néron) as assistant and Miss A.M. Walters (Colette) as courier, and in April by Lieut. Parsons (Pierrot) as second radio operator. Néron was somewhat young for the job, but carried out one or two very efficient sabotage attacks. Pierrot worked well and Colette showed courage and determination in her work, for which she was awarded the M.B.E.

27. Hilaire himself, unfortunately for posterity, is a most unvocal person, and his own reports on his activities are of the briefest. (He indeed once expressed to the writer the view that, once an action was over, it was not worth reporting on). The report attached at Appendix B is, in fact, the only report that Hilaire prepared after his return to England.

28. Philibert, however, has to some extent supplied the deficiency, although his own area was Southern Dordogne, and he was only indirectly aware of what was going on in the rest of the circuit. Further information is in Appendix A, compiled from telegrams and reports received in London during the course of action.

29. Pre-D-Day activity is probably adequately covered by the latter: as to the Post-D-Day period, Philibert reports that the most active regions were those of Bergerac, Sarlat (Dordogne), Nérac, Villeréal (Lot-et-Garonne), Sotorac, Touriac (Lot), and the region that was under Hilaire's direct command covering the Gers département and certain Landes communes. Apart from Nérac and Villereal, activity in Lot-et-Garonne was very small, owing to the inertia of the local commander Beck (real name Guérin).

30. Philibert, who was Hilaire's chief lieutenant during the clandestine period, was responsible for the Southern Dordogne and North-Western Garonne area, where he was working in close collaboration with Bergeret (real name Loupias, Sous-Préfet of Bergerac) the local leader of the Armée Secrète.[24]

31. At D-Day the Das Reich Armoured Division was grouped in the region of Montauban. Early in June the division divided and part tried to make its way towards Dordogne, while the remainder attempted to reach Bordeaux by way of Gers. Each of these parts was completely halted by the Gers and Southern Dordogne[25] groups, railways having been cut and bridges blown up.

32. In reply, the Germans called on the local garrisons, who carried out many punitive sorties, notably at Mouleydier and Pressignac in Southern Dordogne and at Castelnau-sous-l'Auvignon in Gers, where the defenders were under the direct command of Hilaire himself. This latter engagement is briefly described by Hilaire at Appendix B, but the report is chiefly interesting in its oblique reference to the last moment at

which Hilaire himself was in personal command of French troops; at 1700 hours on the 21st June Hilaire's Castelnau Maquis left Condom in column to join with the Maquis of Panjas, the whole forming the Bataillon de l'Armagnac under Capitaine Parisot.

33. The sum total of these activities by the Gers and southern Dordogne groups was to deny to the Germans access to the Normandy battlefield along two lines of approach:

1. Carcassonne–Toulouse–Bordeaux.
2. Bordeaux–Bergerac–Souillac, where they would be astride the Toulouse–Limoges railway.

34. It is estimated that the actions in these two zones cost the Germans about 1,000 casualties and the loss of fifteen tanks, and at least twenty to twenty-five motor vehicles of various types. The losses on the French side must have amounted to about 200.

35. Hilaire and Parisot marched into Toulouse with the Bataillon de l'Armagnac on the 21st August and the bataillon was sent to harry the Germans in the direction of Carcassonne. Later it moved up to Bordeaux and the Royan pocket. Here the bataillon was transformed into a regiment and played an important part during the winter 1944 in the La Rochelle redoubt. By this time, however, it was under the command of Colonel Monnet, Commandant Parisot having been most unfortunately killed by an aeroplane propeller on Toulouse aerodrome.

36. Philibert has given the writer some impressions of the political aspect of affairs after D-Day. As ever in the south-west, the political situation was fraught with difficulty, and, indeed, Philibert and Hilaire themselves adopted diametrically opposed principles, Hilaire having as little as possible to do with the Communists and Philibert keeping in close touch with them. Philibert reports that the Communists as a party refused to act on the 7th June,[26] claiming that the English agents alone had decided (!) to go into action and that this action was premature. They launched a very strong campaign of calumny, but by the beginning of July the F.T.P. groups themselves had almost all become active and their activities became greater and greater until the Liberation. Except for small groups and individuals they mostly had

political aims and kept aside a great part of their ammunition for future activities. The Right-wing O.R.A. groups, comprising mostly officers who up till that moment had had absolutely no activity whatever, behaved in much the same way as the Communists. In both cases, except for individuals or faithful groups there was a sort of revolt against Hilaire's command. Towards the end of July another tendency manifested itself, that of Chefs de Groupes, who preferred to keep their men out of action, to be able later to march into the towns and not to be unjustly accused of having risked the lives of their troops.

37. There were, of course, exceptions to the above rather unhappy picture, since certain Communist groups acted perfectly on the one hand, and, on the other, Hilaire had round him officers more or less of the O.R.A., whose behaviour was impeccable.

38. All this is episodic in relation to Hilaire's achievement as a whole, and this is very well summarised in a note supplied to the writer by the officer responsible for the co-ordination of the work of the circuits in Southern France with the operations from North Africa. He arrived in Toulouse on the 18th September, 1944, and writes:

"The only footnote I can usefully add to your notes on Hilaire is one underlining the extraordinary prestige Hilaire had acquired in South-Western France in the course of two years' work there. There is a legend in Toulouse that the Germans, in 1943, already believed him to be a British General sent in to direct the whole of the Resistance in the South-West.[27] At the time of the Liberation, the whole of the area was in the hands of a series of feudal lords whose power and influence was strangely similar to that of their 15th century Gascon counterparts. Among these barons, Hilaire was, without any question, the most influential. His position naturally created for him a host of enemies. He seems particularly to have been on bad terms with the F.T.P. since most of his material had been given to M.U.R. groups. I believe from those who know the area better than myself that Commandant Parisot's accidental death (at a pick-up operation) was a very great loss to the circuit. His replacement by Colonel Henri Monnet, brother of Georges Monnet, 1939 Minister of Blockade, served to accentuate, rather than smooth over, the political differences in the area.

Colonel Monnet had his eye firmly fixed on the post-war political future. He commanded the Brigade de l'Armagnac, which was formed out of the troops that Hilaire had armed, during the whole of the winter of 1944-45, when it was engaged on the siege of the Island of Oleron. Thereafter he entered General de Gaulle's Cabinet, from which he appears to have engaged in election-rigging for the U.D.S.R. He is now presenting himself as a candidate in the Landes, where there is no doubt that Hilaire's prestige will form an important plank in his electoral platform."

39. The same source was given a verbatim account of Hilaire's famous interview with General de Gaulle on the 18th September. 1944. The story ran roughly as follows:

40. A large official lunch had been arranged by M. Pierre Berteaux, the Regional Commissioner, in honour of the General's arrival. Hilaire, who was at the time unquestionably one of the most powerful men in the South-West of France, was naturally invited to this lunch, but on arrival at the place where it was to be given he was intercepted by Berteaux, who explained to him that General de Gaulle did not wish him to be present at the lunch, but that he wished to see him afterwards in the Commissaire's office at half-past-two. At 2.30 exactly Hilaire presented himself and was shown into a large room in which he found himself alone with the General. He saluted. "Qu'est-ce que vous faites ici?" said the General. Hilaire explained that he was helping General Bertin and Colonel Ravanel. "Non," said the General impatiently, "mais qu'est-ce que vous avez fait?" Hilaire explained the part he had been able to play in forming and equipping the F.F.I. Battalions of the Gers and the surrounding departments. This account provoked an access of rage on the General's part. "Vous n'avez pas le droit de former des bataillons – vous, un étranger. Vous n'avez rien fait." Hilaire explained that in so doing he had been carrying out the orders he had received from S.H.A.E.F. General de Gaulle, shifting ground, next accused him of interference in civil matters. Hilaire admitted that he had done so in a couple of cases where "résistants de la première heure" had been unjustly imprisoned. By this time General de Gaulle was pale with anger. He ordered Hilaire to leave Toulouse immediately and to rejoin his army at Lyon. Hilaire, who is of small stature, played a very passable David to the General's Goliath. "Mon Général, je vous connais comme chef du Comité Français de la Libération

Nationale, et même comme Président du Gouvernement Provisoire de la République, mais pas comme un officier supérieur, et je vous emmerde." "Je vous ferai arrêter!" cried the General. Hilaire replied that he was at the General's disposition in this matter. He explained that he would be obliged to communicate the General's wishes to Allied High Command and to wait for orders from them. His responsibilities in the South-West were not on a scale of which he could divest himself in five minutes. He had, for example, a number of "Jedburgh" teams and Allied Missions on his hands. "Take them with you," cried General de Gaulle. Hilaire pointed out that there were French officers among them. This had no quietening effect at all on the General. "Je vous casserai." he shouted, "Ils sont des vendus, des mercenaires: qu'ils partent avec vous ..." There followed a deadly silence. Finally, Hilaire enquired whether he might leave. The General came round from behind his desk and shook hands, showing him to the door. "Il y a une chose de vrai dans ce qu'ils m'ont dit de vous ... que vons êtes sans peur et que vous savez dire 'merde.' " At the door he offered Hilaire his hand again.

41. Before passing on from the Hilaire circuit it is necessary, unfortunately, to refer to one other matter. Reference has already been made to the fact that Hilaire made many enemies. This was no doubt inevitable in a general way, but in two cases the persons who turned against him were of the inner circle who had worked closely with him during the clandestine period.

42. The first was a Belgian, Maurice Rouneau (or Rendier), a somewhat unprepossessing journalist, who had at one time been Hilaire's second-in-command, but in 1943 had left, or been sent out of the area, had come to England, had been commissioned into the British Army and had been parachuted into Brittany shortly before D-Day. After the Liberation he returned to the South-West and started spreading stories detrimental to Hilaire, until sternly reminded by the Paris office that a continuation of such conduct would render him liable to an action for libel. His motive was quite clearly jealousy.

43. The other was an Englishwoman, Colette. Reference has already been made to the qualities of personal courage which she displayed in her work as courier. Unfortunately, there was another side, and on the 31st July, 1944, Hilaire sent London the following telegram: "Have had to

send Colette back because she is undisciplined, most indiscreet … also disobedient in personal matters. She constitutes a danger to security."

44. Hilaire had had, in fact, on one occasion to place Colette under arrest. Colette's reaction was to attempt to spread adverse reports concerning Hilaire, including allegations that he had been responsible for the torture of miliciens and collaborators. These allegations led to a Court of Enquiry in London, at which Hilaire was exonerated.

45. "Hell hath no Fury …" and Colette's case could be left there without further comment. Unfortunately, a good deal of damage was done, since, in spite of F. Section's efforts, she was allowed early in 1945 to return to the region (though not for long) as assistant to the Press Attaché.

46. To conclude, it is hoped that the account already given and the record of action in Appendix B will demonstrate why Hilaire is regarded by F. Section as one of the most distinguished officers they ever sent to the Field. This view, incidentally, is shared by Colonel Monnet, whom the Judex party met when, in December 1944, they visited the Headquarters of the Demi-Brigade de l'Armagnac, and of whom they formed a very high opinion: he said many nice things about Hilaire, especially regarding his power of leadership, his fairness, his courage, his discretion and his sense of clandestinity.

47. Lieut-Colonel Starr was awarded the D.S.O., M.C., and Croix de Guerre avec Palme. A good account of Hilaire's position in the South-West appears in *Maquis de Gascogne* by Raymond Escholier (Éditions du Miliue du Monde, Genève).

Major Hiller's Organisation.

Operational name of organisation: The Footman Circuit.
Operational name of organiser: Maxime.
Name by which known in the Field: Maxime.

48. Maxime's was one of the most delicate liaison missions with which an F. Section officer has ever been faced.

49. In 1941 Colonel Fourcauld of the B.C.R.A. had started the service Froment, an intelligence organisation which later developed a para-

military wing in the Zone-Sud, known as Froment Action. Both these movements relied on the support of a number of Socialist leaders. Some time later Colonel Vény took over the command of Froment Action, which came to be known as the Groupes Vény. The Groupes were part of the de Gaulle organisation, la France Combattante, and were financed by the Service Froment, to whom they were thus subordinated. Colonel Vény managed to build up an organisation covering the Marseille, Limoges, Lyon, Toulouse and Montpellier areas. It was built up mainly with the help of the Socialists, and in each area there was a Socialist political chief by the side of the military chief; but while being an approved organisation it never became the official Socialist organisation. This, together with the difference in the discipline and organising ability of the Socialists, explains the comparative failure of the Groupes Vény. Militarily, the Colonel's aim was to recruit the largest possible number of men, to organise them up to the platoon level, and leave them unarmed until D-Day.

50. In the winter of 1942, at the time of the formation of the Armée Secrète, the Groupes Vény were ordered to join in the merger. This was done everywhere, but by April 1943 Colonel Vény had withdrawn from the merger, partly from thwarted personal ambition and partly from distrust of the A.S. Security. For a while they had to live by expedients until the Service Froment again financed them.

51. In October 1943, at a meeting of Vény and the Socialist chiefs of the Service Froment, it was decided that they could not continue as a dissident organisation, and representatives were sent off to London and Algiers. Colonel Vény was in agreement with this, on condition that his troops retain their separate existence.

52. At the same time Colonel Vény began negotiations for arms with Jean (Captain Peuleve, an F. Section officer working in Corrèze), without informing the chiefs of the Service Froment, who were opposed to these negotiations. He also failed to inform Jean of the London and Algiers negotiations, or of the fact that he had at least moral obligations towards the chiefs of the Service Froment.

53. This was the situation in January 1944 when Maxime arrived and negotiated an agreement, by which we were to arm and finance the Groupes Vény, who were in turn to attack all our targets. In February

the truth about the Algiers negotiations leaked out, and it was learned that the Froment-Vény organisation had been accepted in the M.U.R. under the name of France au Combat. There were to be F.A.C. representatives at the various echelons of command, but there was to be a complete merger of all troops. Colonel Vény refused to accept this, and the Groupes Vény were split into two rival factions: the supporters of the F.A.C. and the Colonel's supporters working with Maxime, who were promptly accused of being sold to Britain.

54. In February the Colonel and the F.A.C. came to terms and Maxime accompanied the Colonel to Paris for negotiations with the M.U.R. His aim was to try and ensure that the Groupes should retain a separate organisation for security reasons, while at the same time freeing themselves from the accusation of being politically subservient to Great Britain. The negotiations, however, broke down completely when the M.U.R. representative insisted on a complete fusion.

55. In February 1944 Maxime received Barthélemy (see under Châteauroux–Limoges) and Firmin, who had come out to carry out the organisation and supply of Vény groups in the Limoges and Marseille areas respectively.

56. Maxime describes the organisation at the time of his arrival as follows:

> "When we arrived it was an organisation in power rather than in being. In each department there was a chief who was in loose contact with a number of people. There were no arms whatever, no organisation worth speaking of, and, worst of all, neither drive nor offensive spirit, among the leaders, at any rate. Maquis groups were non-existent, owing to lack of money. The chief assets were, that with so rudimentary an organisation, security at the top was good, and the recruitment of reliable people did not offer any problem."

57. By the beginning of June, however, he had armed approximately 600 men in the Lot, 600 in the Lot-et-Garonne, mostly in the North-East of the department, and 200 in the Tarn, mostly around Carmaux, all these areas being, incidentally, good Maquis country. They were all sedentary

elements except for the small Maquis in each department to man a recuperation ground. They had been organised into teams of up to 20 men, each having its own prearranged Maquis site, its own vehicles earmarked, and some small reserve of food and fuel. They had no reserve ammunition, and enough explosives for railway sabotage, but not for road mines.

58. In April he had a number of mishaps. Jean was arrested, then later the Gestapo tried unsuccessfully to arrest two of their helpers in the Lot. In May, German mass arrests in the Lot left them with several of their supporters caught in the bag; but most of them escaped soon after.

59. In May, when they had been promised large despatches of arms, Maxime agreed with André Malraux, to whom he had been introduced by Nestor, to give all surplus arms to the best elements of the Mouvements Unis in the Toulouse area. When the promised arms did not materialise the plan had to be abandoned, and the only people Maxime was able to arm, in addition to the Groupes Vény, were the Groupes Francs of the Tarn.

60. List of Operations:

Date. 1944	Operations.	Containers.	Packages.
February	3	45	10
March	4	46	7
April	9	131	27
May	7	103	33
June	12	342	172
July	14	872*	64
August	11	292	87
September	3	68	6

*Including Daylight Operation (558 containers 14.7.44).

61. On D-Day practically all their troops took to the Maquis, while the Germans held the towns and occasionally sent strong columns out.

62. They found themselves complete masters of the countryside. Their problem was no longer one of security, but of administration.

63. During the month of June shortage of ammunition and explosives, and preparations for possible airborne landings limited guerrilla activity.

64. In the Lot F.T.P. propaganda and organised hostility resulted in the loss of 200 armed men, who went over in small batches. The resulting friction seriously hampered all work. In July negotiations were started through Andre Malraux for the entry of the Groupes Vény into the F.F.I. It was agreed that the Groupes should he placed under F.F.I. command, but that they should retain their separate organisation, and to continue to work with Maxime. Such an agreement had become indispensable in view of the growing general demand for unity under French Command.

65. From July onwards arms began to arrive in large quantities, and they had at last enough ammunition and explosives.

66. On the 23rd Maxime was wounded and Eustache took over. Soon after Sostène and Dick arrived.

67. Towards the end of July Col. Vény decided to merge, not with the C.P.L. as had been agreed with Malraux, but with the F.T.P. A merger was arranged in the Lot, which relieved the existing tension, but did not have time to bear its fruits. In the Tarn and the Lot-et-Garonne the Colonel failed in his attempt, and his Troupes Vény were admitted as such to the F.F.I.

68. From the beginning of August onwards they gradually lost control over the Groupes Vény. The F.F.I. chiefs of the departments concerned were quite willing to take their advice, but either they were too newly in command to have any real control over their troops, or else they were more interested in occupying the towns than in pursuing the Germans.

69. By the middle of August Maxime had armed approximately 1,800 men in the Lot, 1,800 in the Lot-et-Garonne and 500 in the Tarn. In addition he had given enough arms for a hundred men each to the O.R.A. and the F.T.P. of the Lot, the A.S. in the Correze, and a Maquis in the South of Aveyron. Lastly he had armed approximately 500 men of the Corps Franc de la Libération in the Tarn. None of these organisations was under Maxime's control but they all did good work.

70. After the evacuation of the Toulouse region by the Germans, the mission was virtually terminated, orders now being issued by the F.F.I. on a regional instead of a departmental basis.

71. In spite of the difficulties alluded to above Maxime had very successfully carried out his main mission, which was to organise and equip the Vény groups, and get them to carry out the Allied High Command objectives.

72. In the pre-D-Day period one really outstanding sabotage attack had been carried out against the Ratier propeller works at Figeac. This was attacked in January 1944, and the extremely valuable production of variable pitch air-screws was almost completely crippled for the rest of the war.

73. After D-Day the outstanding accomplishments of the group were:

Lot.

74. All the railway lines were cut (this is not attributable to the Vény groups alone) and on the 9th June the Das Reich Division had to leave for the North by road instead of by rail. The Germans made strenuous efforts to repair the Cahors–Brive lines, but only got one troop train through.

75. All local telephone lines cut, including the German Cahors – Paris cable.

76. Various guerrilla engagements took place, particularly towards the end, and the Vény groups took part in the investment of Cahors under F.T.P. leadership, and the half-hearted pursuit which followed. The operation was a complete failure, owing to the incompetence of the F.T.P. leaders, and their unwillingness to take the advice of the Allied officers present.

Lot-et-Garonne.

77. The Agen–Périgueux line cut on D-Day and the cut maintained. The Toulouse–Agen line was cut several times. Local telephone lines were

cut, and the Bordeaux–Toulouse German cable cut on two occasions. In various guerrilla engagements 25 Germans were killed, 22 wounded and 88 taken prisoner, a negligible result due to ineffectiveness in the F.F.I. commanders.

Toulouse.

78. A team of four men supplied with H.E. by the Tarn put the German exchange in Toulouse station out of action. Early in July destroyed the H.T. pylons of the Lannemezan–Portet-St.-Simon line over the Garonne: repairs took 3 weeks. Put seven railway engines out of action.

Tarn.

79. *Railways.*
    Carmaux–Albi line cut 9 times, permanently after the 9th August.
    Carmaux–Rodez line cut 4 times, permanently after the 7th July.
    Albi–Castres line cut 5 times.
    Castres–St. Sulpice line cut 2 times.
    Castres– astelnaudary line cut once.

Telephones.
    Toulouse–Lyon German underground cable cut between Rodez and Albi and never repaired. Also numerous local lines.
    Numerous guerrilla attacks.

80. Maxime summarises the results of his mission by noting that the results obtained were not proportionate either to the number of men or the quantity of material received. He attributes this to various factors:

    1. Delay in sending arms. Arms in quantity only began to arrive in July.
    2. Delay in sending officers.
    3. Delay in the formation of the F.F.I.
    4. Resurgence of the French national spirit; resulting in an unwillingness to take the advice of Allied officers and in the failure of several operations.
    5. Shortage of French officers.
    6. Inter-group and personal rivalries. Most of Maxime's time was

taken up in trying to deal with personal quarrels or political disputes and he met very few leaders who were able to set aside all political loyalties and think only of fighting the Germans.

81. Maxime's "team" consisted of:

Maxime (Major G.F. Hiller, D.S.O.).
Eustache (Captain C.A. Watney), Radio operator and Second-in-Command.
Sostène (Lieutenant Songy) (Aus), Lieutenant.
Dick (Captain Daniels) (Aus), Lieutenant.

82. N.B. The writer has received from a reliable source, a note concerning Vény himself (now General de Brigade Jean Vincent) which it may be of interest to place on record:

"General Vincent, who was in the Resistance from 1942 onwards, always showed personal courage. At the same time, self-interest was his sole criterion in dealing with individuals and groups and he considered the "Groupes Vény" primarily as a means of self advancement. His age and severe wounds prevented him from taking a close interest in this organisation and his efforts were limited to keeping in being a large paper army and advertising it in Resistance circles. His real contribution to the Resistance was more modest and consisted in having assembled and kept together over a long period a number of nuclear organisations."

Appendix A:

ACTIVITIES OF HILAIRE CIRCUIT

July 1943
Organised 28 teams ready for railway destruction and a military group of 1,200 men for guerrilla activity.

August 1943
Poudrerie de Bergerac completely destroyed.

August 1943
At Riscle (Gers) 20 railway wagons containing small arms, 64 railway tanks and a complete train of munitions destroyed.

August 1943
Between Pau and Dax a train of 28 wagons of small arms and ammunition destroyed.

9th August, 1943
German ammunition train destroyed on Toulouse–Carcassonne line.

August 1943
2 pylons on Toulouse–Ak line blown up, interrupting supply and cutting telecommunications with Office National Industriel de l'Asote.

August 1943
Area organised into districts with Headquarters.

19th December, 1943
18 locomotives blown up at Montauban.

18th December, 1943
3 bombs at Milice Headquarters at Agen.

23rd December, 1943
More bombs at Milice Headquarters at Agen with result of German reprisals.

31st December, 1943
Marmande area – 30 locomotives blown up.

December 1943
600 men of Cazaubon Chantier de Jeunesse and 800 of the Naval School
at Castelmorin organised for resistance.

15th January, 1944
4 locomotives, turn-table and points destroyed in the Marmande depot.

22nd January, 1944
Locomotives destroyed as follows: 6 at Le Buisson; 11 at Bergerac; 9 at
Aymet.

19th February, 1944
4 wagons of fulminate of mercury blown up at Libourne.

28th March, 1944
Toulouse powder factory blown up. Result all machine tools out of
order, raw material destroyed: 30 100-h.p. motors and pipe-line also
destroyed.

March 1944
Further Toulouse poudrerie information: dryers and pulverizers in the
shops put out of action: more than 30 motors put out of action.

April 1944
German general killed in attack on German column in Dordogne.

22nd April, 1944
Train containing munitions and German war material attacked between
Bergerac and Ste.-Foy.

26th April, 1944
Further 12 wagons from same train destroyed in station at Lamonzie.

April 1944
1,500kgs of heavy submarine oil burned at Boussens. Factory
temporarily stopped, more oil and 6 transformers destroyed.

April 1944
Further Boussens information: 1 electric distributor destroyed, putting fire-pumps out of action; 150 tons of synthetic lubricant set on fire.

29th April, 1944
Hispano-Suiza foundry at Tarbes attacked. All models and matrices for aero-engine parts destroyed and production reduced by at least 75 per cent. Subsequently confirmed work for Germans completely stopped for at least 3 months.

April 1944
Petrol tanker train derailed at Montrejeau.

13th May, 1944
Lorraine-Dietrich wagon factory at Bagnères successfully blown up.

10th June, 1944
400 men ready.

14th June, 1944
Holds Condom, Nogaro, Eauze, Gabarret.

13th June, 1944
Losses inflicted on enemy in first battle of Agen.

10th June, 1944
All targets (rail cuts and road blocks) successfully attacked.

29th June, 1944
Auch – 150 Germans killed. Official figures.

Appendix B:

REPORT OF HILAIRE ON POST D-DAY ACTIVITIES

Night of the 6th to 7th June, 1944, all men grouped themselves in North and South Garonne, North and South Gers and Hautes-Pyrénées – special sabotage teams started working on railroad cuttings, telephonic and telegraphic destruction, &c.

The maquis was divided into the following districts:

Dordogne and North-West of the Garonne under Philibert.

North-East of the Garonne under Beck and Main Noire.

South of the Garonne (Lot and Garonne) under Gabriel.

Gers divided into two groups, one at Panjas under Capitaine Parisot and the other at Castelnau under my personal supervision.

Landes under Romain.

Pyrénées under Mazencal.

Castelnau was attacked on the 21st June, 1944.

The group was composed of 500-odd men with Stens, rifles, a few Bren guns and grenades. We were attacked at about 6 a.m. by approximately 2,000 S.S. coming in from the North who were using mortars and cannon. By 13.30 p.m., after continuous firing, I decided we could not hold out much longer and blew up the explosives dump. We continued fighting until 15.00 hours when I ordered the retreat towards Condom as the road was sufficiently clear. I lost twelve men killed and a few were lightly wounded. The Germans admit the loss of 437 killed. The village was completely razed to the ground. The men formed a column in Condom which we left at 17.00 hours to join with the maquis of Panjas, the whole forming the Bataillon de l'Armagnac under Capitaine Parisot.

Battle of Estang on the 3rd-4th July, 1944.

The Maquis, now 1,200 strong, was disseminated in the neighbourhood when a column of about 1,000 Germans was signalled. Four companies under Capitaine Parisot attacked this column at Estang. Towards 19.00 hours the Germans retired to the North, intending to return to Mont-de-Marsan and fell into an ambush of two companies who held them the whole night. The next morning at dawn, the Germans sent planes on reconnaissance. These sighted the trapped Germans who had sent up distress signals. F.W., Kondors and Dornier bombers arrived practically immediately and machine-gunned the roads and surrounding fields, endeavouring to destroy the cars and lorries used by the maquis, dropping anti-personnel bombs near Lannemaignan, where many of the men were. We retreated without too great a loss and reformed at Maupas. Our losses were four men and the enemy approximately 150. It is regrettable the Germans shot nine hostages at Estang.

We stayed there three or four days and then moved to Honttanx, finally settling at Averon-Bergelle. By this time the Bataillon was 2,000 strong. This was the main body of the maquis in the district, there were still other groups as shown at the beginning of this report.

On the 14th July a column of about 4,000 men of the "Das Reich" Panzer Division, coming South from Garonne, started scouring the district to destroy the maquis. They attacked the maquis under Gabriel in Lot and Garonne. After a few hours of fierce fighting Gabriel withdrew his men without too many losses. The Germans attacked again at Sos on the 20th July, this time the fight lasted three days.

After that experience the Germans left the maquis in peace as it was much stronger than they had expected. During the next few weeks we received a few more arms and reorganised the companies.

On the 11th August, 1944, having heard that the German garrison, composed of men of the Edelweiss division, were preparing to leave Aire-sur-Adour, Capitaine Parisot attacked the column just outside the town on the morning of the 12th. The attack was most successful, liberating the town with scarcely any damage, inflicting losses on the enemy, who finally retreated to Mont-de-Marsan, and only losing four of our men.

On the 19th August, 1944, on receipt of a report that the German garrison at Auch was leaving, the Bataillon attacked them at L'Isle Jourdain on their way to Toulouse. The battle lasted forty-eight hours, when all Germans who had not been killed gave themselves up. Prisoners included two Colonels, the Captain who made himself known by the cruel treatment of French prisoners. One other Colonel had been killed. The Bataillon lost ten men. We captured several lorries, also petrol and other stores.

During the whole of the period since D-Day various small encounters took place.

As regards battles and encounters undertaken by maquis in Dordogne, where Philibert had to bear the brunt of attack by the S.S. Division "Das Reich," and Pyrénées, reports will have to be obtained from the respective leaders and forwarded later as no details are to hand.

Chapter 11

The Marseille Region

THE OLIVE CIRCUIT

1. Towards the end of August 1941 a group of four organisers left Liverpool to make their way via Gibraltar into unoccupied France. Among them was Lieutenant François Basin, known as Olive. His general mission was to build up Resistance in South-Eastern France, his more immediate and localised "point de depart" being to act as technical adviser to a certain Dr. Lévy of Antibes, who was already active in that area.

2. Olive was arrested by the French police soon after his arrival, but, managing to convince them that he had been repatriated with members of the French military mission after the Armistice, was released and, into the bargain, got himself supplied with genuine papers.

3. At the beginning, Dr. Lévy (Philippe) was extremely helpful, and with his aid Olive was able to establish himself quickly; he was introduced to the heads of Resistance movements and to many influential people, who were later to prove useful. Unfortunately the connection with Philipe did not last and Olive was forced little by little to exclude him from his organisation. He (Philippe) was not satisfied to work with Olive alone, but was at the same time a leading member of the Libération, Combat and Communist Parties; he also developed an inordinate greed for money.

4. Communications, as was normal at this period, were a source of difficulty. Olive was successful in developing a line through Switzerland as early as November 1941 and he was also able to use Marie's (Virginia Hall) channels through Lyon, but both of these were indirect and cumbersome.

5. In January 1942 Olive had received the visit by submarine of Captain Peter Churchill (Raoul), despatched by London on a rapid mission of inspection in unoccupied France, who brought him revised directives. It is interesting to note, in view of later events, that Raoul, on his return, reported with considerable approval concerning a certain Girard, whom he described as the "éminence grise" of the Resistance groups and as having been of great assistance to Olive.

6. In March 1942 Raoul left London again to accompany two wireless operators destined also to enter Southern France by submarine. One of these, Julien,[28] was to work for Olive. He was landed on the 21st April and established contact with London early in May 1942.

7. Before his arrest in August 1942, through a courier (Jean Gogniat) being picked up at the Swiss frontier, Olive had built up thirty-one cells covering the Bouches du Rhone, Var, Basses-Alpes, Alpes Maritimes. Seven of these were designed for sabotage work, the remainder for propaganda, distribution of tracts, &c. Actual sabotage operations were few, in accordance with the policy ruling at this period.

8. Olive. However, was also in contact with all the important Resistance groups of the region, notably Libération (d'Astier de la Vigerie), Liberté (Fresnay) and Libération Nationale (Général de la Laurencie), and in April 1942 he made a distinct contribution to history by enabling

d'Astier to make use of a return passage to England in the submarine which brought Julien to France.

9. Last, but not least, Olive was in close contact with the André Girard (Carte) mentioned above, who was represented as the head of a powerful nation-wide organisation. This contact was fraught with consequences for F. Section.

10. Olive displayed a very high degree of diplomacy in his dealings with Carte. He kept his own organisation entirely separate from the rambling Carte structure, while maintaining close contact with it. He evidently impressed Carte, who was anti-de Gaulle, with the possibilities which co-operation with Olive implied, since in June 1942 Carte agreed to send one of his officers to London to make arrangements for even closer collaboration. In the meanwhile, Olive, in April 1942, had profited by the enforced departure of Frederick (Max Hymans)[29] to send to London a detailed report on his relations with Carte. Unfortunately Frederick, who came through Spain, was considerably delayed.

11. The officer chosen by Carte to visit London was known as Louba (real name Frager). His report convinced the authorities in London that the organisation he represented had tremendous possibilities, and it was decided that on his return to the Field he should be accompanied by Major Bodington (known as Jean-Paul) from Headquarters. This took place in July 1942.

12. It is difficult to arrive at a balanced judgment on Jean-Paul's visit. Symptomatic of one viewpoint is a report made by a Captain Renaudie[30] after the Liberation that the Carte group perpetrated a gigantic buff at this period in order to obtain London support. On the other hand, Jean-Paul was an experienced officer with a wide knowledge of France and the French. The truth is perhaps somewhere between the two.

13. Jean-Paul reported, on his return to London early in September, that Carte had received him at first with a certain reserve, but that this soon developed into cordiality, and that he had agreed surprisingly quickly with Jean-Paul's suggestion that a responsible staff officer should go to London at the earliest opportunity. Jean-Paul met this officer and, though it was never expressly admitted, was convinced that this visit

would afford the first contacts between the French General Staff and
our own.

14. Jean-Paul's Report continues:

> "Meanwhile I had an opportunity to study the Carte
> Organisation. It has been built up carefully by men who have for
> many years been experts in their own particular line and in
> conditions of the utmost secrecy. If there was some delay in
> getting going, it was largely due to the fact that the recruiting and
> careful selection of "troops" had been the main task, in
> preparation for the moment when action was propitious. It is
> because there was an element of surprise
>> (a) at our readiness to give immediate assistance, and
>> (b) at the fact that our organisation was as well defined and
>> extended as it is, that there was a slight time lag.
>
> "A point I wish to make quite plain at the very beginning is that
> after my mission in France, I have no doubt in my mind that the
> French, as represented by the Carte Organisation, that is to say, a
> national movement affecting every stratum of society, are far
> more prepared than is guessed at by the majority of responsible
> persons in this country."

15. He goes on to record that he was particularly impressed by the
purity of spirit, the forcefulness of character and the determination in
the men he met. Equally, by the very wide ramifications he came across.

16. His conclusion was that the work of the Carte and F. Section
Organisations was fundamentally different but, at the same time,
complementary. F. Section agents were now working on a definite plan
aimed at definite targets; the Carte organisation had as its ultimate
object the reinforcement of our invading forces by guerrilla troops. From
the para-military point of view the Carte Organisation could provide
what was virtually the mobilisation on the spot of a secret army; it was
closely linked with the French General Staff.

17. He proposed collaboration between Carte and F. Section of S.O.E.
on the following basis:

S.O.E. to provide –
(1) The possibility of daily broadcasts for instructional and directive purposes.
(2) The supply of liaison material, *i.e.*, internal radios.
(3) The supply of instructional sabotage material, supplemented by material to be stored in various arsenals already prepared, to be followed by more elaborate material, food and other requirements for action by guerrilla forces.
(4) The means of direct contact with London.
(5) Competent instructors in para-military or military warfare.
(6) One of its own W/T. operators.

18. In return Carte would contribute:

(1) The gradual development of direct contacts between the United Nations General Staff and the French High Command.
(2) The placing at our disposal of all the organised forces as known by the National Census then in progress.
(3) The assistance in every department of the Carte organisation, when required, *i.e.*, help for agents, storage of materials, organisation in both zones of para-military organisms.
(4) Use of the internal wireless system.
(5) Use of a considerable network of intelligence useful to para-military and military preparations.
(6) The organisation of liaison and transport facilities where needed.
(7) A sure check on the subversive activities of German agents in France.

19. This proposition was favourably received in London and it was decided to give Carte full support. A "clandestine" radio transmitter, "Radio Patrie," was installed "somewhere in England," to broadcast the Carte messages to French Resistance, and an officer was sent specially from London to take over from Olive his liaison duties with the Carte organisation.

20. This officer, Captain Peter Churchill (Raoul), arrived on the 28th August, 1942. On the 18th Olive had been arrested at Cannes.[31]

21. This arrest was fraught with consequence. Olive, as has already been noted, has displayed great skill in his relations with Carte. Raoul, though he had given evidence of great courage and resourcefulness on his two previous missions, was no diplomat: Carte, into the bargain, had in the meanwhile received the visit of Jean-Paul, and knew that he was now assured of the support of London.

22. On the 5th December, 1942, Raoul sent the following message to London:

> "Please insert Lise[32] who works here gets on plane as Carte hopes to take nine men.
> Limit list again as Carte out of control with temper and power due your polite acceptance his dictatorial wishes. Lise must explain as even Louba fed up and fears bad impression."

23. The plane referred to was a bomber in which it was intended that Carte and a number of his staff officers should come to London. This operation did not, finally, take place.

24. In March 1943 Raoul and Louba were brought to England by Lysander. They related a tale of megalomania and imprudence on the part of Carte (he was apparently wedded to a nation-wide system of card-indexing, which quite naturally led to widespread arrests) which made him quite impossible to work with. Louba, his second-in-command, had finally decided to break with him, and Raoul supported Louba.

25. Carte also reached London at about the same time and a very painful and difficult series of discussions began. Painful, because Carte was indubitably sincere, but difficult – and finally impossible – since his head was firmly anchored in the clouds, and it was impossible to persuade him to relate his plans and dreams to such materialistic considerations of supply, finance and security as of necessity governed the conduct of operations at the time.

26. It was also clear that the rift within his organisation was so deep that he could not be allowed to return to France – we were indeed assured that he would be "bumped off" the moment he did so – and he was

finally allowed to go to the United States, where it was felt he would do relatively little harm.

27. This left Raoul and Loubs, the latter of whom claimed that he represented the concrete as opposed to the abstract in the Carte organisation. In this claim he was supported by Raoul and it was decided that the confidence which had been Carte's should now be extended to Louba. Louba, for his part, agreed to accept the London directives and the London ideas of how a subversive organisation should be managed. This involved the splitting up of the Louba kingdom, which embraced groups as far apart as Mantes, Strasbourg and Bayonne, into self-contained (and, it was hoped, uncontaminated) organisms, capable of working in accordance with London principles and directives.

28. A major plank in this programme was the division of what would be left of Carte's organisation into three main zones:

(1) A Northern zone in the old Occupied France under Louba himself: this stretched from Normandy viâ the Yonne and Côte-d'Or Eastwards to Nancy and it was intended that Louba should concentrate on Yonne and Côte d'Or and gradually pass the outlying portions over to other organisers.
(2) A Central zone under Raoul. He was to be senior liaison officer for the whole area between the Paris – Nancy line and the S.E. Mediterranean coast. He was to he himself primarily responsible for the Haute-Savoie area.
(3) A South-Eastern zone which was to he entrusted to a newcomer, Captain (later Lt.-Colonel) Francis Cammaerts (Roger). Under his inspired leadership this ultimately
became by far the most important of the three zones.

29. Roget had arrived on the 17th March, 1943, in the Lysander, which took Raoul and Louba back to England.

30. The programme was a reasonable one, and might have been successful but for two things. The one was a Colonel in the German Intelligence service whom Louba was in contact[33]: this man represented himself as an Alsatian and an anti-Nazi, but this did not deter him from

appearing at the Hôtel de la Poste at St. Jorioz two days after Raoul's arrived there on the 15th April, 1943, and arresting him and Lise who was with him.

31. The other adverse fact, which was not known until later, much later, was that two of Louba's lieutenants were double agents. These are the notorious Bardet (then known as Roger Chaillan) and Kieffer, concerning whom more will be found (under Paris) at paras. 114 and 115. There is a strong probability that Bardet is the betrayer of Eugène in Toulose[34], and he has admitted to the betrayal of Captain S.C. Jones (Élie), British liaison officer to Louba's circuit in the Occupied zone .

32. Roger had fortunately escaped damaged and was getting to work in the South-East.

Lt.-Colonel Cammaert's Organisation.
Operational name of organisation: The Jockey circuit.
Operational name of organiser: Roger.
Name by which known in the Field: Roger.

33. Roger had arrived on the 17th March, 1943, by Lysander to a reception organised by Raoul. The subsequent arrangements were in the hands of Marsac, who brought him to Paris preparatory to his going South. The next day Marsac, his secretary, and a Doctor who had formed part of the Reception Committee were all arrested and Roger was advised to leave Paris immediately. (He had in the meanwhile entrusted almost all his money to Marsac). This he did and was taken to St. Jorioz, a small village on the south side of the lake about 5 miles from Annecy.

34. This was the Louba group's Headquarters, but Roger's first impressions were not favourable. In the next two or three days he became convinced that the job which he had been given of taking over Raoul's circuit consisted in taking over the job of liaison officer to a highly insecure French-run organisation which, by the absence of its two leaders, had fallen into the hands of a young man who was, in his own words, too young and tactless for the job.

35. (In this Roger was indubitably right, for the young man was Roger Bardet (then known as Roger Chaillan), the "hero" of two somewhat

mysterious escapes from the Gestapo, Louba's right hand man, who later took over from him in the Yonne Valley and who at the moment of writing is in solitary confinement at Fresnes under suspicion of having been a double agent.)

36. Roger met three other people at this time, Lise, Raoul's courier, Arnaud (Captain Rabinovitch) Raoul's radio operator, an efficient but extremely difficult young man who refused flatly to work with him, and Albert (known as Deschamps, real name Floiras) another radio operator who worked efficiently and well with him until the end. This man was one of the two operators whom Carte had sent to England to be trained, as part of the programme for the development of the Carte – London connection.

37. In case time might be thought to be hanging heavily on Roger's hands an emissary also arrived bringing a letter from the arrested Marsac in Paris introducing the bearer as a German Colonel who wished to go to England and who was disposed to be friendly. Against all advice Roger Chaillan insisted on visiting Marsac in person in Paris and in trying to push through the negotiations with the German Colonel.[35]

38. Suspecting a trap, Roger prudently – and luckily – retired to Cannes, where he spent four weeks awaiting developments. At the end of this time Arnaud arrived with the news that Raoul and Lise had been arrested.

39. Faced by all these developments Roger decided to sever all contacts with the old organisation, and to build anew himself. He had the faithful Albert (equipped by Arnaud before leaving with two sets) as wireless operator, and he had selected Pierre Agapov as recruiting officer and second-in-command. He moved his Headquarters to Montélimar.

40. Having neither the men nor the material for industrial targets, Roger's plan was – to establish along the main lines of communications, starting by the coast and Rhone valley, a series of dissociated groups capable of carrying out attacks on these communications, to organise simultaneously a number of reception grounds within reasonable distance of these groups, and to split his region up under area leaders. He decided to limit his activity to the area bounded by the

Mediterranean, the Rhone valley from Marseille to Vienne including the line of communication on the West bank of the river, a line from Vienne to Briançon passing through Grenoble, and down the Italian Frontier.

41. During May, June, July and August 1943 cells were organised and built up, under M. Berruyer in Isère, M. Daujat in Drôme, Jacques Latour in Vaucluse, and in Bouches-du-Rhône under Jacques Langlois[36] for that part between Marseille and Tarascon, and by Henri Vian for the line which runs eastwards from Marseille. Meanwhile, Pierre Berthone (Area Commander) was increasing his groups on the coastal lines between Nice and St.-Raphaël. First contacts were made with the Maquis in the Vercors.

42. By November 1943, with the aid of Pierre Agapov, Roger had built up the skeleton of a very widespread cellular organisation, capable, if it received enough material, of carrying out innumerable sabotage operations against all possible German lines of communication. This question of material was a difficult one, but, slowly progress was made:-

Stores Operations to the Jockey Circuit.

1943.	Operations.	Containers.	Packages.
August	1	7	...
September	3	21	4
October	1	12	2
November	1	11	5
1944.			
January	4	72	28
March	8	156	133
April	8	119	93
May	18	418	278
June	16	466	343
July	10	240	153
August	16	377	171

43. In November 1943 Roger returned to London to report.

44. During his absence in England orders were sent to his circuit, in connection with operations in Italy, for concerted attacks to be made on

their railway targets. These were, for technical reasons, only moderately successful, but 25 teams went into action and delays of up to 48 hours were obtained on almost all lines. Unfortunately, although Roger had made it clear to all leaders that these action messages had nothing to do with D-Day, the sending of these messages did produce rather strong emotional reactions which were followed by disappointment. More unfortunate still, the most successful attack, against a German leave train at Montélimar, involved the death of Daujat, who had remained too near the scene of the accident in his desire to observe the results of his handiwork.

45. Roger's return to the Field in February 1944 was dramatic. The weather became worse and worse, and the aircraft in which he was travelling had already turned back for home when heavy icing developed, two engines caught fire and he and the crew had to jump for their lives. Lesser men than Roger might have been embarrassed by the fact that he was carrying over a million francs and a hundred ration cards, in addition to the more humdrum articles of equipment, but he managed to persuade a neighbouring farmer of his *bona fides*, to make arrangements for the safety of the crew, and within a few days to rejoin his circuit, francs, ration cards and all.

46. Almost immediately new troubles assailed him. A number of arrests occurred in the Berthone groups and these in turn involved Agapov, who disregarded Roger's advice to steer clear of all his old haunts. Agapov appears to have been taken in by one of the Gestapo's simpler gambits, and to have agreed to betray various people, including Roger and one of his assistants, Lieutenant Martinot,[37] on the "understanding" that they would be treated as prisoners of war.

47. (Agapov's case is at present before the courts and Roger has testified in his defence. The final verdict is not yet known.)

48. Whether by coincidence, or as a result of Agapov's arrest, Roger's organiser at Avignon, Jacques Latour, and two of his lieutenants were arrested, and Roger became aware by the middle of April that the Gestapo knew his name, Roger, had his photograph, knew that he had worked in Cannes, Nice, Marseille and Avignon, and had offered a large sum of money for his arrest.

49. During April and May the imminence of D-Day became increasingly felt and most of the civilian administration came over to Roger in a body; at about the same time a second radio operator (Casimir) arrived, giving a direct link with Algiers, and greatly increased deliveries of stores resulted. In each Département Roger had now an officer in charge, a liaison officer in contact with other groups and a small H.Q. staff. This organisation, it should be remembered, was built up on British lines, that is to say, small independent groups briefed to go into action independently against their own specific targets.

50. Roger's report gives a most interesting account of the difficulties which lay in the way of the co-ordination of such an organisation and its French counter-part. This report also gives, better perhaps than a direct statement could do, an insight into the position which Roger came to occupy in the final stages of the Liberation of the South-East of France.[38] It should be borne in mind that the exploits of French Resistance in this region were singled out for special mention by General Eisenhower.

51. To quote Roger (in the form of extracts from his report):

52. "Though I was aware of the agreements which had formed French resistance movements into the F.F.I., I was too fully occupied to realise that the activity they envisaged was so entirely on an army basis. After the landing in Normandy I presumed that we in the South had a two or three months' battle on our hands and considered that my directive of independent action and receptions could work out during this time. The concentration of work in Hautes Alpes was directed on the general lines of communication Briançon, Gap, Veynes, the line Marseille – Grenoble, the line Gap – Grenoble and the line Briançon–Grenoble.

53. "We arranged in this department with the civilian administration to assist with the local distribution of food, as we were cutting all lines of communication and therefore creating a very serious food problem in the towns. This plan that I put into practice personally in this department, I had recommended to other departments, but I soon realised that the F.F.I. had larger ideas. Leaders appeared, called up everyone armed or unarmed and established the strong point of the Ubaye Valley (Barcelonnette) and the Vercors. The story of Barcelonnette

need telling in some detail as it is the story of my official entry into contact with the F.F.I.

54. "On the 7th June a group of men working with me received an order to hand over all their recruits, arms and explosives for the defence of Barcelonnette. As this note was not signed by anyone known to us, nor presented through any regular channels I told my officer to reply that he could not do this. He received an immediate reply saying that if he did not obey orders he would be court-martialled and shot. To this letter I replied myself, saying that there must be some misunderstanding as the men in this area were following a directive issued by Allied High Command and explained my position in the area. I received a letter of apology and a request to visit Barcelonnette. There I met Colonel Zeller (Faisceau), Sapin (Perpendiculaire), Captain Edgar, a British Captain, who had been sent to Maquis from the South-East in March with French Officers and American Officers, and the local F.F.I. leader's. Individually they explained to me the 'Plan Rouge' as follows:-

55. "On the receipt of certain messages the F.F.I. were to unite all resistance forces to divide the South-Eastern territory into three different kinds of zones: "1. Zone du Maquis – Plateaus and mountain areas held as strong points, *e.g.*, Barcelonnette, Vercors and parts of the Ain and the Jura – parts of Savoie. 2. Zone de Guérilla – zones in which Maquis groups were to operate from the mountains and on roads and railway lines without this area being held as strong points. 3. Zone Côtière and Zone d'Occupation Intense – this being a sabotage zone where German occupation was heavy and where Maquis activity was impossible.

56. "They explained to me that this plan was the result of discussions in Algiers and London. They were to establish strong points to be held at all costs. The second zone was more in keeping with my directive, only the Maquis, instead of acting in individual independent bands of ten to fifteen men, was to operate under a regular army system of companies, battalions &c. Only in the third zone was it clear that our directive was identical. The absolute condition of carrying out this plan, which had been agreed upon in Algiers and London, was that it could not last more than fifteen days, so they told me that they had evidence that within fifteen days there would be a landing in the South-East and they had seized Barcelonnette with 200 rifles divided among 800 men and with

only fifteen rounds per rifle. They obviously needed very immediate assistance either by parachute operations or by help from me. I threw cold water on their optimism by telling them that I was convinced that their conception of the position was due to a misunderstanding, that they could not possibly rely on a landing within fifteen days, that they could not rely on parachute operations at any time as there were innumerable factors which would prevent aircraft from coming to them and that I was not prepared to withdraw my material which was being used against German lines of communication in order to waste it by fighting a defensive battle in a cul de sac like Ubaye. Captain Edgar and Colonel Zeller were very depressed by my statement and the other young French officers regarded me as a non-co-operator and as a 'dégonflard'. As their position was critical and the Germans were attacking them from two sides, I agreed to send a small force to attack the Germans in the rear of their main attack over the Col de Vars, but warned them that the troops at my disposal were not men used to fighting open battles and could not obviously prevent the Germans from ultimately retaking Barcelonnette. I advised them to try and modify their plan, though obviously the difficulties once it had been put into motion, fear of reprisals and fear of losing the support of the civilian population made their position extremely difficult. When I returned to my headquarters in the Hautes-Alpes I found a number of telegrams awaiting me, telling me to put all my men and material at the disposal of the F.F.I. and explaining that from now on I was senior liaison officer with the F.F.I. in Regions 1 and 2.

57. "The very nature of the French military commanders, of their war training and their desire for 'gloire' and particularly of their very understandable desire to reinstate in the eyes of the world the greatness of the French army made it impossible for them to fight the hit-and-run warfare that I advocated. Unfortunately, the relief force which I sent to relieve Barcelonnette arrived too late, they had to carry their material over the mountains over a distance of 40 miles, and twenty-four hours later Barcelonnette fell.

58. "The result of the fall of Barcelonnette and our new position in relation to resistance was that I moved to the Vercors, which was the locality chosen for zone HQ. It was essential in this position that I should be with Colonel Zeller who had been given the command of

Regions 1 and 2. It must not, however, be thought that this command was either universally known or accepted, but at the same time it was obvious that he was the only man with sufficient tact to overcome political difficulties and gain some semblance of unified command.

59. "The most important problem before us was the part that we could play in relation to a possible landing on the Mediterranean coast. It was clear that we could not neutralise entirely the coastal defences and that because of the arrests that my organisation had suffered in the Alpes Maritimes we could not even go a long way towards sabotaging guns and defence installations, but we immediately set people to make plans of German mine-fields and to prepare themselves to act as guides for advancing troops. It was obvious that the coastal defences were not strong enough to resist penetration by a determined force and it was equally clear that, in spite of all our difficulties of organisation in the F.F.I. we could clear the roads and block the Germans in their garrison towns, so that an immediate advance to Grenoble along the Route Napoléon was possible. We reckoned that the maximum time necessary to get an armed force to Grenoble was seven days. There was nothing new in this scheme, but we could not get any form of hint which would help us to muster our forces and allow us to ration our material, particularly ammunition, for the landing date. We had received orders to act and had to go on using up our material. Wireless communication proved useless to obtain an answer to this problem, so, at the end of June, I sent out Major Marten, a member of a Jedburgh team, to carry our reports to A.F.H.Q. It appears that he discussed the matter so thoroughly with them that on security grounds he was not allowed to return. We then decided that Colonel Zeller, who had been appointed general by General Koenig should go himself.

60. "Meanwhile a military mission consisting of Major Long and Captain Houseman (British), Capitaine Volume (French) and Lieutenant Paray (American) had arrived to take charge of military liaison with the Vercors authority, and Pauline (Christine Granville) had arrived as liaison officer to work for me and to investigate possible relations with foreign elements in the German Army.

61. "From the 6th June onwards the Vercors was attacked several times, both in the North and the South; each time the Germans had suffered

very heavily, proportional losses being at least a hundred to one, and had been thrown back. We had been sent heavy daylight deliveries of material and many night deliveries, and the area was at last well armed. In the Ain and Jura we were also receiving much material, and throughout region one, the 'Plan Rouge' was working so well that the Germans were extremely worried. Everywhere we threatened their main line of retreat, which was the Rhone valley.

62. "From the 20th June they had realised that sabotage activity was being directed from our strong points and they decided to reduce these strong points. They attacked deeply in the Ardèche and caused severe dislocations. They then attacked the Ain and made the F.F.I. withdraw into the hills. The same process was going on throughout the South-East and South-West. We had been instrumental in preventing reinforcements from reaching the Normandy front, the German garrisons were tied up almost without supplies or communications in a few towns, and the morale of the German forces in this part of the world was visibly falling. Poles, Czechs, Russians and Serbs had been persuaded to desert, to sabotage their weapons and to fight against the Germans. The biggest menace to the Rhone valley communications was the Vercors where we actually had 3,000 men under arms, but with the surrounding defences this number was doubled. The geographical advantages of the Vercors made it almost impossible to attack with infantry alone.

63. "From the 10th July the Germans started using air bombardment against us, particularly against our reception ground at Vassieux, which we were trying to make into a landing ground. For ten days they bombed us, and on the 19th July their main attack started, carried out by two divisions assisted by the Air Force and by airborne troops. They landed sixty gliders and attacked every approach to Vercors, using aircraft against the defences. It became clear that we could not hold out and that the only way of avoiding 100 per cent. massacre was for the army of the Vercors to 'explode' into the woods and make their way to neighbouring departments to reform. At this point I persuaded General Zeller, who had been waiting to be picked up on the Vercors landing ground, that it would be failing in our duty to remain there since the rest of region one, and particularly region two, needed our instructions badly. Also he was expected to go to Algiers as soon as possible, which would quite obviously not be possible if he remained in the Vercors.

64. "On the morning of the 21st July we left and set up our new headquarters at Seyne-les-Alpes. A short time after Colonel Zeller left for Algiers and he also was prevented from coming back. He was replaced by Colonel Constant (de Saint-Sauveur), who only arrived on the 12th August and did not bring with him, even then, any definite instructions about D-Day action, but came with a mission to settle the political difficulties of region two.

65. "At Seyne-les-Alpes I received missions: for the Alpes Maritimes and the Var, Major Gunn, Captain Halsley and Commandant Chasuble (Sorensen); for the Vaucluse, Basses-Alpes and Bouches-du-Rhone, Major Goldsmith, Commandant Amlot; for the Hautes-Alpes, Major Purvis, Captain Roper and a French Commandant; for the two Savoies, Major Green and Major Hunter; for the Italian Frontier, Major Hamilton and Captain O'Regan. I also received three American operation groups and five other Jedburgh teams and a group of six French instructors from the Drome. The work done by all this personnel was invaluable, but in most cases they had only a fortnight or so in which to do it. If they had arrived by the 15th May they would have solved all local F.F.I. problems as their presence alone united the various resistance elements. As I had received no answer about the plan for the advance on Grenoble, I decided to prepare forces as if this was going to be carried out.

66. "The one point on which my directive and that of the F.F.I. had been similar, was the necessity of attack on lines of communication. The results of these attacks had been more successful than anyone could have hoped, all German forces were bottled up in garrison towns, and troop movements only took place in large convoys, which generally arrived at their destination only after fighting three or four small engagements and losing a few vehicles. Apart from the coastal defences the only German troops that remained mobile in the area and who might have presented any danger to any invading forces, were the two divisions who had been engaged against the Vercors. The only line where the Germans could move with any kind of freedom was the Rhone valley. I made plans for making quite certain that the F.F.I. could handle any attack on the Route Napoléon which might come from the Rhone valley, but the main danger seemed to be the unknown quantity of troops in Northern Italy who might attack over

the Alpine Passes and take the troops advancing on Grenoble in the right flank. It was believed that the Germans had, if necessary, seven divisions in North-Western Italy for such an operation. To prevent this, the military missions were given the frontier passes as their main target.

67. "Around the 1st August orders were given to the F.F.I. to save all ammunition and material possible and to annoy the Germans rather than to attack them, to make them feel that they were still bottled up. This was done in order to make sure that materials would be available to defend the Route Napoléon and the airborne troops' landing grounds if necessary. Meanwhile the resistance troops in region one had managed to assume sufficient unity to assure effective action. Colonel Bayard (Descours) provided the necessary skilled military directive and the work of M. Farge, Commissaire de la République, a very able, energetic and diplomatic politician had undisputed authority deriving directly from General de Gaulle.

68. "In region two (Marseille region) we were faced with a very different picture. From the middle of July to the middle of August I was almost entirely occupied with the very tiresome internal affairs of this region. The military chief, Levalles, had given Sapin (Perpendiculaire) carte blanche from the 6th June to work out the 'Plan Rouge' from a base at Barcelonnette. After the fall of Barcelonnette he turned against Sapin and without interviewing him or letting his military chief, Colonel Zeller, know, he issued a kind of papal bull in which he denounced Sapin, called him a traitor and told all the Maquisares to come back to the towns.

69. "These instructions created confusion in all ranks of the F.F.I. and this confusion was increased when Levalles was arrested. Maxence (Juvenal), the political and civilian F.F.I. chief, now claimed, and assumed, complete military command. He was an inveterate enemy of Sapin and showed no inclination to try and reach a compromise. At this point there was a severe split in policy. Maxence and many M.U.R. and F.T.P. leaders claimed that the big towns, Marseille and Avignon, should be heavily armed. On the other hand, they had no constructive proposals to make about how this should be done, or what the people of these towns would usefully do with arms. The resistance in the

country was achieving concrete results, though they were divided through lack of leadership and varied directives. Algiers had the matter in hand and were sending out new F.F.I. commanders. Meanwhile, the matter was further complicated by the arrest of the D.M.R. 'Circumference' and the quite unjustified suspicion that was attached to him when he was released. The situation then became as follows:-

70. "Sapin controlled important mountain forces in the Alpes Maritimes and the East of the Basses-Alpes. The Durance valley was left without a leader, but I was near enough to this area to be able to give a directive to local leaders, and the West of region two was very largely under the influence of the S.A.P. headquarters run by Pierre Michel. At this point, Algiers sent Colonel Widmer as D.M.R., Commandant Amiot as D.M. Vaucluse and Basses-Alpes, and, finally, Colonel Constant as F.F.I. commander with an extended regional command, but all this happened too late to change the situation to any extent.

71. "Just after the arrival of Colonel Constant, on the 13th August, I was arrested by the Gestapo at Digne, but, by this time, the Germans were so convinced of the strength of the F.F.I. that, when the landing took place on the 15th, their whole effort was directed at evacuating their forces along the Rhone valley, and in all the garrison towns the German troops were ready to surrender. For this reason, as we had foreseen, the road to Grenoble was open. As we were not sure whether the landing forces were sufficiently in the picture, Major Gunn drove down to Draguignan to put them 'au courant.' They agreed to follow him if he would lead them up the road in his civilian car and in this way they arrived at Grenoble almost without firing a shot. The garrison at Digne, Gap, Sisteron and on the Italian frontier were mostly made prisoners by the F.F.I.; the Germans were ready to surrender to anyone, small boys of 14 and women of 60 were to be seen with anything up to twenty German prisoners in tow.

72. "The Germans showed symptoms of wishing to attack across the Italian frontier, but the F.F.I., with the aid of the Allied Mission, effectively destroyed the roads and made it impossible for all motor vehicles to take part in an attack, so the Germans merely occupied the frontier to protect their own flank. While the invading army had been making up its mind to advance up the Route Napoléon, Major Fielding,

Commandant Sorensen and myself were being released from the hands of the Gestapo by the courage and brilliant initiative of Pauline.

73. "We were released just in time to welcome the liberation army on its arrival at Digne and to continue in its wake through Gap to Grenoble. From Grenoble I was called upon to go on a tour of the West bank of the Rhone, to give General Patch's orders to the F.F.I., who were to protect the right flank of General de Montsabert's army group who were attacking Lyon from the West and North-West. This tour was to prove to me that the effectiveness of the F.F.I. action which I had myself seen in the East and which had allowed the American Armies to arrive in Grenoble in seven days almost without fighting, was just as great in the South-West for, far from there being any threat to the flank of General Monsabert's army corps, his work had been largely done for him by the F.F.I. In the Ardeche alone they had taken as many as 16,000 prisoners and there was no menacing German unit South of the line Bordeaux, Moulins, Paray le Monial. I handed General de Montsabert's instruction for the sending of F.F.I. units to attack the German retreat along this line to local Commanders.

74. "Returning to my area I found that the military missions were thoroughly in control of the Italian frontier situation, which, on the Italian side, was being particularly well handled by Major Leonard Hamilton, and after a quick tour of my area, I returned to London."

75. Roger's work begun in circumstances of great difficulty, had thus been brought to a triumphant conclusion. For his service in France he was awarded the D.S.O., Légion d'Honneur and Croix de Guerre.

Other Circuits.

76. The Olive–Raoul–Roger succession was, of course, not the only circuit in the area, though it was by far the most important. Brief mention has already been made of Henri Sevenet in the Montagne Noire in 1944, the brothers Newton (Arthur and August) made a short stay in the Le Puy area in 1942, as also had Major and Mme. Lechène on a Propaganda mission. Gilles (Lieutenant Coppin) had for a time installed himself in Marseille, and Major Goldsmith had also put in a brief appearance, during the course of which he had been instrumental in arranging the escape of General Chambre to North Africa.

216

77. In late 1942 Félix (Captain Sydney Jones) had been sent to investigate certain contacts which had been notified to London, and it was on the basis of his report that Bernard (Captain C.M. Skepper) was sent to the Marseille area in May 1943. Unfortunately, the contacts which he had been given were more inclined to propaganda than for action, and Bernard found the task of organisation for sabotage very difficult. By February 1944 he appeared to be making progress and declared himself able to attack his D-Day communications targets. Unfortunately, in May 1944 he, his radio operator Laurent (Captain Steele) and his courier Gaby (Mrs. Plewman, sister of Flight-Lieutenant Brown-Bartrolli, organiser in the Cluny area) were all arrested.

78. The most important of Bernard's contacts had been Pierre Massenet, Prefect of Marseille. Mme. Massenet was a personal friend of Bernard and is closely in touch with the affairs of the circuit. When corresponding with the Paris office she has always asked that she should be addressed c/o Commodore W.R.D. Crowther, R.N., Marine Nationale, Marseille.

79. In March 1944 a dropping operation brought Firmin (Major Boiteux, M.C., M.B.E.) back to France. He had already carried a long and successful mission in the Lyon area (see Lyon, paras. 9-24) and his present purpose was to be put in contact by Maxime (see Toulouse, paras. 48-81) with the Vény groups in the Marseille area.

80. It may be interesting to quote Firmin on what he found there:

> "I was sent to France to work for Colonel Véni, who claimed to have 3,000 men in the Marseille region and a Maquis of 300 men in Nice region. This was untrue. Here in a few words is the position as I understood it; it took me three months to grasp it and I do not yet know if I got it straight.
> "The Socialist Party had been doing passive resistance since 1940. Towards the end of the war they realised that if they did not do more active work they would not be recognised by the different resistance movements, so decided to organise their newspaper readers on military lines. It was decided to ask Colonel Véni, a member of their party, to do this; but Véni's head swelled and he claimed the men as his own and when he received nine British

officers, to organise his three groups of Limoges, Toulouse and Marseille, Véni's head swelled still more.

"When I arrived at Marseille it was due to the 'mauvaise entente' which already existed between the Socialist Party and Véni, that I received such little help, and whatever help I did receive was very reluctantly given. It was not till after the 6th June, after I had been wounded and Captain Dussard, who was Véni's representative in Marseille, had been killed, that I received a great deal more help, although, even then, the Socialist Party only helped me in undertakings which would later reflect glory on their Party and which would serve as propaganda, and it is to be noticed in speeches made by their leader, Gaston Deferre, and in the numerous articles on their activities that mention is never made of the help given to them by the British Government. On the contrary, Deferre appears to have organised my three Maquis of Plan d'Aups, Trets, and Allauch all on his own!

"Although reluctant myself to work with a political party, after the death of Captain Dussard I was compelled to do so as I needed the men to accomplish my mission. Although I then received much more help it was far too late to do much. I was put in contact with groups at Toulon and region; I sent in a few reeeption grounds, but received no stores in that area."

81. The good Vény (now Monsieur le Général de Brigade Jean Vincent) does not, indeed, seem to have impressed at all favourably any of the British officers who worked with him.

82. In spite of all these set-backs, Firmin's groups did successfully sabotage all the telephone targets they had been given, his two Maquis of Trets and Allauch successfully attacked convoys on the roads, his teams at Marseille did very well in street fighting, and took many prisoners. They also, incidentally, fed about 500 people daily for a week and were able to stop a certain amount of looting by placing armed men in food factories.

83. After the fighting was over Firmin had an interview with Général de Montsabert, who suggested that he form a "Groupe Franc" with his men. This he did and believes that they were the first to be incorporated into the French Army with the 7ème Régiment de Tirailleurs and

Algériens. He had got together 200 men from his Trets and Allauch Maquis and his Marseille groups, and they kept their own officers and N.C.O.'s.

84. Firmin's file contains a full report on the activities of his Maquis groups by an L. Svirinovsky, chez Mme. Caprile [of] Marseille. This might be a possible source of further information.

85. Firmin was assisted by Horace (Captain Cohen, M.C.), a very competent wireless operator with previous resistance experience, having worked in the Paris area and narrowly escaped arrest in the break-up of the Robin circuit in April 1943; also by Aleric (Lieutenant Aptaker) as arms instructor. Aleric was destined to spend quite an appreciable part of his time as prisoner of the Communists! Julien and Paul were also sent to help him from Algiers.

Appendix A:

ACTIVITIES OF ROGER CIRCUIT

31st July, 1943
A number of railway wagons destroyed. (Area unspecified.)

20th July, 1943
All lines to Italy cut for 4-7 days from impeding troop movements.

July/August 1943
20 locomotives, 20 tankers and 150 greaseboxes attacked and put out of action along the South coast.

27th November, 1943
150 men organised and ready at Valensole, with arms and stores.

November 1943
Six derailments successfully undertaken in the Rhone valley and between Marseille and Nice.

November 1943
Assistance in sabotaging material given to Italians after the Armistice.

November 1943
Destruction of the viaduct at Anthéor completed.

November 1943
Passive resistance encouraged at Saint-Auban and production cut to 30 per cent. as a result, and diminishing weekly.

November 1943
Minor sabotage on railway bridge at Carnoules, causing an engine to break through.

November 1943
Petrol dumps sabotaged with water and abrasives.

8th December, 1943
Railway A target destroyed near Montélimar. An iron bridge blown up and traffic held up for a day and two nights. A German leave train destroyed and 60 casualties caused.

December 1943
Further A targets on railways dealt with. Tunnel at Manosque, two targets at Montélimar, and one each at La Coucourde and Cagnes.

4th March, 1944
36 locomotives successfully attacked and put out of action in depots at Avignon, Miramas and Veynes.

March 1944
Electric station destroyed at Briançon.

March 1944
Filters and transformers sabotaged at Saint-Auban, with result of reducing production of alumina, to 10 per cent.

March 1944
2 German leave trains derailed on P.L.M. at Soyons (Ardèche) south of Valence.

11th March, 1944
8 locomotives and 5 petrol tankers destroyed at Porte-lesValence.

March 1944
A repair crane destroyed in the same place, by unbolting it.

26th March, 1944
20 locomotives destroyed at Valence.

15th April, 1944
Teams ready in Drôme, Bouches-du-Rhône, Basses-Alpes.

15th April, 1944
54 locomotives destroyed at Avignon, Veynes and Miramas.

22nd April, 1944
Rail cuts organised at Aspres/Veynes and Draguignan.

3rd June, 1944
Organised a minimum of 2-3,000 men.

10th June, 1944
Cut all telephones; no through trains.

14th June, 1944
Briançon and main roads attacked.

29th June, 1944
All traffic in Hautes- and Basses-Alpes cut.

Chapter 12

The Lyon Region

LYON GENERAL

1. Lyon as befits its size and importance, has always been a centre of Resistance activity, more particularly so as far as F. Section is concerned, before the German occupation of Southern France. It was notably the Headquarters of Virginia Hall (Marie), whose valuable activities have already been described and whose influence on the whole early history of the British circuits in France was so great.

2. Whereas Marie's activities had their influence almost everywhere where an F. section circuit was at that time in being, there had existed from an early date a circuit with the Lyon district as its own particular objective.

3. On the 23rd August, 1941, Lieutenant (later Captain) J.G. Duboudin, known as Alain, left Liverpool and arrived in the South of France on the 19th September. His mission was to build up an organisation in Lyon and its neighbourhood, of which the importance was obviously very great. In the early stages his only means of communication with London was through Marie, but in April 1942 he was given a radio operator, Lieutenant Zeff (known as Georges 53), and conditions became easier for him.

4. It is impossible to assess with any hopes of accuracy the work which Duboudin carried out between the time of his arrival in September 1941 and his return to England in October 1942. According to his own report, in May 1942, he had contacted a number of different resistance organisations, amongst whom he had started to form teams. On his return to London he claimed that he had organised a large number of teams over a large area and that transport on a considerable scale was available. The Coq Enchaîné organisation, said to have connections with President Herriot, was stated to be working exclusively for Alain. He stated that he covered eleven Départements: Loire, Haute-Loire, Saône-et-Loire, Jura, Rhône, Ain, Savoie, Haute-Savoie, Drôme and Ardèche, and that men under his control numbered 8,000-10,000.

5. But all this was Alain's testimony as to his own activities. In the meanwhile other, less complimentary reports had been reaching London. Alain had quarrelled with Marie, and Gauthier distrusted him. More damaging still was a later report put in by Valérien (Major Cowburn).

6. Quite apart from this, there was evident confusion in the Unoccupied Zone, and particularly in Lyon, where Alain and Marie had their own organisations and where Gauthier also had an important part of his own widespread groups. To cope with this situation London sent to the Field in May 1942 Captain V.H. Hazan (Gervais) to act as co-ordinator and to unravel the tangle into which things had fallen. Unfortunately, although in his own way he was a first-class man, and from August 1942 till June

1943 proved extremely efficient and popular as chief instructor to the Carte group, he did not possess the qualities required for the position of co-ordinator, and did nothing to lessen the prevailing confusion. In July 1942 Major Bodington also took a hand and, it would appear, took the wrong decision in confirming Alain in his command of the Lyon area.

7. In October 1942, however, Alain was recalled to London and instructed to hand his circuit over to Captain Boiteux (Nicolas), who had been sent to act as his assistant in June 1942. Even in this, however, Alain ran true to form and refused to divulge to Nicolas either his contacts or the localities where his arms and explosives were hidden, the latter being particularly ungenerous of him since Nicolas ever since his arrival had been particularly active in the organisation of receptions of material which he had, in duty bound, turned over to his superior officer, Alain. Alain was also shown later to have taken credit for work which had, in fact, been done by Nicolas.

8. With his return to London, Nicolas was left in charge of his own organisation and such portions of Alain's groups as he could run to earth.

Captain Boiteux's Organisation.

Operational name of organisation: the Spruce Circuit.
Operational name of organiser: Nicolas.
Name by which known in the Field: Nicolas, Robert, Jean and Charles.

9. Nicolas' brief was to act as technical adviser to Alain, and he was parachuted to the Field on the 2nd June, 1942. His arrival was not without incident; he himself was dropped uneasily close to the village of Anse, and a fellow-officer (Patrice)[39] who was dropped with him landed most inappropriately on the roof of the Police Station, the occupants of which gratefully received him into custody. Nicolas himself escaped a like fate by the skin of his teeth.

10. Nicolas and Alain soon found themselves at cross-purposes, and already by the end of June Nicolas was applying to London for permission to work separately from him. This was not granted, and they went on working together till Alain's departure in October 1942.

11. At the same time, however, Nicolas did continue to keep his own section of the organisation reasonably watertight, which was natural enough as he occupied himself almost exclusively with the reception and storage of material and with training.

12. When Alain left for London, Nicolas was left in sole charge. A fortnight later the Germans marched into Unoccupied France and the true value of Alain's paper army was made manifest. On the arrival of the Germans in Lyon they had been seized with panic, and many of them had thrown their arms into the river. When the time came for action Nicolas found that most of his teams had either been arrested or had taken fright. They had been full of promises, but at the first sight of danger their bluff had been called.

13. This was not the end of his difficulties. Georges 53 had worked for Nicolas soon after his arrival and had been replaced by Grégoire (Captain P. Le Chêne). He also was an extremely competent and conscientious operator, but on the 9th November he was arrested by the Gestapo. He was in due course replaced by Captain Borosh (Marius), but direct contact was not re-established till May 1943.

14. In the meanwhile Nicolas had been building up his own organisation of really reliable men, and very valuable it proved, since the direct connection can be traced between the early efforts of Nicolas in 1942 and 1943 and the outstanding success of the Maquis centred on Cluny against the Germans in the Liberation period in 1944.

15. His chief Lieutenants in this organisation were Raoul Léger, Joseph Marchand and Jean Régnier. Of these, Marchand and Régnier later came to London, where they underwent a period of training, and returned to the Field. Régnier to carry out an extremely sucessful mission in Chalon-sur-Saône and Marchand, who was faced with much greater difficulties, to endeavour to organise resistance in St.-Étienne.

16. Marchand was one of the first to join Nicolas and to work for him in the organisation of the reception of stores. He had been in Resistance from the beginning, but thereafter never wavered in his adherence to the British organisation. On arrival in England he was commissioned

in the British army, was promoted to the rank of Captain and was awarded the D.S.O.

17. His services were very great, and his particular value lay in the fact that it was through him that Nicolas was able to report on his return to London that he had established contact with various groups in the Maquis with total effectives of approximately 1,000 men. Most of these groups were organised by Marchand, and it is from these groups that the Cluny–Charolles Maquis trace their direct descent.

18. Nicolas' report was thus a mixture of good and ill.

19. A considerable amount of sabotage had been carried out, but owing to Gestapo activity, non-co-operation by Alain, chicken-heartedness by the Coq Enchaîné warriors and ordinary consumption by use, there were no stores left. On the other hand, although Nicolas himself was too badly blown for him to remain, his group survived, with Marius as leader and means of communication with London, and – most important of all – the following groups were organised and prepared for action when materials were available:

St.-Rambert-en-Bugey under M. Flamand, who was arrested a week before Nicolas' departure in August 1943.

Villefranche (Monsol). The leader, M. Bouricaut, had also been arrested and replaced by M. Ducoin.

St.-Etienne under H. Pointu.

St.-Gengoux-le-National under Jean Louis Delorme, who apart from being in command of the camp had several teams in the Mâcon district who had been doing a lot of sabotage.
Cluny, comprising three camps at Lugny, Salornay and St.-Bonnet-de-Joux. These were under the direct supervision of Marchand. Their discipline was very good and much sabotage had been done.

20. Nicolas, who, ever since his arrival, seemed to have specialised in hair-breadth escapes from the Gestapo – to the extent on one occasion

of having his foot grabbed by one of them and leaving his shoe in the German's hand – arrived back in London full of zeal to continue the fight, and in March 1944 was parachuted back to the Field to carry out a mission in the Marseille area. For his work on these two missions he was awarded the M.C. and the M.B.E.

21. Marchand, who came to London with Nicolas, also volunteered for a further mission. His report is interesting in that it sketches in the political background against which their activities had been carried on. In view of the mentality it reveals their efforts appear even more meritorious.

22. He recalls that, when it was evident that Alain's organisation was non-existent, Nicolas and he decided to obtain the assistance of elements belonging to other groups. Accordingly certain active sections of Combat and Franc-Tireur came over to them. But this aroused keen opposition on the part of the heads of these organisations, firstly, because of the contacts with the Coq Enchaîné, with whose politics they did not agree: they next refused to co-operate on the grounds that they would not agree to receive directives from the English. At the same time parts of these groups complained that they had no means for action at their disposal and it was decided to give Franc-Tireur one stores operation. This was received perfectly, but the use to which it was put passed entirely out of Nicolas' control, and it became evident that he and Marchand would have to continue to rely on the teams which they had already recruited and which were, in fact, sufficient for the targets which they had been specifically assigned.

23. Even in this they were not left undisturbed, as the Carte group, with their objective of the formation of a secret army with the three Gaullist groups under the same command, began tempting Nicolas' teams to go over to them. Worse was to follow, since with the dissolution of the French Army some of the material which the army had collected was passed over to the Gaullist groups, and these were now in a position to offer material to Nicolas' groups, combined with the argument "Remain French and free from the Directives of the English."

24. In spite of all this, the British organisation survived, and Marius was left holding the fort in preparation for the final stage.

Flight-Lieutenant Brown-Bartrolli's Organisation.
  Operational name or organisation: The Ditcher Circuit.
  Operational name of organiser: Tiburce.
  Names by which known in the Field: Tiburce and Toto.

25. Tiburce arrived in October 1943 to supervise the Maquis groups already mentioned and to attack on D-Day German railway and road traffic from Chalon, Mâcon, Paray-le-Monial in Saône-et-Loire and Ambérieu in Ain. From Marius, who had been keeping things warm for him and who acted as his radio operator, he learned that no contacts existed in Ambérieu or Paray-le-Monial, that the Maquis groups now consisted of two Maquis of fifty each under the command of Jean Louis Delorme at St.-Gengoux and one of 100 near Cherny under the orders of Jean Renard, Georges Malère and André Argnet.

26. These four men had been enrolled by Marchand, and were to prove of infinite value to Tiburce as long as they were free or alive. Shortly after his arrival he was joined by a young Englishman, known as Thomas who had escaped from a concentration camp and who became his lieutenant.

27. Tiburce, like other British organisers, had orders to avoid contact with the A.S. and F.T.P., but noticed that, although the A.S. leaders did everything to interfere with his work, the French had no confidence in them, accusing them of Fascist tendencies and their leader, Ferrant, of having fought against us in Syria in 1941 and of being a great admirer of Marshal Pétain. The result of this, and of the mistakes they made, was that more and more people wanted to work with Tiburce.

28. In December Marius left the Lyon area, and communications thereafter were handled by Ibis, a locally-trained operator, who was not satisfactory. The result was a great dearth of material, a situation not remedied till the arrival of Jacquot (J. Litalien, an American) in May 1944.

29. Meanwhile, in April, two further helpers had arrived, one of them, Chico (Captain Archambaut) had been asked for by Tiburce to take over his contacts near Ambérieu, the other was Porthos (Jean Régnier), who had returned to London with Nicolas and Marchand, and was now to carry out a final mission in the Chalon s/Saône region. In May

Dieudonne (Captain d'Artois) arrived and was put in charge of the Charolles–Paray-le-Monial region.

30. On D-Day they were able to arm about 200 men in Saône-et-Loire, who immediately started attacking in small groups. Attacks on rail traffic were soon successful, and from the beginning the lines Lozanne–Parcy, Mâcon–Cluny, Cluny–Chalon, Cluny–Paray were cut and never used again. The Mâcon–Chalon and Paray–Montceau lines were attacked every day in several places. Several dozen bridges were destroyed, including nine between Villefranche and Tournus.

31. Incorporation in the F.F.I. after D-Day brought an order from General Koenig that Capitaine de la Ferte (the Ferrant referred to above) was to be sole Departmenatal chief in Saône-et-Loire. Tiburce describes him as a "nice boy, honest, brave, an ideal 2nd Lieutenant, never able to command more than a Company, distrusted politically by the average man, envied and distrusted by the political organisations (M.U.R., F.T.P.), ex-admire of Pétain, ex-enemy of ours, without ideas of his own, without prestige or authority." Orders, however, are orders, and forces were joined, the Department being divided into four military zones: Cluny, Charolles, St. Gengoux, La Clayette. More arms and material began to arrive, and all German convoys inside the triangle were attacked.

32. Up till then the F.T.P. had kept apart, inactive: they said they had no arms, so when on the 14th July Tiburce received 36 planes he gave them enough arms for 300 men, on the undertaking that they would join the battle. He then decided that three regiments should be built up, one at Cluny, one at Charolles and one at St.-Gengoux: he also tried to organise a Departmental H.Q. for Saône-et-Loire with Ferrant, Dieudonne and an F.T.P. representative to plan Departmental action. Tiburce reports that in spite of Dieudonne's efforts this plan did not work, "the task of making a leader out of Ferrant proving too much even for Dieudonne, and the task of getting the F.T.P. to fight proving impossible." So when at the beginning of August he received another 36 planes, Tiburce felt compelled to refuse further arms to the F.T.P.

33. As the stores position improved so did numbers grow. Below is the record of stores delivered to the group, from the early Nicolas days to the final stages under Tiburce.

Date.	Operations.	Containers.	Packages.
1942.			
August	1	8	...
October	3	18	4
1943.			
April	2	10	1
September	3	35	1
1944.			
February	3	57	12
March	2	31	2
April	3	30	7
May	4	45	13
July	4*	487	26
August	5*	570	41
September	3	826	22

Including Daylight Operation (14th July and 1st August).

34. Thus, although conflicting claims are possible on other points, there is no doubt of the crucial contribution which the British organisation made on the Stores side.

35. Early in August 3,000 Germans attacked Cluny with guns, armoured cars and planes. The battle lasted 14 hours and at the end of it the Germans fled, leaving behind two 47-mm. guns, two armoured cars, several trucks and more than 400 dead. The F.F.I. lost 12. From that day until the end no German entered the Cluny–Charolles–St. Gengoux triangle except as a prisoner.

36. The F.F.I. by now had more than 3,000 men well enough armed and well enough trained, especially those trained by Dieudonne, who had started a school for N.C.O.'s at Charolles. He had also arranged for a remarkable network of telephone posts throughout the territory which proved most valuable.

37. Attacks now began on traffic on the main roads Mâcon–Chalon and Paray–Montceau, the F.F.I. being reinforced by the arrival of S.A.S. and Jedburgh teams. Every day some 20 to 50 German vehicles were destroyed.

38. But the group had more ambitious schemes in mind. They delivered Roanne. One of their battalions started attacking between Villefranche and Mâcon, and later took Villefranche in co-operation with French armour with the 7th Army, taking 5,000 prisoners. On the 8th September attacks were mounted on Mâcon, Tournus, Sennecey and Chalon. At Mâcon the Germans fled before the attack, at Tournus the F.T.P. never came and Sennecey was captured, with considerable loss, by evening. Thereafter the F.F.I. acted as Infantry to the French tanks in the taking of Chalon, Montceau, Le Creusot, Paray-le-Monial, Autun and Chagny. 900 of their men were enrolled for action with the 7th Army.

39. Tiburce's Report concludes: "From the 6th June to the 8th September we fed all the civilian population beside our own men. In all I armed 5,000 men ... I claim that we were the only fighting force in Saône-et-Loire, that only our teams, and I include there those of Porthos (Jean Régnier) did any sabotage work, and that because of us Saône-et-Loire can take a prided place in Resistance. I wish London had understood earlier how keen we were, and how we were placed to be much more useful to the defeat of the Germans than much-vaunted regions like Haute-Savoie and Ain."

40. He goes on to cite two special heroes, Jean Renard and Jean Louis Delorme, concerning whom Marchand will be able to give full particulars.

Captain Régnier's Organisation.

Operational name of organisation: The Mason Circuit.
Operational name of organiser: Porthos.
Name by which known in the Field: Porthos.

41. Porthos arrived late in the Field with a mission to build up a sabotage organisation round Chalon s/Saône. In view of the shortness of time available, Tiburce made over to him his own contacts in the Chalon neighbourhood.

42. Porthos was accompanied by an extremely competent radio operator, Flavian (Captain Jaurent Singer), who, as subsequently appeared, in addition to his wireless work did some successful organisational work on his own account.

43. That their joint contribution to Resistance in Saône-et-Loire was no small one is shown by the statement of stores which they were able to receive during the short time they were in the Field.

Date. 1944.	Operations.	Containers.	Packages.
April	4	71	17
May	7	114	30
June	4	84	29
July	4	41	25
August	3	90	36

44. Porthos and Flavian arrived on the 3rd March and made contact with Ange, who put them in touch with Jean Louis Delorme in the Chalon Region. The necessary arrangements were made with Tiburce and work began.

45. The scale of Porthos's organisation was perhaps not a very large one, but all that Porthos did was done most competently. As far as communications went, Flavian proved outstanding, setting up six or seven separate transmitting stations, and training no less than eleven locally-recruited operators, some of whom were made available for other circuits – a most valuable contribution.

46. With a view to organising the disruption of enemy communications on D-Day, Porthos formed and trained a number of sabotage teams: by D-Day he had built up one of the most efieetive sabotage networks in France. When the order was given, all the railway lines in his area were attacked and enemy traffic was reduced by 80 per cent. Telecommunications between Paris and Marseille and Lyon and Mulhouse were kept almost permanently cut; an important refinery at Les Thélots was put out of action. Six important road and rail bridges were blown up, notably the bridges at Étang-sur-Arroux, Blanzy and Louhans.

47. Porthos supplied both A.S. and F.T.P. with arms, on condition that they would conform to his directives. Relations with the A.S. were always harmonious, but it took all Porthos's diplomacy and persuasiveness to bring the F.T.P. into action. He was finally successful, however, and in one operation they destroyed over 400 miles of railway.

48. In addition to his valuable work as radio operator and trainer of radio operators, Flavian at one period found himself in sole command of a Maquis of 350 men at Cruchaud near Buxy.

49. From D-Day onwards they both devoted themselves to the organisation of guerrilla action in conjunction with the F.F.I. Porthos took part in several actions against the enemy, notably at Laives in August and in the fighting for the liberation of Chalon-sur-Saône where he particularly distinguished himself, being one of the first to enter the town.

50. In the meanwhile, that pillar of the whole British effort in the Lyon–Cluny area, Marchand, had returned to the region in October 1943 to develop a circuit in the St.-Étienne area.

Captain Marchand's Organisation.
Operational name of organisation: The Newsagent Circuit.
Operational name of organiser: Ange.
Name by which known in the Field: Ange.

51. Ange's activity until August 1944 was to be greatly hampered by the unintelligible messages sent and received by his W/T operator, and this was the chief reason for his only receiving seven dropping operations in nearly a year.

52. The St.-Étienne area had suffered badly from arrests, but Ange found three good local lieutenants, and organised sabotage in St.-Étienne, including an attack against the St.-Chamond steel works and the total stoppage of production in an important Duralumin factory at Rive-de-Gier.

53. In early June 1944 Ange's supply dumps in the Condrieu–Rive-de-Gier area were captured by the Germans, with the result that, when the guerrilla messages were sent to him on D-Day, the 1,000 men he had at his disposition had to be reduced to 150-200 men, who formed a Maquis at Montbrison. On the 5th July he successfully received a stores operation, and began to attack the railways between St.-Étienne and Roanne.

54. Guerrilla action included the killing or wounding of 150 Germans and G.M.R. at Lérigneux, and an attack on a German convoy on R.N. 86 when eighty of Ange's men had unexpectedly to face 2,000 Germans; they attacked all the same, killed many and were enabled to escape by an Allied air attack on the column.

55. There is no doubt that Ange would have achieved outstanding results had it been possible to send him more material.

56. Of the officers mentioned above:-

Nicolas (Major Boiteux) has been awarded the M.C. and M.B.E.
Ange (Captain Marchand) has been awarded the D.S.O.
Marius (Captain Borosh) has been awarded the M.C.
Tiburce (Flight-Lieutenant Brown-Bartrolli) has been awarded the D.S.O.
Dieudonne (Captain d'Artois) has been awarded the D.S.O.
Chico (Captain Archambaut) has been awarded the M.C.
Flavian (Captain Jaurent-Singer) has been awarded the M.B.E.

57. There has been some administrative delay in the case of the award to Porthos (Captain Régnier), but he will doubtless by now have received his M.C. It would be desirable, however, to refer to Marchand before discussing this with him.

58. So much for the Alain–Nicolas–Marius–Tiburce succession. Mention must now be made of certain other entirely independent Resistance streams, rising from independent sources, which all combined at the end to make this one of the most effective Resistance areas in France. There were four main lines: 1. Xavier (Lieut.-Colonel Heslop), working with Colonel Romans in Ain and in liaison with Cantinier (F.F.C.) in Haute-Savoie; 2. Théodule (Captain de Brouville), who built up a powerful organisation in Jura and Doubs and extending as far as Dijon in Côte-d'Or; 3. Lucien (Captain de St.-Génies) around Dôle with remnants of the Carte group; 4. Gaspard, the French chief of a French organisation, who threw in his lot with Hector (S/Ldr. Southgate) and to whom a mission under Hubert (Captain Farmer) was sent.

Lieut.-Colonel Heslop's Organisation.
Operational name of organisation: The Marksman Circuit.
Operational name of organiser: Xavier.
Name by which known in the Field: Xavier, Louis.

59. The origins of Xavier's second mission go back to July 1943, when messages began coming through from Berne concerning several groups in Haute-Savoie, which were asking for an organiser to be sent to them. F. Section, as it happened, was at the time working in close conjunction with the London representatives of the O.R.A., a French Army Organisation of Giraudist tendencies, and an extension of the proposed mission, to make contact with a local leader, D'Osia, operating in Haute-Savoie, was agreed upon. Subsequently the B.C.R.A. also became interested, and the mission became the first joint mission to be mounted by F. Section and the B.C.R.A. in conjunction.

60. Xavier was the British officer assigned to the operation, his mission being to represent the Allied High Command and convey their directives to the Haute-Savoie Maquis groups, which represented a new and growing element in the resistance battle against the enemy. The French officer who was to be Xavier's counterpart was Cantinier (Lieut. Rosenthal), and special mention is due to him for the loyalty of his co-operation.

61. Xavier and Cantinier landed in France from a Hudson aircraft on the 21st September.

62. On the 17th October they were back in London, where in a hectic 36 hours before returning to France they reported on the first part of their mission. Xavier related how, immediately on arrival, they had been told that the group in Haute-Savoie, which they were to contact, was in a state of disintegration, and that nothing would be gained by a visit at that time. Instead, a tour of inspection was arranged in other areas, notably in Ain, Isère, Savoie and Haute-Savoie. The party consisted of Cantinier and Xavier, accompanied by representatives of the local leaders, and the tour appears to have been in the nature of a triumphal progress. As representative of the Allied High Command, Xavier conducted as minute an inspection of the camps as time permitted, and brought back a long list of grounds for the reception of materials.

63. London accepted the revision of the mission, and Xavier and Cantinier returned as an inter-Allied mission to control Maquis of all political complexions in Ain, Isère and Savoie.

64. Xavier, incidentally, had been briefed by F. Section to organise small self-contained groups on British lines for purposes of sabotage, as a *pis aller* if the security of the Maquis groups made it impossible to work with them. This had been done, and was to prove a valuable adjunct to the larger work.

65. More important still, Xavier was sent in October a radio operator, Gaël (Captain D. Johnson of the U.S. Army), who worked admirably and, in addition to his radio work, very ably seconded Xavier in his task. The fact of possessing such a link was a tremendous asset to Xavier, for, although Cantinier was able to use B.C.R.A. channels, their system was cumbersome and slow compared with the direct F. Section line.

66. And so began the series of operations, through which Xavier was to render such signal service.

Date. 1944.	Operations.	Containers.	Packages.
January	2	15	10
February	5	142	11
March	11	309	56
April	11	280	166
May	8	171	97
June	2	468*	24
July	3	223	103
August	6	597*	71
September	2	134	1

Including Daylight Operation (25th June and 1st August). In addition, a certain quantity of arms was delivered by Dakota.[40]

67. This material was put to good use; the list contained in Appendix A will give an idea of the sabotage accomplished by the circuit. Noteworthy are the attacks on the extremely important S.R.O. Ball-Bearing works at Annecy.

68. By January 1944 there were nine Maquis camps in Ain, consisting of 520 men, and three *corps mobiles*, fairly well armed. Good transport was available, and the district south of Nantua was practically controlled by them. By March a force of some 700 men was in control of the Glières Plateau in Jura, but were heavily attacked by the Germans, who lost 500 killed and 700 wounded.

69. By May Cantinier had separated from Xavier and was in charge of Haute-Savoie: Xavier had about 1,300 men in Ain and Jura. By July he and Cdt. Romans had under their direct control some 5,500 men, fully armed, and were working in close conjunction with Lieut.-Colonel Belleroche, Sous-Chef militaire of Region R.I., who transmitted Allied directives, received through Xavier, to the military delegates of all regions under his command.

70. In addition to the 5,500 there were a further 2,500 men in training battalions who were unarmed, and 2,500 more who could be called upon for training at any time.

71. It was the policy of Romans and of Xavier to refuse to arm anyone who had not volunteered to fight. In other words, there was no general mobilisation of man-power in their area. All armed groups had 2,500 rounds of Bren ammunition, 150 rounds per rifle and 5 magazines per Sten. In addition H.Q. held a reserve of 30,000 rounds of Bren and 60,000 rounds of sub-machine gun ammunition.

72. It was all needed.

73. Training was intensive, lasted 15 days and included large-scale manœuvres. Discipline, particularly fire discipline, had become extremely good.

74. Action on D-Day was quick and effective, and by the 12th June Xavier reported that the towns of Oyonnax, Nantua, Hauteville and Bellegarde were held by the Maquis. On the 13th he reported that rail traffic was completely cut on the Culoz–Ambérieu, Bourg–Lons-le-Saunier, Lyon–Bourg, Culoz–Bellegarde lines. Road traffic throughout the area had been interrupted, but not completely cut. As a result Colonel Romans and he had had to take over the administration of the

civilian population's food supplies and finances "under military law and in the name of de Gaulle."

75. Naturally the German reaction was severe and immediate, and by the 16th Xavier reported that Bellegarde had had to be evacuated after four days' fighting. They were being attacked in force from three sides, German losses being 400 killed, their own 60. Even so they were continuing to interrupt German traffic on the Lyon–Besançon road and the Lyon–Ambérieu–Mondane railway. Their arms situation was critical, but they still contrived to hold under their control the area Ouannax–Nantua–Hauteville.

76. This was of vital importance, as it was within this area that the two daylight operations took place, bringing them 420 containers on the 25th June and 468 on the 1st August.

77. In July Xavier returned to London to report, was personally invested with the Croix de Guerre by General Koenig, extracted some heavy machine guns from the Supply Department, and was all ready to fly with them to this area in a Dakota aircraft, when bad weather intervened and his return to France was delayed by three weeks.

78. This was extremely unfortunate, since, although it is not possible to state with conviction that his presence during this period would have avoided all the difficulties that had arisen, he found on his return that political difficulties were rife, a certain Grégoire (real name Farges), a political commissaire sent from Algiers, having accused Romans of trying to take civil powers without authority. Romans was also at cross-purposes with Colonel Bayard and Belleroche.

79. On the purely military side, however, all remained well apart from a shortage of material. When, therefore, on the 14th August the action messages for Southern D-Day came through, action comparable with that of the 6th June was carried out.

80. On the 23rd August, 1944, Belleroche ordered attacks on Bourg, Ambérieu and Lyon but Xavier and Romans considered the moment inopportune, as the Germans disposed of considerable armoured units. On the 24th August, 1944, he spent a day with Cantinier in the Haute-

Savoie now liberated, and operating against the Germans at Col de Tamie. The Germans now started to leave Ambérieux and Xavier succeeded in splitting them between Ambérieux and Chalamont and cleared the aerodrome. On the 25th August, 1944, they entered and cleared the Pays de Gex and chased the Germans to Morez, making their first contact with the Americans on the 27th August, 1944, at Bourgoin, to whom he gave valuable intelligence on local conditions. With them, he proceeded to Montluc, but they were driven back to Meximieu, which they held for 48 hours until reinforced. Although requested to go on by the Americans, he was unable to do so after Bourg, as he had not the necessary transport. They remained, therefore, to mop up.

81. On the 4th September, 1944, Xavier visited the Prefet at Bourg, with Colonel Romans, who was received coldly, political difficulties again showing themselves. Xavier's mission was now complete except for the mobilisation of 2,000 men on General Koenig's orders to continue the fight in the North, and these were sent to Pontarlier, but fresh political troubles developed and they had to withdraw. Colonel Romans, who had been in London, now returned, and he and Xavier continued their recruiting for the North. In between times, Xavier organised the Dakota transport service between his area, and London. But the political situation worsened, Colonel Romans was arrested and Xavier ordered to leave France by Farges. He therefore toured his area to make final settlements and returned to London via Paris, where he saw General Koenig and arranged for steps to be taken for Romans's release.

82. So, rather unhappily, ended a supremely successful mission. The Judex party when it reached Lyon in November was very kindly received by Farges, who apparently regretted his high-handed treatment of Xavier, and Xavier has since been awarded the Légion d'Honneur. Romans, of course, was duly released from gaol, and is now very actively engaged in the Centre de Propagande du Maquis, 22, rue de la Faisanderie, Paris.

83. The officers sent from London to the Marksman Circuit were:

Xavier (Lieut.-Colonel R. Heslop), D.S.O., Legion d'Honneur, Croix de Guerre.

Gaël (Captain D. Johnson) of the American Army, his extremely competent original radio operator.

Parsifal (Major Parker), R.A.M.C., D.S.O., of whom Xavier says: "Soon after he joined me we were very heavily attacked and chased for several weeks in the mountains and woods. Major Parker got all his wounded away to safe places and continued to organise field hospitals wherever possible, under the most difficult conditions. He carried out his work with total disregard for his personal safety and without sparing himself; his irrepressibly cheerful personality helped his wounded enormously, and the people working with him. I cannot write too highly of the courage, ability and fine personality of this officer."

Bayard (Lieutenant Nornable), M.C., a courageous and efficient instructor.

Yvello (Lieutenant Veilleux) a French Canadian and a very competent radio operator and Elizabeth (Miss Rochester), courier.

Captain de Brouville's Organisation.

Operational name of organisation: The Treasurer Circuit.
Operational name of organiser: Théodule.
Name by which known in the Field: Théodule, Albert and Pat.

84. The roots of this organisation go back far into F. Section history. In September 1942 Dominique (Captain B.D. Rafferty) had been parachuted to work near Clermont-Ferrand and had developed contacts in the Dijon and Montbeliard areas. In April 1943 he had been joined by César[41] (Captain H. Ree), who had followed up the Dijon contacts, which he had handed over in June 1943 to Bob (Captain J.A.R. Starr) and Gabriel (Lieutenant J.C. Young), and had occupied himself especially in building up an extremely successful circuit in and around Montbéliard.

85. In July 1943 Bob had been arrested, having been betrayed by a double-agent, Pierre Martin, and César had brought Gabriel to Clairvaux for safety. Here he was joined by Pedro (Lieutenant Jean Simon, also known as Cauchi and Claude), who had arrived in June from London and was to make up for Gabriel's lack of French by doing outside work, while Gabriel, who was also a radio operator, ensured contact with London. Pedro made an auspicious start by liquidating Pierre Martin,

but in November 1943 Gabriel and his courier, Paulette were arrested in the Pauli sawmill at Clairvaux.[42] In February 1944 Pedro was shot dead by the Gestapo in the Café Grangier in Montbéliard.

86. Meanwhile (to telescope a long and dramatic story) César had had his epic fight with a Feldgendarme, and had taken refuge, wounded in Switzerland. Luckily, however, he was able from there to supervise the continuing activities of what was left of his own and Pedro's circuits and to report to London that there were still elements capable of being developed, if an organiser was sent to them.

87. In the Jura–Dijon portion, which had been particularly Pedro's responsibility, the choice fell on Théodule.

88. Théodule had already been working for some time in Resistance. He had been third-in-command to Colonel d'Osia in Haute-Savoie, and in that capacity had received and hidden Flight-Lieutenant Griffiths, Captain of an aircraft which had been brought down while on an operation to the Pimento Circuit. Griffiths had been favourably impressed by him and had reported that he would be an extremely useful recruit for S.O.E. When, therefore, they came back to England together in February 1944, F. Section had successfully laid hands on him. After a very brief refresher course he arrived back in France in April. He was followed, fifteen days later, by Paul, his radio operator (Edwin Poitras of the United States Navy), of whom he speaks most highly.

89. About mid-July he was joined by José (Captain Georges André), coming from Switzerland, who became his extremely efficient second-in-command, and in June (on the eve of D-Day) by Émile (Captain Georges Millar), to whom he assigned the task of co-operating with Boulaya (Colonel Barthelet) in attacking the important rail network in the Besançon–Belfort–Vesoul–Gray region. The history of his exploits there belongs to the Strasbourg area, but Théodule's verdict may be here recorded:

"I shall never be able to pay adequate tribute to his work. Calm, far-seeing and showing exemplary sang-froid, he mounted sixty-two attacks in three weeks against the railways of the region, including the sabotage of the station at Besançon, two turntables,

242

the destruction of which immobilised seventy-seven locomotives, being blown up and sixteen charges being placed under the points, which were all demolished. Petrol trains were attacked with Bazookas. &c., men were killed at his side and he himself was nearly captured five times; a fine soldier."

90. But to return to Théodule. His work on the organisational side was outstanding. Arriving in mid-April he found only three of César and Pedro's lieutenants vaguely maintaining (so he says) a semblance of activity. They were Pierre (Pierre Larsennieux of Lons-le-Saunier), Henri (le petit Henri of Arinthod, Jura) and Gutt (Auguste Grancher of Pont de Poite, Jura). This "vagueness" had not apparently been completely aimless, since Théodule was able to report through Berne a week after his arrival that about fifteen Gestapo agents had been killed at the beginning of February, ten locomotives had been destroyed at Mouchard, two derailments had been carried out, pylons and goods station cranes had been attacked: on the 1st April three locomotives had been attacked at Dôle, a track repair train and some locomotives at Dijon.

91. With Théodule's arrival, May was a fruitful period of organisation. By the beginning of the month all preparations were made for cutting the Dôle–Dijon, Dôle–Besançon, Dôle–Lons-le-Saunier and Dôle–Pontarlier lines. When this programme was put into action rail traffic ceased in the area: the canals were similarly dealt with.

92. Théodule's circuit was divided into the following main groups. In the South (St.-Amour) a sabotage group under Henri Claire. Further North the Lons-le-Saunier sector under Commandant Louis of the A.S. furnished a further nucleus for sabotage and guerrilla work for the region between Lons and St.-Claude. This was placed under the command of Pierre. Further North still the Frontenay–Poligny–Arbois region was under the command of Captain Gilles.[43] Further North again solid groups at Mouchard under Mathieu and at Dôle–Auxonne under Georges Michelet of the F.T.P., later replaced by Paul of the same persuasion. West-South-West of Dôle was Lucien (de St.-Genies), of whom more later.

93. These groups established, the crying need was supplies. Here is the record:

Date. 1944.	Operations.	Containers.	Packages.
May	3	60	19
June	2	48	18
July	2	36	12
August	16	373	108
September	9	582	165
October	1	48	4

94. These figures speak eloquently of the tragedy which befell resistance in this part of France. Just when supplies were most urgently needed, June and July 1944, the shortness of the summer nights made it impossible to deliver them – either from England or North Africa – and Théodule found himself in the invidious position of having to disobey an order coming to him from Xavier (Lieutenant-Colonel Heslop) in the Ain to set up ambushes on the roads in his district.

95. But the rest of the programme was duly carried out and, although for about a week after D-Day Théodule lost contact with most of his circuit, he learned later that everything had gone according to plan, that the great majority of railway lines were unusable, that the underground cables had been cut except at Dijon, that telephone, telegraph and high tension lines were for the most part out of service.

96. Then came the incorporation of the British circuits into the F.F.I. under General Koenig, and Théodule received orders to collaborate with Orcia. To this end Théodule handed over the command of his southern groups (650 well-armed men under Gutt and Henri Claire) to Commandant Louis and Colonel Belleroche, the D.M.R. The Dijon groups under Georges André were placed under the general command of Commandant Guy (A.S.), although they retained their autonomy and worked closely with the S.A.S. group, Houndsworth; they comprised 750 well-trained and armed men. Émile worked in intimate collaboration with Boulaya and Ligne, the D.M.R. Théodule and Orcia aimed to set on foot a force of 3,000 men.

97. This project was realised only in part owing to the ever prevailing insufficiency of stores, but general insurrection was organised throughout the Dijon–Besançon–St.-Amour triangle, and the Germans

were given no peace. The region was cleared of Germans with the exception of Mouthe, Pontarlier, Dôle and Besançon, which proved indigestible morsels for the F.F.I. with their limited means.

98. Contact being established with Allied troops, Théodule and Orcia began the organisation of F.F.I. shock troops to fight with General Delatre de Tassigny's army. He was beginning to get this under way at the camp at Val d'Ahon, thanks to a large daylight delivery of stores at Lemoy, and 1,200 men of the group were fighting with the army, when Théodule returned to London.[44]

99. Théodule and Émile were both awarded the D.S.O. for their work during this mission.

Captain de St.-Genies' Organisation.
Operational name of organisation: The Scholar Circuit (known locally as Radio Patrie).
Operational name of organiser: Lucien.
Name by which known in the Field: Lucien.

100. The early history of this group is that of the Carte organisation, with which F. Section first made contact in 1942 (see under Marseille). This group had widespread contacts throughout France, and when the split came and Paul seceded from Carte to be officially recognised by London as Carte's successor, certain groups, disliking Paul, remained outside the new group and sought to renew direct contact with F. Section through Switzerland.

101. These elements were known to London as the Mesnard group, after their leader, although it appeared that this leadership fell to Mesnard very largely owing to the fact that he had his Headquarters at Annemasse and that he was the man who, in consequence, was able to maintain the liaison with London. His organisation, however, showed welcome signs of wholeheartedness and adherence to F. Section principles and directives, and from October 1943 efforts had been made to send them an organiser from London.

102. On the 18th March, 1944, Lucien and his radio operator Odette (Flight-Officer Yvonne Baseden, W.A.A.F.) were parachuted into South-

West France. Lucien was an escaped French P.O.W. – although he was naturalised English just before starting his mission – and an outstandingly fine officer. He quickly contacted Leroux (Charles Alluin) who had taken over the circuit after the arrest of Mesnard in February. Leroux reported that he had 300 men directly under him in Bouches-du-Rhône and that, apart from this, the group consisted of 300 men in Aude, Hérault and Aveyron, 20 in Haute-Loire, and groups of 100 and 200 in Maquis at Dôle. Morale was low owing to lack of materials.

103. The plan was to divide the organisation into three, South-East, South and North, and, although one group was split by the Germans, including the one, unfortunately, from which trained wireless operators were to be drawn, reorganisation under the skilled direction of Lucien was well under way by D-Day.

104. The stores position had also been improved, culminating in a large-scale daylight operation on the 25th June:-

Date. 1942.	Operations.	Containers.	Packages.
August	1	6	...
1943.			
January	1	5	...
March	3	67	31
April	5	58	8
May	5	72	19
June	2	423	10

105. Then came tragedy. A boy carrying a wireless set from the daylight operation was caught by the Germans and talked. The same day a party of Gestapo surrounded a certain house in the outskirts of Dôle, Lucien was shot dead, and Odette, Leroux and others were arrested and taken away. Odette has since returned, but Leroux has not.

106. So ended, sadly, a mission full of hope. Lucien was a really first-class organiser, and his circuit, from a late start, had already certain notable actions to its credit. On the 27th May the Solvay works at Tavaux had been put out of action by the drying-up of the Rhone –

Rhine Canal; on the 3rd June the records of the S.T.O. at Dôle were destroyed, and between D-Day and the 10th June the Telephone Exchange and the Despatcher at Dôle were completely destroyed, the Strasbourg – Paris underground cable cut, and many attacks were made on rail and telephone communications between Dôle and Dampierre.

107. In August, apparently, contact with the group was resumed, since four stores operations took place and over 300 containers were delivered.

108. One post-liberation story requires mentioning. In February 1945 the Judex II mission was visiting Captain Ree's circuit in Montbéliard, when it was learned that Robert Graf had just returned from a Concentration Camp in Germany. An officer was detached from Judex II to interview him and M. Mayor concerning the circumstances of Lucien's death, which had taken place at "Les Orphelins," a house occupied by M. and Mme. Mayor on the Graf property, the Grafs being prominent cheese manufacturers. M. Mayor received him, and introduced M. Graf as having worked with the circuit. When, therefore, the usual papers concerning the circuit were supplied by the F. Section Paris office to the D.G.E.R., a reference was made to M. Graf as having placed his house at the disposition of Lucien for his Headquarters.

109. Then came the return of Odette and of Mme. Mayor from Germany, and a first-class row, since they maintained firmly that Graf had been a notorious collaborator with the Germans, and had had no knowledge at all of what had been going on at "Les Orphelins." Meanwhile, Graf, in some mysterious manner, had obtained a copy of the D.G.E.R. statement, and had had it photographed and inserted in the local papers to prove his patriotism. The indignant ladies became more and more vociferous, and have only been silenced (temporarily perhaps) by a letter being written to Mme. Mayor pointing out that the error was entirely due to the action of her husband in introducing Graf to the British officer.

110. A very local storm in a teacup, but echoes doubtless persist.

111. Captain de St.-Genies was given a Posthumous Mention in Despatches and Ft/O Baseden the M.B.E.

Gaspard.

112. It has been related elsewhere (Châteauroux, Limoges) how Gaspard, head of a French organisation, made contact with Hector (S/Ldr. Southgate) and besought him to let him have the supplies, which he was unable to obtain through his own French channels. This Hector did, on the usual conditions, and the Gaspard organisation has a number of notable sabotage exploits to its credit, including the attack on the liquid oxygen works at Massiac and the burning of a stock of 40,000 tyres at the Michelin works at Clermont-Ferrand.

113. At the end of April 1944, therefore, F. Section sent Gaspard a mission consisting of Hubert (Captain, later Major, Farmer), Hélène (Nancy Wake), courier, and Roland (Captain Rake), wireless operator.

114. On the 20th May Roland made contact with London and reported that they were in touch with Gaspard, that his organisation had immense value as a fighting force, was situated in strategic centres in the Le Puy, St.-Flour, Aurillac region, but had absolutely no stores and was in dire need of arms.

115. The short summer nights made it difficult to deliver to so remote an area, but the following was achieved:-

Date. 1944.	Operations.	Containers.	Packages.
June	8	150	163
July	2	19	14
August	6	113	41

116. Meanwhile Hubert reported that Gaspard's groups included:
3,000 men at Mont Mouchet.
1,250 men between Fridefont and Viaduc de Garabit.
2,500 men at Le Lioran.
1,000 men at Fix-St.-Geney.

117. Apparently these large concentrations were a mistake, more particularly in view of the lack of armament, and heavy losses were suffered when the Mont Mouchet Maquis was attacked in force.

Gaspard reported that he could muster 15,000 men against the Germans' 20,000. According to Hubert, the attackers numbered 10,000, and Maquis losses were 1,200. On the 21st June Hubert also reported attacks against the Chaudesaigues and Fridefont Maquis, which had been dispersed with heavy losses.

118. Thereafter effective contact ceased till the 17th July, when Hubert, who had received a new W/T operator, appeared to have re-established himself. On the 29th July he reported groups at Pontgibaud, Sauxillanges, Ambert, Thiers, Giat, La Peyrouse, St.-Gervais, Aigueperse, Forêt de Cuireis, Ygrande, Besson, Vallon, Cérilly and Deneuille. Activity was considerable and included the blocking of a tunnel on the Moulin–Montlucon line by blowing up two trains inside it. St.-Hilaire was taken over and there was a succession of minor skirmishes; men were always available, but materials were always the limiting factor.

Appendix A:

ACTIVITIES OF MARKSMAN CIRCUIT

October 1943
50 camps of 70 men each organised in Ain.

7th November, 194
Annecy – 1 truck, 3 motor-bicycles and 1 cycle-taxi seized from the Germans.
10th November, 1943
Two pylons blown up on the Ugine–Annecy H.T. line and all factories in the Annecy area put out of action.
11th November, 1943
Explosion and damage caused in the house of a denouncer at Allinges.
11th November, 1943
Bioge – water and electric pipes destroyed.
12th November, 1943
120 cheeses seized at Grand-Bernard.
12th November, 1943
A collaborator shot.
13th November, 1943
A pylon on the 45,000-volt H.T. line Cluses–Le Fayet destroyed.
13th November, 1943
Schmidt-Roos ball-bearing factory at Annecy blown up and 2 transformers set alight. Probably out of action for 3 months.
27th November, 1943
46 camps of 30 men each organised in Isère.
4th December, 1943
Second attack on Schmidt-Roos at Annecy: 2 transformers blown and fired, oil tempering installations fired, 9 blanchard and Cincinnati type grinders destroyed. Official result – factory entirely stopped and several millions of francs' worth of damage done.

December 1943
2 electrical motors driving saws at Durrafour sawmill at Neyrolles (Ain).

December 1943
Railway cuts accomplished in Ain.

December 1943
3 lorries captured – 1 with load of tyres, 2 with petrol (one a 5-ton lorry) – Ain.

2nd January, 1944
9 camps totalling 500 men now completely equipped in Ain, complete with 20 lorries, 8 cars and 9 motor-bicycles.
15th January, 1944
Stand-up fight with G.M.R. 4 of the enemy killed, 10 wounded and a lorry blown up.
22nd January, 1944
Bellegarde – 12 locomotives attacked and 1 German Lieutenant killed and 4 collaborators kidnapped.
January 1944
16 railway locomotives destroyed as follows: 5 at Annecy, 3 at Laroche, 2 each at Bonneville and Le Fayet, and 1 each at Vovray, Évires, Seyssel and St.-Giffre – all in Haute-Savoie.
January 1944
Turn-table put out of action at Laroche.
January 1944
7 Germans killed in ambush, area unspecified.
January 1944
36 locomotives attacked in Ain, as follows: 12 at Bellegarde, 11 each at Bourg and Ambérieu and 2 at La Cluse.
January 1944
Briffant sawmill at Main blown up.
January 1944
2 German officers killed, 2 German lorries destroyed and 6 Germans killed in ambush; later 3 more Germans in ambush.
Up to 24th January, 1944
34 locomotives destroyed as follows: 11 at Annemasse, 4 at Laroche, 2 at Annecy, 1 each at Rumilly and Marignier (all in Haute-Savoie) and 19 at Ambérieu.

26th February, 1944
S.R.O. ball-bearing factory at Annecy attacked and 2 transformers put out of action, also 3 big rectifying machines. Only 10 per cent. of personnel working.

26th March, 1944

2 trains derailed (area unspecified) enabling a convoy of departees for Germany to escape.

26th March, 1944

100 men armed in Jura Maquis.

25th March, 1944

Railway line sabotaged in 2 places (area unspecified).

1st April, 1944

2 railway demolitions (area unspecified).

April 1944

3 railways kept out of action near Bourg–Ambérieu.

April 1944

600 men fully armed in Ain Maquis and a further 500 outside it. 250 men in Jura Maquis, of whom 100 fully armed.

April 1944

Losses inflicted on the Germans, &c., in Glières attack as follows: 250 Germans killed, 400 wounded, 50 Milice killed.

15th April, 1944

Power plant sabotaged and German stores set on fire at Ambronay (North of Ambérieu).

April 1944

Concentrated attacks on all railway lines. Results: 3 German troop trains, 1 Milice train, 3 war material trains and 1 oil train all derailed. 3 engines sabotaged.

22nd April, 1944

2 German 77 mm. guns captured and gun crews wiped out.

29th April, 1944

500 Germans killed and 700 wounded in Jura Maquis battle.

27th May, 1944

12 Milice killed, 38 wounded in attack on a camp.

3rd June, 1944

45 Milice killed. 130 wounded in fighting at Nantua.

3rd June, 1944

11 locomotives and a turn-table knocked out at Bellegarde.

10th June, 1944

Two locomotives, control-tower, and turn-table sabotaged at Ste.-Claude (Jura).

June 1944

Feldgendarmerie (area unspecified) successfully stormed.

June 1944

Sixteen locomotives, control-tower, turn-table and catch-points sabotaged at Bourg (Ain).

June 1944

Turn-table at La Cluse, catch-points at Oyonnax, Nurieux and Bellegarde all sabotaged.

6th June, 1944

Fifty locomotives, two turn-tables and machine-shop sabotaged at Ambérieu.

June 1944

Railway line Bourg-en-Bresse–La Cluse–Nantua–Bellegarde reported out at forty-two points.

17th June, 1944

Traffic completely cut in the following places: between Culoz, Ambérieu, Bourg and Lons-le-Saunier; between Lyon and Bourg; between Culoz and Bellegarde.

June 1944

German losses in attack: 34 killed, 35 prisoners.

June 1944

Railway bridge, engines and catch-points blown up during evacuation of Bellegarde after four days' fighting.

18th June, 1944

Remaining engines at Ambérieu knocked out and a train derailed on the Lyon–Amberieu line.

24th June, 1944

A train derailed in a tunnel at Bellegarde.

Up to 18th June, 1944

Saône-et-Loire rail sabotage of varying degrees on the following lines: Dijon–Modane, Mâcon–Chalon, Paray-le-Monial–Montceau-les-Mines.

1st July, 1944

Intermittent sabotage on the Lons–Bourg, Lons–Besançon, Lons–Champagnole lines in the Jura.

1st July, 1944

Five engines and a turn-table blown up at Lons.

1st July, 1944

Forty-five Germans killed and three taken prisoner.

1st July, 1944

Fifty Germans killed and wounded in an attack on Bourg.

9th July, 1944

Two break-down cranes put out of action (area unspecified).

Appendix B:

ACTIVITIES OF TREASURER CIRCUIT

Between January and the end of April 1944
Jura – Fifteen Gestapo agents killed.

Early February 1944
Mouchard – ten locomotives destroyed and two derailments caused, resulting in a twenty-four-hour stoppage.
February 1944 Bouchard – high tension lines and goods-station cranes attacked.

1st April, 1944
Three locomotives at Dôle and a track repair-train and some locomotives destroyed at Dijon.

May 1944
Three locomotives, one electric line and three rail cuts (ares unspecified).
20th May, 1944
Two canal-lock gates blown up at Dijon.
20th May, 1944
Ammunition depot blown up at Dôle.
10th June, 1944
Teams for sabotage in Dijon and Dôle areas.

June-July 1944
Nine locomotives and the signal-boxes destroyed at Is-sur-Tilles: these cannot be repaired till after the war.
June-July 1944
Three barges burnt and two lock-gates blown up on the Canal de Bourgogne.
June-July 1944
Underground cables, telegraph lines and station water supplies destroyed in the Chaigny, St.-Seine l'Abbaye and Auxonne areas.
June-July 1944
Five locomotives and a turn-table destroyed in the locomotive depot at Besançon. The Tunnel Du Roche in the same area blocked by derailing a train.

June-July 1944
Points blown up on the Besançon–Dijon line at Frasnois.

June-July 1944
High tension lines, telegraph lines and station water supplies destroyed in the Dôle area, and a lock-gate on the Rhone-Rhine canal kept out of action.

June-July 1944
Seven locomotives, water-pumps and a coal-elevator destroyed at Lons-le-Saunier; all points cut and the Passenans tunnel blocked for several weeks by two derailed trains.

June-July 1944
Twelve Germans killed in a battle in the Clairvaux area.

19th June, 1944
Complete destruction of a German ammunition depot at Crugey near Dijon. Between 700 and 1,000 wagons of Flak, Infantry and Aviation munitions were stored there, estimated at 1,000 tons, supplying all the airfields in the South-East. The explosions lasted four days and the flames from the entrances destroyed a nearby cement factory.

During July 1944
Sixty-four rail cuts effected on the lines from Besançon to Vesoul, Dôle and Belfort.

July 1944
18,000 litres of petrol destroyed in the same area.

Appendix C:

ACTIVITIES OF SCHOLAR CIRCUIT

May 1944
Solvay chemical works at Tavaux (Jura) put out of action.
May 1944
Rhone-Rhine canal drained, stopping all traffic and cutting off supplies to the above-mentioned works.
May 1944
A force of 100 Air Force officers and n.c.o.s orgainised, complete with motor vehicles and ready to attack.

June 1944
"Fiches de recensement" for conscript labour destroyed at Dôle.
June 1944
The telephone exchange and despatcher at Dôle station destroyed.
June 1944
The underground cable from Strasburg to Dôle cut.
June 1944
Railway lines cut and telephones destroyed in the four main Dôle areas and in Bruyère and Lin. A railway bridge on the Dôle–Dampierre line, 7 kilom. North-East of Dôle destroyed.
June 1944
Railways on Jura kept constantly out of action. German prisoners taken.

Notes to Part II

[1] A grand old lady, mother of Henri Sevenet who worked with Lionel and left France in April 1943 for the United Kingdom; he returned to the Field in September 1943 and was killed by an enemy bomb while fighting with the Montagne Noire Maquis in July 1944.

[2] Incidentally, in the rush, he laid his lights on the wrong ground and the aircraft, when it took off, fouled some telephone wires, several yards of which were found trailing from it on arrival in England. The pilot on this operation was Squadron-Leader Dufour.

[3] This operation, rightly regarded as a considerable achievement, consisted of two containers, and offers an interesting contrast with the 800 or so containers dropped in one daylight operation in much the same area to Hamlet (Major Liewer) in July 1944.

[4] Flying-Officer E.M. Wilkinson.

[5] It was to this farm that Valérien had been taken by Max Hymans and George Noble on being parachuted to the Field on his first mission in September 1941. On the 16th March, 1946, the writer received a notification from Max Hymans, Secrétaire-Général à l'Aviation Civile et Commerciale, Ministère des Travaux Publics et des Transports, that it was intended to hold a memorial service at Tendu to Chantraine towards the end of April or the beginning of May.

[6] Hector completely deceived the local Gestapo who first examined him and it was not till some weeks later, in Paris, that his identity was betrayed to them. He passed through Fresnes and Buchenwald, was liberated by the Americans, and is now resident in Paris.

[7] Lieutenant A.P. Shaw, posthumously Mentioned in Despatches, 21st June, 1945.

[8] This appears slightly embittered. Hector had visited the Maquis and had been impressed by it.

[9] O.G. = Operational Group, an American type of Commando. S.A.S. = Special Airborne Services.

[10] Of which 1,248 were delivered in two daylight operations.

[11] Of which 1,248 were delivered in two daylight operations.

[12] Major Liewer used the pseudonym Staunton throughout the period of his association with the British.

[13] Including Daylight Operations (413 Containers on the 14th July).

[14] Lieutenant Pertschuk was also known as Perkins.

[15] See under Marseilles, paragraph 10, *et seq.*

[16] See under Paris, paragraphs 114 and 115.

[17] See under Chateauroux-Limoges, paragraph 4.

[18] He did leave in April 1943, underwent further training and returned to the Field in September 1943 to build up Resistance in the Tarn-Aude region. In this he did extremely

258

well and the successes of the Montagne Noire Maquis are largely due to him. He was killed by a bomb during an attack on the Maquis by German aircraft in July 1944.

[19] M. Piercy.

[20] The S. phone, an apparatus for ground-air conversation.

[21] Later, as Ambroise, to return to the Field as radio operator to Captain Benoist on his last mission.

[22] Later, as Abelard, to take over the Troyes circuit from Major Cowburn.

[23] He had become Deputy Mayor of Castelnau-sous-l'Auvignon near Condom, passed as a gentleman farmer and was much respected.

[24] Loupias has written a book "Messages Personnels" describing events in Southern Dordogne, to which the reader is referred.

[25] Other circuits also participated, as noted elsewhere.

[26] It is a pity that Hilaire is not available to check the accuracy of this statement, since it is he who told the writer some time ago that it was precisely the Communists who bore the brunt of the early fighting, whilst the raw levies of the other complexion were being armed and trained. Perhaps his remark relates to the beginning of July, by which time his account and Philibert's would agree.

[27] They put a price of 10 million francs on his head dead or alive.

[28] Lieutenant (later Captain) Newman.

[29] See the Unoccupied Zone, paragraph 5.

[30] A member of the Carte organisation, now resident in Cannes.

[31] He was released in November 1942, continued to work for a time in the Le Puy area, and returned to London in the summer of 1943.

[32] Mrs. Sansom, Raoul's courier.

[33] Known then as Colonel Heinrich – real name Verbeck.

[34] See Toulouse and South-West, paragraph 8.

[35] The Colonel Heinrich (Verbeck) already refered to.

[36] Jacques Langlois represented the best elements of the Louba circuit and Roger had complete confidence in him.

[37] An American officer sent from London with the main objective of helping Roger to organise the Valensoie Plateau for large-scale receptions of parachute troops.

[38] The writer met General Zeller in the late summer of 1945 when he paid high tribute to Roger's work at this period.

[39] Lieutenant Sheppard.

[40] As was a film of the Normandy landings, which was shown in the local cinemas amid enormous enthusiasm.

[41] See under Strasbourg.

[42] He had, apparently, been given away by Benoit (Captain Maugenet, a Frenchman with a British Commision) who had just arrived in France by Lysander to join him, and had been arrested by the Gestapo almost immediately.

[43] A great friend of F. Section, but at present understood to be in prison. The reason is not known, although an amiable failing for smuggling watches over the Swiss frontier may be responsible.

[44] The subsequent results were not entirely happy, although this really forms no part of the present history. In February 1945 the writer met a very discouraged Georges André, who had just ceased to command his battalion in the line, and was most disgruntled at the way it had been sent unfledged into battle near Colmar. The equipment of these troops was not nearly so good as those of regular units, and losses were very heavy.

Index

260